Asbury Theological Seminary Series in World Christian Revitalization Movements

This volume is published in collaboration with the Center for the Study of World Christian Revitalization Movements, a cooperative initiative of Asbury Theological Seminary faculty. Building on the work of the previous Wesleyan/Holiness Studies Center at the Seminary, the Center provides a focus for research in the Wesleyan Holiness and other related Christian renewal movements which have had a world impact. The research seeks to develop analytical models of these movements, including their biblical and theological assessment. Using an interdisciplinary approach, the Center bridges relevant discourses in several areas in order to gain insights for effective Christian mission globally. It recognizes the need for conducting research that combines insights from the history of evangelical renewal and revival movements with anthropological and religious studies literature on revitalization movements. It also networks with similar or related research and study centers around the world, in addition to sponsoring its own research projects.

It is uncommon to find a study in revitalization that emerges from the world of a pastor ministering within a racially divided inner city congregation which also builds upon such formidable foundations as an in-depth analysis of the malaise of contemporary Western civilization, based upon its modern and post modern ideological and philosophical underpinnings. And, from that grounding, it is a study that proceeds to offer a cogent diagnosis of an (if not the) intellectual problem lying at its epicenter. This is precisely what Peter Bellini's study entitled: *Participation: Epistemology and Mission Theology* sets forth.

The author identifies that challenge as the demise of a concern for ontology amid a preoccupation with epistemology which, as he demonstrates, characterizes the philosophical consensus dominating that civilization, particularly since the Enlightenment. It is also extraordinary to have set forth as a valuable resource for remedying that dilemma an Eastern ascetic theologian, who is further shown to provide resource for rethinking a theology of mission for the present day, viewed within the parameters of the theology of John Wesley. Bellini's work addresses all of the above, and does so within the framework of recovering the apostolic concept of participation in Christ, from the standpoint of what he calls a Radical Orthodox perspective.

In short, this is a study that does not stop with a cogent cultural evaluation and critique, but also offers a prescriptive response. He finds in Maximus the Confessor a "participatory view of ontology, in continuity with a Christological ontology of participation", which has special relevance for the global Christianity of the twenty first century. Following Maximus, as well as Wesley's prevenient grace, Bellini champions a worldview that discerns within every culture some "point of similarity" or contact, "however vague, wounded or fallen," with the universal witness of the Holy Spirit. That witness, to which the work of the Revitalization Center at Asbury is dedicated, is, in our author's terms, "to conform culture, and its society, to the image of Christ." It is this theme, and its articulate exposition, that commends Bellini's study as an entry in this Series.

J. Steven O'Malley
Director, Center for the Study of World Christian Revitalization Movements
Editor, The Asbury Theological Seminary Series in Pietist and Wesleyan Studies

Participation

Epistemology and Mission Theology

Peter J. Bellini

*The Asbury Theological Seminary Series in
World Christian Revitalization Movements in Pietist/Wesleyan Studies. No. 2*

EMETH PRESS
www.emethpress.com

Participation: Epistemology and Mission Theology

Copyright © 2010 Peter J. Bellini
Printed in the United States of America on acid-free paper

All rights reserved. No part of this book may be reproduced, or stored in a retrieval system or transmitted in any form or by any means, electronic, mechanical, photocopying, recording, scanning or otherwise, except as permitted by the 1976 United States Copyright Act, or with the prior written permission of Emeth Press. Requests for permission should be addressed to: Emeth Press, P. O. Box 23961, Lexington, KY 40523-3961. http://www.emethpress.com.

Library of Congress Cataloging-in-Publication Data

Bellini, Peter J.
 Participation : epistemology and mission theology / Peter J. Bellini.
   p. cm. -- (Asbury Theological Seminary series in world Christian revitalization movements)
 Includes bibliographical references (p.   ) and index.
 ISBN 978-0-9819582-9-3 (alk. paper)
 1. Missions--Theory. 2. Philosophy and religion. 3. Knowledge, Theory of (Religion) 4. Participation. I. Title.
 BV2063.B42 2010
 266.001--dc22
                                2009048621

Contents

Introduction 7

1. Some of the Problem 15

2. Deflationary Ontologies: An Epistemological Crisis within
   Modernism and Postmodernism 27

3. An Ontology of Participation: A Radical Orthodox Proposal 69

4. Participation in the Logos *(Metousia Logo)* and
   St. Maximus the Confessor 95

5. Participation in Grace *(Metousia Chariti)* in John Wesley's Theology 111

6. Participation and Some Implications for a Theology of Mission 129

7. Conclusion, Contributions and Questions 177

References Cited 181

Introduction

He himself is before all things, and in him all things hold together (Col. 1:1).

This work endeavors to imagine a vision of epistemology that is compatible with Christian theism and its soteriological work in theology, specifically a theology of mission. Historians of philosophy and theology differ in locating historically the break between theology and philosophy and ontology and epistemology. Some locate the bifurcation in Aquinas and the distinctions that he made between the scope and function of philosophy and theology. Others, like me, tend to locate the bifurcation in later High Medievalism with Scotus and Ockham and innovations like the univocity of being and nominalism, and do not interpret Aquinas's philosophy-theology distinction in such mutually exclusive terms. In consonance with Eastern Christian tradition and certain attempts at retrieving and remixing patristic sources, such as Catholic Ressourcement and Radical Orthodoxy, I am compelled to believe that theology and philosophy are done best together and ultimately if done right have each other's best interests at heart. Von Balthasar often spoke of the servant nature of knowledge.[1]

As Christianity contextualized within Hellenism in its first four centuries[2] it sought to keep its faith and witness consistent with Scripture, as its theology missionally and apologetically spoke the language of faith with philosophical congruence and critical commensurability. This contextualization is best exemplified, but not solely, in the symbols of our faith, specifically the Nicene Creed. Theology has had to bear witness not only to the Spirit and to the church, but also to the world. In preparation for departure, this work seeks a degree of philosophical compatability between an epistemological vision, Christian theism and a theology of mission. As a point of departure, this research is making an assumption, maybe unfounded, untested, or not proven, that Christian theism has held implicitly or explicitly to some form of ontology in its understanding of God and to some form of ontology in its understanding of creation, a de facto ontology of God and creation.[3] A Christian notion of God and creation has involved some view of ontological realism that includes the existence of God and a separate creation (non-pantheistic), that both God and creation have a degree of definable natures and qualities, and that God and creation have a relationship between them, which is analogical. The problem with this kind of talk is that the stock on ontology has gone down considerably since late Medievalism and has gradually deflated through modernism to virtually nothing today. If the concept is used at all, it is in terms of "things" and the classification of "things," an instrumental materialist view, or as merely linguistic analysis. This ontological deflation has been taxing on systems of knowledge that have had to carry this unbearable load, and the repercussions have been nothing less than systemic Western atheism[4] and the enthroning of autonomous reason as an empire over "lesser" forms of knowledge. Christian theism and theology need to recover its ontological sensibility and its influence on epistemology. This can begin by positing a theo-ontology that is Trinitarian and a creational ontology that is analogical to its Creator in which God is both transcendent and immanent in relation to God's creation.[5]

Christian mission and communication, as well as the nature of epistemology, demand that theology and practice be conveyed faithfully and specifically within a contextual framework. Currently, we are situated in a so-called post-everything world that is postmodern, post-rational, post-real, postcolonial, post-Christian, post-Western, post-Communist, post-American, post-writing, etc. world that is calling the church to rethink and remix its theology and examine its epistemological concerns and claims. Some movements[6] may feel that a particular epistemology need not be contended for, and the whole preoccupation over the last five-hundred years about getting our head screwed on straight before our heart can understand properly is not necessary. Canonical Theism, one such movement, is correct that we do not need to contend for any one particular or one right epistemology in a foundational way before we can believe or even theologize. There is a certain theological latitude that allows us "to think and let think" concerning epistemology, to borrow from John Wesley. However, I am not contending for just one particular or foundational epistemology in terms of justifying the canons of faith for the church, but this endeavor seeks *an* epistemology, and maybe several, that is compatible to Christian theism for theological and missiological purposes and the need for contextualization. We do not need here a fundamentalist canon of knowledge, but no theology or canon of faith can claim epistemological immunity or neutrality. Even a claim of knowledge based on the canons of faith can be construed as a type of social epistemology in terms of being based on a tradition, be it research, virtue or canonical. I have no qualms with this, but we cannot claim epistemological immunity. One way or another we will make knowledge claims.

From Liberation theology colonizing Marxism to Fundamentalism canonizing Enlightenment rationalism, Christian theology and theology of mission have often adopted modernist epistemologies into their systems without much prophetic critiquing. Much of the epistemic DNA that birthed the behemoth of modern atheism remains within the foundations of many Christian theologies. Postmodernism, as well as other recent schools of philosophy, in turn, have analyzed modern epistemologies and their claims to pure and foundational reason and have found them corrigible and wanting. Postmodernism has offered a variety of epistemological solutions through the study of semiotics and hermeneutics. Some of these solutions are compatible with Christian theism, while others are not. Part of the problem is that postmodernism has not fully rid itself of its modernist vestiges. In fact, they often borrow each other's clothing because they wear the same size. Theological correctives have attempted to identify and rectify some of the negative effects that modernist epistemologies have had for both the church and those that have heard the gospel.[7] Further work remains to be done to close the gap between epistemology and Christian theism, specifically mission theology. At this time, the author onlyknows of two other published works that deal with epistemology and mission theology besides this one.[8] Further research is needed in this field that will examine epistemology and its relationship and impact on ontology, theology, Christian theism, and specifically mission theology.

In light of an epistemological crisis[9] that has intensified since the advent and development of postmodernism, this research attempts to offer a sound ontologically based epistemology that can be implemented within theology and specifically within a Christian theology of mission both locally and globally. The hypothesis is that modernism has deflated ontology, and has disconnected it from God, and has inflated epistemology to a role of first philosophy. It is then necessary to implement a sort of ontological[10] critique of some of the influential epistemologies within modernism that highlights this trend of deflation. The result of modernism's overemphasis on autonomous reason, when applied to mission theology, has often been mission practice under the cover of Western hegemony reproducing both evangelism and oppression within the same missionary enterprise.

An important note to make early on concerning the terms "modernism" and "postmodernism," both terms are worn out to the point of being catch phrases and buzzwords for every argument *ad nauseum* to the point that they may not mean too much anymore. Besides, even when they have been used, they are often slippery words that are difficult to grasp with any great degree of certainty. These terms will not be used in an exhaustive sense but in part by giving particular examples that may reflect or highlight these two periods or sensibilities. Also in this critique of both, this studydoes not want to make any wholesale claims of condemnation or praise. They are too complex for such simplistic appraisals, though they will be addressed from a critical standpoint. This work will cite some of the problems with modernity, but it is not an appeal to do away with all that modernity has brought us. Individual freedoms, civil rights, sensitivity and respect for the individual, the prevenient grace of God even in the contractual State (even though we moved away from covenant to contract), technological progress, computers, and especially Amazon.com are just a random sampling of reasons to applaud modernity. When using the two terms, I am trying to keep in mind all that has made them abstruse, fluid, nebulous, and easy game for reductionism. Use of the term "modernism" then is primarily defined by the ideas and impact of Continental Rationalism, specifically Descartes, British Empiricism, specifically Locke, Hobbes, and Hume, the Enlightenment, specifically Kant, and Phenomenology and Existentialism, specifically Husserl, Kierkegaard, Heidegger, and Sartre. Use of the term "postmodernism" is defined primarily by the ideas and impact of Foucault, Derrida, and Baudrillard.

This research will survey and examine some of the highlights of both modernism and postmodernism in order to uncover some of the symptoms and causes of this epistemological crisis and its impact on theology. It will also investigate three cases that exhibit how this crisis has affected modern mission adversely and has contributed to Christendom's missionary collateral damage of colonization, exploitation, westernization, truncation and distortion of the gospel. Along with my own analysis, this work will consider a critical theological framework posited by Radical Orthodoxy in order to examine a deflationary-nihilistic trend in modernism and postmodernism. The argument is that the epistemological crisis is truly an ontological crisis, a deflation of ontology, or a series of deflationary ontologies, and even further a theological crisis. The side effects of modernism's bent towards atheism have been a virtual elimination of the Divine and transcendence and a deflation of ontology. One way to approach this problem is a return to and a remixing of ontology as it relates to epistemology and theology. An *ontology of participation* in transcendent being, specifically God's being is one such approach. Such an ontology is a vision[11] that depicts reality as the created order "suspended"[12] from the transcendent[13] God and dependent on God for its very existence and nature. Creation is not an autonomous realm but participates in God who gives it meaning, purpose and order. Creation is called to gaze continually upward for all that it is and will be, a radical revival of the transcendent and transcendence. This work reflects an ontological vision that informs knowledge. Epistemology is not an isolated or closed discipline but is inspired and shaped by the creational context which participates in the *logoi*[14] or in the workings of God's will. All of creation is in an analogical relationship with God, and as a part of creation, we know as we and all things participate in God. Knowing is a factor of being related to God.

This research has attempted to develop the Radical Orthodox model of ontology into one that would have epistemological and theological bearing, as well as take on a more Christological form for the purpose of application in mission. One of the key contributions brought to this study is an attempt to modify the Radical Orthodox *metousia Theou,* or participation in God, into a more Christological construct, a *metousia Logo*, a participation in Christ the Logos, and then to apply it to mission theology. In searching historical theology at the crossroads of Platonic participation and Christian Incarnation, this model draws from the ancient Byzantine theologian and monk Maximus the Confessor (580-662) and his theology of the Incarnation and the *logoi.* Maximus' theology of the *logoi* is participatory in nature and Christocentric in its focus and purpose. It serves as a philosophical-theological bridge between a philosophical and Neo-platonic ontology of participation and a theological and even Christological ontology of participation.

Anticipating the need for a robust theology of mission that will do justice to Maximus' liturgical sweep of cosmic history, I found it helpful to look to the founder of Methodism, John Wesley in order to flesh out some of the soteriological and missiological implications of an ontology or onto-epistemology[15] of participation. The study argues that there are many similarities between the two saints, drawing some comparisons between Wesley's theology of grace and Maximus' understanding of participation in the *logoi*. The compatible visions of these two men are integrated into an onto-epistemology and theology of participation. Participation could be incorporated into a theology of mission with sanctification in the image of Christ or *theosis* as its goal with Maximus, and both can contribute to constructing a soteriology that is directed towards *theosis*[16] or sanctification in the image of Christ. A soteriology, or cosmic theology whose thrust is sanctification as new creation, can be instrumental to informing and directing a theology of mission.

In the final chapter, I examine the impact of an onto-epistemology of participation on four areas of mission theology, the Trinity, creation, the Incarnation and the new creation. Mission begins with the mission of the Trinity (*missio Trinitatis*). The church, through its baptism into and participation in Christ's death, burial and Resurrection, is called to participate in mission with God. The church discovers that through creation's participation in God, there is a universal witness of God through creation in the context of culture. As the Spirit of Christ seeks to incarnate the message of the gospel into a particular cultural context, so the church co-working with God explores what critical contextualization looks like in each unique setting. When the Word becomes contextual flesh and dwells among the people, the Spirit comes and exegetes the will of the Father in grace and truth, embodies it, and applies it locally within a specific cultural framework. God's grace affirms and builds upon God's universal witness through the *logoi*. The Word informs the remnants of a local, cultural grammar that still echo God's revelation and intention in creation, law, and redemption. The prophetic work of the Spirit that comes to convince the world of sin reveals similarity, dissimilarity and lapse from the gospel, a process that is discerned and witnessed to by both the local and global church as the gospel is shared.

Finally, the message of cosmic transformation[17] in Christ is presented in a holistic way that involves a comprehensive understanding and offering of salvation (*soteria*). The role of the Holy Spirit in mission takes a primary place, as the Spirit seeks to bring persons and communities to Christ through the person and ministry of Christ that are offered universally. The mission and goal of the Spirit, and thus the church is nothing less than the universe transformed into a new creation in the image, or icon, of Christ.

Notes

[1] In Von Balthasar's *Theo-Logic: The Truth of the World,* he describes the subjective , personal or contextual dimension of knowledge requires a posture of receptivity and servitude if one is to apprehend what is to be known.

[2] Adolf Harnack, and others who have followed his lead, posited a thesis that Christianity was corrupted by Hellenism through Platonic syncretism. Surely, there were many grave errors within Constantinianism and examples of Platonic syncretism, such as certain doctrines of Origen , but this writer's holds that the church was able to contextualize the Gospel within the site of the Greco-Roman world with a greater degree of success than Harnack would acknowledge, specifically in the symbols of faith like the Creed. See Jaroslav

Pelikan's *Christianity and Classical Culture* for a balanced treatment of Christianity's encounter with the classical world.

[3] Of course Scripture does not speak specifically in such philosophical terms, but nonetheless, there are ontological implications to the existence of God and creation.

[4] David Bentley Hart addresses the latest incarnation of the modernist specter of atheism in *Atheist Delusions*. I believe that atheism and nihilism are the two most contagious and powerful epidemic and fatal diseases that the postmodern world has inherited from modernism and are really the only true challenges to Christianity today besides its own practical hypocrisy.

[5] In *The Named God and the Question of Being*, Stanley Grenz constructs a worthy Trinitarian Theo-Ontology that follows a similar trajectory as this work.

[6] As of late, Canonical Theism, under the direction of William Abraham and others, feels that Christian theism does not stake any claim or have any interest in any particular epistemology or the right epistemology in order to support itself, to which I would agree. However, this movement would even make the claim that the Apostles and the Church Fathers did not give us an epistemology when they gave us the canons of faith. Of course, the early Christian tradition could not have modern concerns in mind, but I do believe that it did step on epistemological territory when it hammered out the symbols of faith for example. "Credo" is an epistemological claim. I do not think it is possible to claims epistemological immunity.

[7] Works like *Transforming Mission* by David Bosch and *Missiological Implications of Epistemological Shifts* by Paul Hiebert have been two such seminal works.

[8] Hiebert's *Missiological Implications of Epistemological Shifts* and *To Stake a Claim* edited by Andrew Kirk and Kevin Vanhoozer.

[9] From late medievalism into modernism and postmodernism, epistemological, or knowledge-oriented issues, have driven much of philosophy, and autonomous reason has come under heavy scrutiny and condemnation for its failure to deliver truth, knowledge, justification and certainty. Epistemology has become the first question in philosophy, or what is called "first philosophy".

[10] Metaphyics has been sort of a rational stepchild of theology, and with Scotus, became a field of its own with its attempts at natural theology. Ontology then became a subdivision of metaphysics pondering the science of being, even the being of God. Thus, philosophically and historically there is a natural connection between ontology and theology, not that theology should be replaced or defined by ontology, hence Heidegger's indictment of onto-theology, but that ontology should be defined by theology, a theo-ontology. I believe the way of ontology is the philosophical reconnection with theology, but first epistemology must recover its ontological moorings.

[11] The vision of *methexis,* or participation, finds its origins in Plato and has its later developments in Middle and Neo-Platonism. Participation in this sense is an onto-epistemological picture of reality in which particular things participate and are truly known in their ideal forms, which are in turn united in the Good. Many of the early church fathers would rework this framework in order to understand the relationship between Creator and creation. Participation then takes on a similar role as covenant.

[12] "Suspension" is a term found in Radical Orthodox metaphysics that depicts the participatory connection between creation and God. I am using this usage as well as extending the metaphor to describe the dependent nature of created being upon the transcendent, that it finds no ground or foundation in itself, either ontologically or epistemologically.

[13] Above all in reconnecting creation to Creator, I am pushing for a revival of transcendence. I will use the words "transcendent" and "transcendence" frequently in reference to

being, either that which is outside of self or that which is outside of the world. By these terms depending on context, I may mean alterity as transcendence as in the difference of the other outside of self, or I may mean phenomenological transcendence, that which is outside of, external to, or above the subjective consciousness, empirical ego or natural standpoint horizon, or I may mean a theological transcendence in term of outside of, external to, or above creation or the world in terms of the Divine (God's absolute otherness), or both its phenomenological and theological sense. Usage and interpretation will depend on the context. I will also use the words "transcendental," referring at times to Kant's critical usage and those after him who use it as such, or at times in the Aristotelian and medieval sense of the transcendentals (being, unity, truth, goodness, and beauty). Context determines usage.

[14] *Logoi* is the plural form of *Logos* which can mean "word" or "reason." St. Maximus used *logoi* to signify the reason or purpose of being of a thing according to God's plan.

[15] Onto-epistemology refers to an epistemology that is dependent on and shaped by an ontological relationship or its relationship with being. In modernism and postmodernism, epistemological constructs are often central to a vision of reality in which autonomous reason, semiotics (signs) or hermeneutics take on an ontological role. Ontology becomes deflated, and epistemology is inflated. No longer is ontology related to the transcendent or to God but is enclosed in an epistemological construct. In an onto-epistemology, knowledge is relational to being, in this case an analogy of being, and to God.

[16] *Theosis* is a theological term frequently used in Eastern Christian thinking that refers to the process and final state of being made like God. Although not synonymous with the term sanctification, it is comparable, and thus I use them together. I also use the term *theosis* "comparably" with Christ-likeness. These terms also are not synonymous or formally equivalent.

[17] Throughout the dissertation I employ a theological grammar that draws from Eastern Christianity. In this case "cosmic transformation," my term, is a general theme used by Maximus the Confessor and other Eastern theologians to convey the idea of God's concern for the whole of creation, and his desire to bring forth a new creation through the Incarnation and redemption in Jesus Christ.

Chapter One:

Some of the Problem

He himself is before all things, and in him all things hold together[1] *(Col. 1:17)*

A Case of an Ontology of Violence

Fifteen years ago, I began to serve as the pastor of an inner city church that was dying and ready to close. In order to discern the hand of God and to turn the church around, I realized that we had to target new people groups like the growing African-American contingency that inhabited the community not only to "save" the church but also to be where God was already moving in God's mission field. The congregation, which was white, middle-class and had moved out to the suburbs in the 1960s, became disconnected from the community and was driving in from the suburbs to attend church. In trying to reach African-Americans, I sought to implement many structural and cultural changes in the church, good old contextualization.

Things got tense when I removed the sacred cow, the Warner Sallman picture of a lily, whiteJesus that hung over the altar table and had been there for years. Its presence was legendary in that church. I let the disgruntled parties know that we do not know the color of Jesus' skin, but as a Semitic man from the crossroads of Africa and Asia, he probably was not lily white. I also let them know that portraying Jesus so overtly as white may not be relevant and even a hindrance to African-American seekers. I was then informed that Jesus was white and that was a fact. Some of the ensuing conversation fell along the lines of "Jesus couldn't be black because he was God." The implication was that being black was inferior to being white. These insights were part of a whole host of other comments that fit into a larger narrative of race that they embraced. They were suspicious of anyone who darker than they were, including me the Pastor, and they were frank in vocalizing it. They also felt that their racial homogeneity was an essential element to the nature and life of *their* church and needed to be canonized and preserved as much as the apostolic faith itself.

Local church epistemology was shaping a theory of race that was hindering God's mission. This line of thinking is not new. It was similar to the ideology that kept blacks enslaved over a century ago. Freed slave Henry Bibb records in his narrative how blacks had little opportunity for moral education. There were no Sunday schools for blacks, and the only Bible exposition heard by slaves was one that divinely legitimized the dreadful institution of slavery and proclaimed eternal judgment for those that refused to obey their masters (Bibb 1999:17). A theory of race and enslavement institutionalized, and perpetuated in the narratives of the dominant culture.

Kelly Brown Douglas calls the church in Bibb's experience "slaveholding Christianity." Slaveholding Christianity operated out of a theology that upheld and justified the institution of slavery and was centered on a white Christ (Douglas 1994:10). The white Christ allowed for others Christians to be enslaved and construed Christianity in a way that made it compatible with slaveholding (1994:12). Douglas recognizes that this system was undergirded by a "wider ideological structure which presupposed that hierarchical relationships between human beings were divinely ordered" (1994:10).

Even Thomas Jefferson, whose pen codified for the United States the equality of all men in the *Declaration*, was part of that ideological institution. Douglas cites Jefferson for espousing black inferiority in his claim that the white race possessed more beauty and nobility than the black race (1994:11). Cornel West also cites Jefferson for claiming that blacks are inferior to whites in "memory, reason, and imagination" (West 1982:62).

West traces the doctrine of white supremacy and racism to modern discourses that are based on a rational epistemology that has characterized scientism since the Enlightenment. West writes, "...the very structure of modern discourse at its inception produced forms of rationality, scientificity, and objectivity as well as aesthetic and cultural ideals which require the constitution of the idea of white supremacy" (West 1982:47). West uncovers the epistemological roots of the modern discourse in Cartesian scientific philosophy and Greek ocular metaphors that promote and encourage the "activities of observing, comparing, measuring and ordering the physical characteristics of human bodies," quantifying, qualifying and evaluating (1982:48-49). Cartesian philosophy granted the perceiving subject a value-free position of quasi-omniscience through supposedly innate ideas that brought order to the observed world, a world that rested as object before the knowing subject. Descartes' method was mathematical exactitude serving the goal of developing a science that represents the observable world.

Greek ocular metaphors and classical ideals of beauty and proportion were used by Descartes to give his philosophy the position of the "mind as the mirror of nature," an inner eye of all-knowing (1982:53). According to West, Rene Descartes' epistemology was foundational for modern science, and even gave way to other alleged sciences that were developing at that time around ethnicity and anthropology. Certain pseudo-sciences sought to apply the "classificatory categories and the descriptive, representational, order-imposing aims of science into natural history" (1982:55). Thus, the category of race as denoted by skin color in the modern sense became the means of classifying human bodies as early as 1684 (1982:55).

West continues to describe the influence rational epistemology had upon white supremacy and racism in the chapter entitled "a Genealogy of Modern Racism" from the book *Prophesy Deliverance!* (1982:47). Much of that discussion goes beyond the scope of this study, but the point is clear. The institution of slavery in the West is an example of an epistemological breakdown that has affected the Western world as well as the Christian missional enterprise with its temptation to fall into cultural imperialism. West recognizes that a certain rational totalization created a hegemony that oppressed and marginalized. He locates the institution of modern Western slavery in modern epistemology. Of course, the causes of slavery are manifold and involve a complexity of issues. However, this writer agrees, at some level, with West that a crisis in epistemology, at least in part, is connected with Western slavery and other hegemonic institutions.[2] Philosophers such as Friedrich Nietzsche (1844-1900) and Michel Foucault (1926-1984) have also emphasized the role that modern epistemology has played in exploitation, power and control. Rationalism becomes a tool crafted by a people group for its own purposes at the expense of another group that is considered to be less than rational and less valuable. The Cartesian *Cogito,* "I think therefore I am," creates an ontological, individualized space that is defined by a thinking subject, and a thinking subject defines all ontological space. Autonomous reason, reason detached from ontological participation in God or anything transcendent, plays God, and makes the rules.

This example of rationalism and slavery is one example of a larger problem of epistemology taking on metaphysical proportions. Many call it an "epistemological crisis" (Kirk 1999:157). However, it is a conclusion of this research that a breakdown in epistemology is merely a symptom of a deeper problem, a problem that is an ontological problem with epistemological and theological consequences, consequences that extend from philosophy to theology to the practice of mission.

Deflated Ontologies and Closed-Systems

In the past Christian theology of mission has often adopted its epistemologies from the periods of the Scientific Revolution and the Enlightenment. As reason and science advanced technology in the Western world, so also Western nations exercised their power through the conquest and colonization of other nations in the Eastern and Southern hemispheres. The church, which often operated out of the same rationalism and positivism, was often mixed-up with the state in the same type of exploitation. However, since the advent of postmodernism, modern, foundationalist epistemology[3] has been seriously challenged in its high claims to objectivity, certainty, and totality. Postmodernism has provided a much needed critique of modernism's claims of pure autonomous and absolute reason and thus its conquests. Yet in terms of constructing epistemologies that are compatible with a scriptural worldview of God and the created order, postmodernism has often come short.

In attempts to tone down the exaggerated claims of modernism, postmodern epistemology has often reduced reality to a closed-system in which God is locked out of our everyday world or not needed. One of the consequences of modern epistemology has been the virtual canonization of atheism across academic disciplines and even with public life and popular culture. I feel that one of the reasons for making atheism a type of natural given is that modern epistemologies have reduced the understanding of reality to a closed, self-sufficient, natural system that is understood through a singular lens of the text, language or the sign, or a total matter of hermeneutics or interpretation.[4] A single category or epistemic device, such as "the text," "power," or "the sign" is employed to explain all of reality. In a closed-system, epistemology, specifically hermeneutics, takes center stage and any sense of transcendence or ontology of transcendence is "deflated" or excluded,[5] what I call deflationary ontology. For example, we see this in some forms of hermeneutics that follow Heidegger's or Derrida's deconstructing the whole of Western metaphysics,[6] in which it seems that every structure of transcendent being is deflated and reduced to text, sign or code. Epistemology and subjective hermeneutics end up taking on the role of "first philosophy," which has traditionally been occupied by metaphysics. This research assumes the importance and precedence of ontology in informing epistemological concerns.

What happens when ontology is detached from God and is located in epistemic structures, like the *Cogito,* the transcendental ego, the analytic of consciousness in phenomenology, or in the text or the sign? What happens when ontology is detached from God and collapses under its own weight, a weight that is grounded in nothingness?[7] Transcendence, in the true sense, is drained into immanence and a quest begins to find certainty, meaning, and truth in the centrality of epistemology. The Western world enters into a crisis of certainty about what is. Ultimately, the issue at hand is an *ontological* crisis with epistemological repercussions. Being, or other ontological categories, cannot be supported (or is denied) and shrinks into its modes of apprehension, epistemic construals groping to shape the ontological structure that is no longer there, a sort of virtual epistemology reifying ontology.[8] Radical Orthodox thinker Conor Cunningham identifies this breakdown in terms of nihilism, an ontology of nothingness that traces its genealogy from the end of Scholasticism to postmodernism (Cunningham 2002).

The genealogy may look something like this. From Scotus' univocity of being[9] to Ockham's nominalism,[10] to Descartes' *Cogito*, to Kant's epistemic dualism[11] and categorical imperative,[12] to Nietzsche's will to power,[13] to Derrida's closed ontological text,[14] and to other closed hermeneutical systems developed in postmodern thinking, epistemology has sought to ground reality in reductive foundations and non-foundations that ultimately hang from an ontology of nothingness, a *meontology,* a univocity of non-being (Smith 2003:186-187; see also Cunningham 2002:xv,240).[15] While looking back on such a genealogy of pure, autonomous reason, Foucault may unearth hidden power plays, but Cunningham uncovers the DNA of such a genealogy, nihilism. According to Cunningham and other Radical Orthodox scholars, the modern and postmodern univocity of being offers a groundless ground that roots every rational structure in nothingness. These rational structures become closed and self-referential in that they are closed to any ontological transcendence and thus resort to their own sign system or language game for meaning or even deferral of meaning. James K.A. Smith calls such a closed-system an "ontology of immanence," immanence in this sense implying also implosion (Smith 2004:187-188). Ultimately, it seems that the only logical possibilities are theism or pantheism, or nihilism, the latter two being the results of univocal being. Radical Orthodoxy understands the dilemma as theism or nihilism.

The results of closed-system hermeneutical epistemologies "hanging" from ontologies of nothingness are manifold. The first is nihilism itself (Milbank 1990:278) (Cunningham 2002: xiii). The created order, and specifically rational systems, within a univocity of being that is separated from a transcendent God, no longer participate in God in an ontological sense. The created order is then immanently dependent on its own being, which apart from God in a traditional view of creation is *ex nihilo* or *nihil*. Any order cannot hold together, but becomes an autonomous closed sphere that implodes under its own ontological nothingness. Like a collapsing black hole, nothing can sustain. No semiotic structure can ultimately hold up but is swallowed up in the void. Nihilism is prophetically a philosophy of death.

The second result of a univocal, closed-system is nihilism and an ontology of violence (Milbank 1990: 279). John Milbank notes that many philosophers within the geneaology of nihilism interpret all metaphysical and ontological claims as violent. If, according to Nietzsche, a hermeneutic of suspicion concerning knowledge and power is necessary to unlock the meaning of Western epistemology, then every view is inherently violent. Every claim is violent, and every claim is a claim to power. There can be no notion of true difference. Violence totalizes everything. Violence as a wafare *a priori*, becomes the key analytic to unlocking the suspicious intentions of those who claim knowledge. A power play is necessarily subterranean to any construct. Nihilistic ontologies of violence inevitably produce competing systems of ratio-empirical geo-politics that wrestle for hegemony. For Milbank and a growing Radical Orthodoxy, outside of an ontology of peace, and an *analogia entis*[16] that would communicate such an ontology of peace, violence, or a will to power, becomes an accurate descriptor for the motive behind the pursuit of knowledge. The third result of a closed-system is a denial of the existence or relevance of anything that is categorically metaphysical, or anything comparable, or any supra-categories or realist categories, including God, metaphysics, being, the transcendentals,[17] the supernatural, universals, essence, substance, transcendence, immaterial realitiy or anything that is not material. I am not claiming here the whole assortment of medieval scholastic devices, but somehow knowledge must connect with *some-thing*, whether it is visible and/or invisible. The denial of the visible in terms of denying some form of realism and the invisible, the non-material and the transcendent have been problematic for philosophy and theology for the last few hundred years. Christian theism that holds to a real creation cannot but hold to some form of realism.

What happens when theology, and specifically a theology of mission, is based on an epistemology without an ontological base in the transcendent? A Western rationalist epistemology that has been foundational to the development of culture, science and industry over the last 400 years has also given rise to racist, colonialist, and imperialist political regimes that have exploited peoples in Africa, Southeast Asia, Latin America and in other places throughout the two-thirds or majority world. Further, this same epistemology has been foundational to Western Christian mission theology and practice, and the results are mixed.

South African missiologist David Bosch (1929-1992) showed how a hegemonic sense of reason and science in the Enlightenment was adopted into the church's theology as the measure of truth, thus setting the bar of certainty too high for absolute verification (Bosch 1991:262-345). Truth became the equivalent of fact, and fact was propositional, logical and, most of all, judged by the human subject using accepted canons of reason. Faith and reason were placed side by side and increasingly it was faith that would have to pass the test of reason (Bosch 2002:269).

As a Western hegemony of anthropocentric ratio-empiricism sought its destiny in possessing the earth through systems of colonization, the church's mission program came to resemble a similar type of science as it replaced traditional evangelism with a *propagatio fidei per scientiam*[18] mission's program, i.e. Leibniz's propagation of Christianity through science or knowledge (Bosch 2002:271). Theology declared itself to be a science founded on Western rationality, which prized itself above other forms of knowledge and culture (Bosch 2002:269). Western rationalism created a hegemony of scientism[19] and technology that enabled colonialism and Christianity to go hand in hand as exploitation and evangelism (Bosch 1991:303-305). The Enlightenment created hegemonies along the lines of the "civilized," who felt it their duty and a service out of their superiority to conquer and civilize the "uncivilized" (Bosch 1991:305,312). Within that same hegemony of reason, it can be seen that difference does imply violence, a "rational" violence which may be understood as the hidden drive behind global manifest destinies.

As mentioned, Nietzsche and Foucault offer a will-to-power hermeneutic for the entire Western rational enterprise, which is an indictment that we must address. It is not only an indictment but also a prophecy. It becomes prophetic because the Western genealogy of rationalism leading to nihilism if perpetuated can only interpret "difference" within an ontology of *violence* (Milbank 1990: 278).[20] Such an ontology is violent on two counts. The first count is that power takes on an *a priori* status. The second count is that power as *the* hermeneutic takes on totalizing status not allowing for any differing claims. Such an indictment may not hold against all theology and mission, but there is enough evidence to take heed. Theoretically, this hermeneutic is more penultimate, as Milbank interprets this "will to power" assessment of history as one that does not allow difference due to the totalizing claim of such a hermeneutic (Milbank 1990:278). It may be descriptive to a great degree, but prescriptively Milbank seeks other options that will not necessitate such a violent *a priori*. I will explore the option of participation in depth in the second chapter.

Missional Impact

As I noted above, not all modernism is bad. It has brought us many blessings as well as cursing. In terms of the great modern mission movement, many have come to Christ, the gospel has spread and churches have been planted. However, the effort at times continues to be tainted by a pragmatic, rationalistic and instrumental scientism that can produce militant technologies of imperialistic, racist, and ethnocentric ideologies and practices that value Western cultural expressions and semiotic systems over those that express cultural "difference." A triumphal theology based on a Western construal of reason often went hand in hand with the geo-political triumph of Western colonial powers. Non-Western culture was seen as inferior, and the doctrine of *tabula rasa*[21] was implemented (Hiebert, Shaw and Tienou 1999:19). This doctrine stated that nothing could be salvaged from non-Western culture. There was no universeral witness of God and point of contact for the gospel. The missionary would have to start with a "clean slate." Wherever this occurred, people groups and nations were converted for the wrong reasons and often with the wrong methods, by foreign or exploitive means, and often converted to a gospel of rational propositionalism, Western syncretism. Split-level Christianity[22], a dualism of Western Christian form enveloping non-Western indigenous meaning, was the result of a gospel that ignored indigenous culture and pretended to begin with a *tabula rasa* (Hiebert, Shaw and Tienou 1999:19-21). The Western mission project involved negating traditional worldviews and colonizing the mind (wa Thiong'o 1986:3; see also Comaroff and Comaroff 1991). Totalization[23] of worldview left no room for contextualization during the bulk of the modern mission period.

Some Biases along the Way

I will lay my cards down up front. I am a Christian. I am an ordained Elder and Pastor in the United Methodist Church. I am a theologian at heart and by trade with a strong philosophical bent. My Christianity is a gathering from the storehouse of treasures old and new, in that I place a high value on Holy Tradition, including the Scripture, the apostolic faith, the symbols of faith, and all things canonical. Although I feel a strong affinity for traditional expressions of the faith within Eastern Orthodox and Catholic Christianity, I am an evangelical Methodist that is baptized in the Holy Spirit as in the Pentecostal-Charismatic idiom. Spiritually I have a passion for experiencing the transcendence of God within creation and through the indwelling fire and power of the Holy Spirit. These and other influences are my biases from my overall standpoint.

Specifically, one key assumption in this research is that ontology influences epistemology; whereas in many modern and postmodern systems, epistemology takes center stage without ontological considerations. Epistemology makes a significant impact on theology, and theology impacts practice, especially in mission where theology is most practical. Often epistemic foundations for theology are borrowed uncritically and taken wholesale. Only later do students of mission find flaws and problems that arise in the practice of that theology. This research will evaluate modern thinking, particularly Descartes, Kant, Husserl and postmodern thinking specifically identifying various ontological problems that affect epistemology and hermeneutics. In the fact that my critique focuses on ontology and how ontology informs epistemology, it is helpful to note that my perspective addresses some continental[24] currents of epistemology more than those of the analytic tradition.[25] It does not mean that this research is void of analytical concerns. The implications touch on many facets of analytical philosophy, and some of my claims indicate the need for virtue, proper participation (playing off Plantinga's idea of function), the recognition of fallibilism, and the context of knowledge within a research or canonical tradition. Having said all of that, my philosophical approach is primarily from a continental sensibility that is aware of the developments of phenomenology over the last one hundred years and combined with remixes of classical and medieval metaphysics and strong convictions from the Nicene symbol and Eastern Christian and Wesleyan theological traditions. Following cursory ontological critiques of modernism and postmodernism, this research analyzes and evaluates these movements through the theological framework of Radical Orthodoxy[26] as part of an ontology of *participation* and a solution to the onto-epistemological problem in modern and postmodern thinking. This move reveals my theological predilection towards all philosophy.

This work attempts to develop more theologically the Radical Orthodox model of an ontologically based epistemology of participation by incorporating some of the work of St. Maximus the Confessor and John Wesley. The Radical Orthodox "participation in God" (*metousia Theou*) ontology has some of its roots in Platonism and Neoplatonism. Maximus the Confessor attempted to extract the concept from its Neoplatonist moorings and transplanted it in *Logos*-based thinking (*metousia Logo*). Maximus' *metousia Logo* model of participation along with the Incarnation and other Eastern Christian soteriological themes will be examined, including *theosis* and cosmic restoration. These pursuits reveal that the heart of Christian theology is located in its soteriological efforts and specifically in terms of holiness

Further soteriological consequences will be developed from Wesleyan theology and its version of "participation" found in universal grace and Wesley's *ordo salutis*.[27] Maximus and Wesley are employed to bring a theological and Christian shape to this universal category of ontological participation, as I go on to examine how the *missio Trinitatis* has utilized this universal category as a vehicle for the gospel and can do so today in a theology of mission. Although I believe the true beginning of all things is the Word, I know that incarnation and mission involve the flesh and contextualization, and hence the needs to find a supracultural and universal witness of God in creation not just in theology but also in philosophy, and not just Western philosophy but in wisdom cross-culturally.

In the concluding chapter, my passion as a missiologist, pastor, evangelist, and disciple-maker are made practical, as some implications for a theology of mission will be proposed based upon an onto-epistemology of participation, as a model for identifying, analyzing, and theologizing around a universal witness and moving to Christocentric critical contextualization of the gospel. A Christian ontology of participation needs to reflect the Triune nature of God. *Missio Trinitatis* will give shape to a mission theology that highlights three key elements: creation, Incarnation and new creation. A high theology of creation recognizes the universal witness of the Logos in creation to all cultures. A centralized theology and methodology of the Incarnation provides the grounds for contextualization of the message for the purpose of cosmic deification through Jesus Christ. A theology of new creation in Christ manifesting a realized and hope-filled eschatology will provide direction and content to the church and its mission.

Notes

[1] All biblical quotations from the New Revised Standard Version, unless otherwise noted.

[2] Clearly, hegemonic epistemology is partly to blame for the evil of slavery. A multitude of socio-political and economic factors can be cited, but hatred in the heart towards fellow human beings stands above all others.

[3] Foundationalism is a type of epistemology which is built like a house. It requires a foundation which can be justified by self-evident truths (strong foundationalism) or basic beliefs that can be reasonably admitted without self-evident proof (weak foundationalism) in order to build a justified and defensible system of knowledge.

[4] A "closed-system" is a philosophy, specifically ontology, that is unconnected to transcendent being. I frequently use the term "closed-system" for those epistemological constructs that interpret reality in singular and sometimes plural terms that lack transcendence, external reference, or an ontological basis in the larger created order and are often subject to reductionism, totalization and the fallacy of self reference.

[5] Hans-Georg Gadamer is a twentieth century figure who represents this transition of epistemology to hermeneutics. Hermeneutics somewhat becomes first philosophy. Gadamer identifies the site of ontology within a historical and linguistic tradition. Gadmer's rejection of positivism, historicism, or any Hegelian unfolding of pure objective spirit and his recognition of the situatedness, conditions, and pre-understanding in our interpretive efforts are a significant breakthrough. However, is the existential location of *da sein* expressed in language all that is to be understood in our interpreting? Again, ontology is deflated of its transcendence.

[6] Hans-Georg Gadamer is a twentieth century figure who represents this transition of epistemology to hermeneutics. Hermeneutics becomes first philosophy.

[7] Though some 'theological phenomenologists' like Jean-Luc Marion believe that God is without being and seek a phenomenological analytic like "givenness," this writer holds a basic belief that God exists in an analogical sense to our existence and has created all things. Without an ontological reference to God, *nothing* can exist, hence *nothingness*. I hold this belief to be basic based on a responsible faith that understands that this knowledge is an interaction of a fiduciary experience that is connected with reasonable evidence in scripture and creation that is gathered and processed from the proper function, reliability and virtue of the individual and the community-tradition of the church within God's created

order that has faithfull transmitted, witnessed and practiced the truth of the apostolic faith in the resurrected Christ as a holy canonical tradition.

[8] In other words, epistemology tries to do the work of ontology or becomes a ruse for ontology.

[9] In medieval theology predication or statements of attribution or relationality concerning God and creation were said to be univocal, analogical or equivocal. Univocal statements signified that what was said of God and creation was the same or of "one voice." Analogical statements signified that what was said of God and creation were analogous or similar or comparable to a proportion but not the same. Equivocal statements signified that what was said of God and creation were not equal or even similar but different in nature. Aquinas held that talk of being in the created order and being in God are analogous, while Scotus held that being was a predication equally shared by God and creation. Both God and creation have being in the same way. With univocal being, being was raised to a category above God in that both God and creation shared in it.

[10] Nominalism is the notion that universals exist only in name and not independently from particulars or in particulars.

[11] Kant separated how we know things. We cannot know the thing in-itself (noumena). We can only know the thing through perception as our minds give shape and meaning to it (phenomena).

[12] For Kant, the categorical imperative was the absolute moral law, the "ought to" or duty of the individual acting for all humanity that defines all rational, moral conduct for all.

[13] Nietzsche understood all knowledge claims as merely an assertion of power.

[14] Much has been said and misunderstood about Derrida's famous dictum that "There is nothing outside of the text." In Derrida, the text defines reality or rather is the sole reality. My claim is that he gives the text ontological status in doing this. I concur with a textual nature of mediation, but if the text or linguistic mediation is not somehow connected to the Logos, then it is grounded in or suspended from nothingness.

[15] Cunningham turns Scotus' univocity of being on its head. Since the created order cannot have being apart from God as its own attribute, that is univocally, then ultimately the created order does not have being but non-being or nothing. Cunningham calls the offspring ontologies of Scotus' univocity of being, "meontologies," meaning ontologies that take *nothing* and make it into a *something*. Meontology is the heart of nihilism.

[16] Latin for "analogy of being"

[17] The transcendentals for Scholastics, like Aquinas, were the one, the true, the good, and the beautiful which are all derivations from being.

[18] Latin for "Propagation of the Faith through Science"

[19] Scientism is a term describing the often exaggerated confidence and faith placed in the empirical sciences to arrive at absolute knowledge, incorrigible certainty, to solve all human problems, or to attain a unified knowledge of everything.

[20] Milbank plays off of the postmodern attraction toward difference and uses it as a critique of Nietzsche and post-Nietzschean thinkers who hold that all knowledge claims are assertions of power or violence. Milbank calls such a totalization an ontology of violence. Since *all* claims are said to be violent, then there is no *difference*. Different claims are really all the same, violent. Milbank claims that with many post-Nietzscheans, difference is violence, and this goes against the postmodern appreciation of difference. Milbank turns to Christianity for an ontology of peace.

[21] Latin for "clean slate." Used by empiricists like John Locke but was applied to missiology to point out that nothing of the receptor culture could be used in the sharing of the

Some of the Problem   25

gospel. Mission was to start with a "clean slate" and eliminate any cultural points of contact.

[22] The notion that converts are often not converted at the worldview level and may convert to a foreign cultural form of Christianity on the top or outer level, but the bottom or deeper level of conversion at the worldview level may go untouched. Thus, one finds the proverbial villager who responded to an altar call, sings Western hymns like "Victory in Jesus," has a rational, propositional adherence to Christianity but at night visits the witch doctor for healing or th shaman for exorcism.

[23] In areas of needed plurality, when a theory or practice is said fully to account for, explain, reduce or dominate, what "All is this or that," leaving no other account, explanation, or voice, it can be said to totalize, totalization.

[24] Here is a brief overview and an oversimplification. Philosophy has frequently been divided into two camps, analytic and continental. Analytic philosophy is more prevalent among Anglo-Americans and is preoccupied with explanation, specifically employing logic and language in foundational, coherent, or pragmatic forms of epistemology, though most analytic philosophers are foundationalists. Continental philosophy, of course, is prevalent on the European continent and is preoccupied with interpretation. Thus it is immersed in hermeneutics, semiotics, and critical theory. The two schools have different interests and methodologies and rarely converge (Richard Rorty has been an exception).

[25] My opinion is that analytic philosophy generally represents more of the "science" of philosophy, and continental philosophy represents more of the "art" of philosophy. I feel that analytic philosophy, in spite of recent developments, is still too bound in Cartesianism with its reduction of philosophy and the "knower" to mathematical reason, cognition, and the individual. Continental philosophy seems to be more fluid in its operations, especially in its working with ontological problems like being and non-being, and, for me, is a more conducive language to talk about the interaction between philosophy and theology, rather than the restrictive confines of analytics. I will, in part, use Radical Orthodox thinking as a framework for doing ontology. Although this movement originated as a British movement, it engages continental thinking in continental fashion.

[26] Radical Orthodoxy is a theological movement out of England headed by John Milbank that attempts to define Christianity in theological terms as opposed to sociological, critical, political or otherwise foreign frames of reference. The proponents of the movement are well-versed in Continental philosophy, particularly French phenomenology and highly conversant in Postmodern philosophy as well. One of Radical Orthodoxy's main thesis is that Duns Scotus' proposal of univocal being was the origin of an autonomous creation apart from God and a systematic demise of philosophy and theology into nihilism over the next six hundred plus years.

[27] Latin for "order of salvation."

Chapter Two

Deflationary Ontologies: An Epistemological Crisis within Modernism and Postmodernism

For 'In him we live and move and have our being'; as even some of your own poets have said, 'For we too are his offspring' (Acts 17:28).

As we stand at the beginning of the twenty-first century, we are at a crossroads between or even an overlapping of two worlds, the modern and the postmodern. Truly, we have a foot in both worlds, as modernism has not fully left us, and postmodernism is not a pure breed. Since a claim is that postmodernism was birthed out of the rational excesses of modernity and still bears that rational image, some identify it as "hyper-modernity" (Best and Kellner 1991:30). Yet some understand that postmodernism also marks a radical break from modernism (Merquior quoted in Best and Kellner 1991:29). The old paths and paradigms do not take us where we want to go any more, and we look on them with suspicion. Postmodern thinking is opening up the door to an entirely new vision of reality, which represents an epochal shift from the old to something boldly new.

For example, French postmodern philosopher Jean Baudrillard believes that we are in such a shift now. In his remixing of the Marxist dialectic, Baudrillard understands the historical succession of the image as a "precession of simulacra," that begins with a sacramental representation of the real in medieval times and degenerates in our time to pure simulacra or hyperreality,[1] in which the sign replaces reality and is more real than the referent (Baudrillard 1983:11). For Baudrillard, the shift into hyperrealism is seismic. It marks the end of the symbolic (Lane 2000:35-40), the end of production (Baudrillard 1999:99), the end of history (Horrocks 1999:16 and Best and Kellner 1991:133), and the beginning of the fourth order of simulacra, the fractal stage in which value is recycled and history is reversed on itself, an apocalyptic countdown (Horrocks 1999:21). It is Baudrillard's contention that we are now immersed in this fourth order. Baudrillard's eschatological view of postmodernity is thus more apocalyptic.

At these crossroads of the modern and postmodern, many feel forced to hold fast and defend the old foundations, while others will critique and tear down old structures which impede and move on to more comprehensive models of the new world. This crossroads has divided philosopher and theologian alike. It is my estimation that postmodernism has for a greater part, broken down the epistemological foundations of modernism. Yet only to establish a different sort of rationalism that continues to deflate the nature and value of reality.

This chapter will examine the deflation of ontology by observing the highlights of some modernist epistemologies and some of the critiques that have been leveled against them. Postmodernism has waged the most brutal war against epistemologies of certainty. Are postmodernism's claims valid? Is postmodernism the answer to some of the epistemological problems that we face in a theology of mission? The sampling of epistemologies and ensuing critiques are cursory and in no way exhaustive.

An Ontological Evaluation of Modernism

Descartes and the Enlightenment

For Christians, a good deal of our theology and missiology has been built upon the epistemological foundations of the Enlightenment (Grenz and Franke 2001:29). The main grid through which this research will be analyzing the Enlightenment will be its explicit and/or implicit views on ontology or its theory of being because its implications have traditionally been linked to transcendent reality and to God. The hypothesis is that the Enlightenment tended to focus on epistemology, or theories of knowledge, for certainty rather than focusing on ontology or theories of being; thus, either ignoring ontological reality or reducing it to epistemic constructs. As a result, in theology we move away from the reality of God to how certain we are of our knowledge of God, and then to "how do we know that we know," and how efficiently can we "prove" this knowledge. This ontological critique of modernism is, of course, one reading of the story and one approach to the problem.

According to Grenz and Franke, Enlightenment epistemology or foundationalism, like constructing a building, offers the certitude of a strong foundation. This foundation "consists of either a set of unquestioned beliefs or certain first principles on the basis of which the pursuit of knowledge can proceed. These basic beliefs or first principles are supposedly universal, context-free and available, at least theoretically, to any rational person (2001:30). Reason would offer a self-evident foundation for building a total understanding of reality.

Missiologist David Bosch also seeks to interpret this shift from ontological premises to epistemological self-evident foundations and claims of certainty. He reads the Enlightenment worldview through seven contours with various missiological implications. One is the undisputed primacy of reason, the Cartesian claim - *Cogito ergo sum* (Bosch 1991:264).[2] Whereas in medieval thinking being or ontology took precedence over epistemology, in Descartes it is reason that has primacy. Descartes, through methodological skepticism, sought to find an Archimedean point upon which the universe could be moved and thought he found it in reflective reason.

Before opening fire along with Bosch on Descartes, it is important to recognize that Descartes has been the fall guy for many things that he never did, said, or intended, and I may be contributing to this at some level unaware. Descartes was not an atheist, a demon, an egotist, or any of the other caricatures that have been created. Descartes, symbolically, has come to signify all that is wrong with hyperrationalism, the Enlightenment, and modern individualism[3]. Descartes was an accomplished Renaissance man with interests in math, physics, astronomy, optics, psychology, philosophy, theology and other fields. His motives in the *Meditations* were actually spiritual, theological, and scientific, although his proof of God came after the proof of his own existence[4]. When speaking of Descartes, as do others, I mean to indicate the work of the person, and more so, the consequences of his work posthumously. References here to Descartes are used more symbolically than personally in terms of the development and consequences of his work in his lifetime and after, Descartes as both the symbol that he has become due to the impact of the *Cogito*, shorthand for the dictum *I think therefore I am*. The following quote from the "Third Meditation," that follows the *Cogito* revelation in the "Second Meditation" sums up the *Meditations on First Philosophy* that is that once Descartes was able to establish his own existence through a sort of ontologism of defining himself as one who doubts, he was able to establish God's existence by ontologism, as a perfect being.

> Altogether then, it must be concluded that the mere fact that I exist and have with me an idea of a most perfect being, that is, God, provides a very clear proof that God indeed exists (Descartes 1998:97).

All of that said, there are many consequences of the *Cogito*, but the three most far reaching are the beliefs that all of reality can be known with mathematical certainty through reason, and that the autonomous rational subject is the authority to determine that certainty, and that being can be reduced to a method of thinking. Again, in making Descartes somewhat of a symbol of his time, Bosch also indirectly connects the *Cogito* to the missional impact created by the hegemony of Western rationality in terms of this equation: Rationalism plus Civilization equals Colonization plus Exploitation.

The second contour in Bosch is that the Enlightenment created a *subject-object scheme* (Bosch 1991:264). The human mind (*res cogitans*) was seen as detached from the world (*res extensa*), which it sought then to analyze and understand. The world could be studied as an object of research independently and impartially, and as a result one could analyze, formulize, quantify, and monopolize the object of study. Autonomous human reason became the ontological ground upon which the rest of reality is built. Cartesian dualism not only helped to form the basis for modern empirical sciences, it was also imported by the church in the form of objectifying the mission enterprise and its receptor cultures (1991:264).

Bosch's third contour is that the belief in purpose and even mystery within science is replaced with a rigid cause-effect scheme (1991:265). Causality removes the teleological questions of metaphysics and life, resulting in schemes of determinism and mastery. For the early church fathers up to Thomas, cause and effect was connected ontologically to the purpose and will of God in the *logoi* and *telos*[5] of things as ordered by the free act of God. In the Enlightenment project, purpose is replaced with causality.

The fourth contour is that the Age of Reason brought with it an infatuation with progress, which was believed to result from mastery over nature and the uncivilized (1991:265). Reason further applied beyond the physical realm to the social realm would become a geo-politics of reason Machiavellian style that valued expediency over morality and justified exploitation overseas (1991:266).

The fifth contour is that there is an unresolved tension between "fact" and "value" within Enlightenment thinking. Science held the belief that its knowledge was "factual, value-free and neutral," that somehow knowledge is without a knower; "it is knowledge without a knowing subject" and hence cannot be disputed (Bosch 1991:266). On the other hand, value is based on individual opinion, belief, and preference to which religion is assigned. Yet, religion has come under the bar of reason and presented itself as a science and operated missionally on the basis of principles and laws that justified colonization rationally.

Bosch's sixth contour is the confidence that every problem can be solved (1991:266). Reason's mastery of nature's laws guarantees solutions in life. There are no holes, gaps or mysteries in the conquest of nature, just continuous upward progress, and civilizing the world became the white man's burden. The problems of the universe are not metaphysical or ontological but scientific and ultimately pragmatic. The final contour is that the idea of the emancipated, autonomous individual became the ultimate authority of truth (1991:267). Faith in the individual, in freedom and in autonomous reason superseded faith in God and society.

Through science's discovery of the laws of nature and the power of reason, the secrets of the universe would be unlocked, and humanity would no longer at the mercy of nature, no longer to be encompassed by arbitrary mystery and uncertainty. These benefits, scientific discoveries, were to be accompanied by the great new gift of power, power to control natural forces and to turn them, in Bacon's phrases, to the 'occasions and uses of life,' and the 'relief of man's estate'" (Willey 1953:15). Alexander Pope, in an "Essay on Man," claimed reason has the power to subdue nature (Pope 1951:200). Pope's epigram on Newton summarizes the spirit of the Enlightenment best, "Nature and Nature's laws lay hid in night: God said, *Let Newton be!* And all was light" (1951:203). Newton stole the Promethean fire and illuminated the medieval mind to grasp the workings of the divine. Newton and the whole Enlightenment ate the fruit which fell from the Cartesian tree and opened up the eyes of reason to a *New Atlantis.*[6]

Descartes

Each of these contours described in Bosch is shaped by the seismic shift from ontology to epistemology that is epitomized in Descartes. With the dictum *Cogito ergo sum,* being, in this case a particular instantiation of the self, "I am," is defined by thinking, "I think." Since Descartes sought to think in universal terms and took the role of philosophizing on behalf of us all, then "I am" meant everyone's "I am" and everything's "It is."The ontological question is answered epistemologically by a thinking, individual subject situated in its own assumed acontextual, autonomous self-reference. Prior to William Ockham (ca. 1287-1347), ontology was often prioritized over, provided grounding for, and informed epistemology. Epistemology did not stand on its own or as first philosophy but was intrinsically connected to being as apprehended by the active intellect. However, with Descartes' *Cogito,* ontology is reduced to the thinking subject, the phenomenological ego or autonomous pure reason. Thinking identifies and defines being, thinking in terms of specifically the context-detached subject autonomously thinking in vacuum or attempting to do so. Descartes turns classic and medieval ontology upside down. All hangs from autonomous reason, as opposed to any form of ontological transcendence. God and the rest of the world could only be established once the *Cogito* was founded.

Descartes would open the door for Kantian dualism, the transcendental ego of the German idealists like Fichte, Schelling, and Hegel, and the phenomenology of Husserl, Heidegger and the post-structuralists, and other movements that would further deflate the transcendent, that which is above or outside of the transcendental ego, the empirical ego or the empirical world. This Cartesian inversion of being and thinking intensely advances the collapse of ontology into a closed system of individuated pure reason and subjective consciousness which will eventually express itself in other closed-systems in which linguistical, semiotic, and hermeneutical reductions become conditions for totalization. A "closed system" here associated with Descartes is a totalizing system or theory that is separated from transcendent ontology, specifically divine transcendence, and places at its center the *Cogito*. Of course, Descartes is no atheist, nor is he seeking to deify the self, in fact he sought grounds for greater certainty in all things including our knowledge of God. The problem is that methologically the thinking self is prior to all things including God. The point made is a wholesale condemnation of hard, autonomous rationalism. An autonomous closed-system of individualistic consciousnesses then takes a transcendent and ontological function to explain its vision of reality, a totalizing effect. The world is established on the innate ideas of the ego.

Modernism consists of many narratives, but one narrative is that of the actualization of"self-will."The autonomous reason of the transcendental ego being quasi-defied and its will being the *zeitgeist* of history incarnate in the *ubermensch* may not be dots connected by a razor straight line, but in some way the dots do connect. Following Descartes, the work of epistemology would take center stage for the next four hundred years. Like a dying star collapsing into a black hole, ontology is swallowed up in the Cartesian critical self and nothing can escape its pull. Reason and the individual become the primary elements for a foundation that will build the modern Western world, including the shape of the modern mission project.

As we continue our tour of modernism, we note that the innate rationalism of Descartes is answered by British empiricism. Empirical philosophers like Locke opposed Cartesian innate ideas and focused on the external, empirical world and the data obtained by the sense as the source of knowledge – "Nothing is in the mind that is not first in the senses." Science would advance as a ratio-empirical discipline in the Enlightenment, not one of pure reason. The development of the empirical sciences along with the moral and political developments of Locke, Kant, the French *philisophes*, and others in the areas of the state, the indivudal, freedom, and other civil right would be significant in arming the West to expand its interests and influence over the colonial world.

Science provided the impetus for progress, but progress at times means encroachment. The empirical measuring of the sciences helped to size up the power and wealth of nations, as well as the "inferiority" and poverty of other peoples in a Western imperial and missional enterprise to colonize, civilize, and evangelize. The inflated esteem and sense of importance of Western nations made small and insignificant those who were "unenlightened" and could not compete. Enlightenment science and reason easily became tools for conquering and mastering nature and for nation conquering and nation building within a metanarrative of manifest destiny. The empires of the West grew in part out of a strange brew of the advancement of Christendom and belief in a scientism and its technological fruits that would develop the underdeveloped. Industrialization and the wealth and exploitation of nations would occur where the hegemony of reason was enthroned, and Christianity flourished right alongside, leaving a wake of colonization (Stanley 2001).[7]Again, the narrative offered here is not Descartes' but more the symbol of Descartes.

The narrative however continues. In terms of the theological, empirical science as a function of naturalism also did its part to detach creation from the transcendent, not necessarily as atheism but at least in terms of deism and the functionality of the connection between God and nature. Deism was *the* theology of the Enlightenment. Newton and others discovered the laws that nature obeys, and scientism found a sufficient reason to convert *creation* into autonomous *nature*. Ontologically, nature became a closed system, meaning that in the study of nature no exterior causes would be considered because they could not be observed, quantified or measured. Nature could become an object of conquest for competing ratio-empirical regimes, which in modernity were ultimately expressed as nationalism and imperialism. God distantly watched while the fittest survived by discovering and claiming nature's embedded secrets and trophies of triumph. With a deist God on the sidelines of heaven and Kantian reason enthroned in the earth dictating morality, "Might makes right" could be justified.

With the inflation of science's authority, the universe became reduced to a self sufficient, closed-system without the need of God's "intervention". Scientism deflated the transcendent species of creational ontology into an organic machine of internal perfection apprehended by pure reason. As this collapse was further impelled by Lockean representational ideas,[8] Hume's causal ordering,[9] and Kant's structural categories,[10] epistemology fell more and more into a crisis of identity and certainty, and the task of verifiability piled high. Epistemological participation in the transcendent is severed, and in dying it closes in on itself groping for incorrigible validation, justification and certainty that is self evident in the epistemic structures themselves. Meaning became more and more a horizontal quest. Later twentieth century analytic philosophy and continental postmodernism would tear down Cartesian strong foundationalism, and postmodernism would dismantle the *Cogito* as any type of substantial view of self.[11] Ultimately, the Cartesian *Cogito* could not hold the universe and God together, and in the process would deflate ontology of any transcendence.

Kant

With Kant's critical philosophy, we begin to understand more the nature of this crisis. Kant sought to limit the use of reason and rightfully so. He did so by analyzing metaphysics as a science or in terms of science. Kant believed that metaphysical notions could not hold up under empirical and rational scrutiny beyond antinomies. Kant built upon Descartes who, basically, made conscious-thought transcendental. The formation of knowledge originates with the transcendental thinker, and there can be no metaphysical knowledge beyond this phenomenological horizon. Kant understood knowledge as the joint product of sense intuition from experience wedded with rational conceptualization and constructs that are built into the subject. In this sense, Kant represents a synthesis between Cartesian innate ideas, Leibnizian pre-ordained harmony and the British empiricists' notion of experience and sense data. Knowledge begins out of experience and is shaped by the cognitive faculties. If what is thought to be known is not experienced or in the senses, it cannot truly be known by reason. It is sense intuition that initiates or awakens the faculty of cognition to action and reason. Without experience derived from sense intuition, there is no knowledge, let alone transcendent or metaphysical knowledge. We have no (sense) object that correlates to metaphysics or even a transcendental idea (Kant 1990:212). The only transcendental analytic is the *a priori* pure categories of reason themselves that give shape to experience.

Kant recognized the need for external, empirical sensation, as well as the category of the thinking ego. The Cartesian *Cogito* cannot truly master the universe through its innate ideas of the true nature of things and the dualism of mind and body. For Kant, Descartes' ontological collapse of being into thinking, and the *Cogito* becoming the Archimedean point upon which to 'build back up all' of reality which he had doubted, is really just a transcendental cognitive grid of categories, which subjectively shape the phenomenal world that appears to us. Knowledge's categories are transcendental to knowing.

In reconciling Continental rationalism with British empiricism, Kant posits that things cannot be known in-themselves (*noumena*) only in the sense-intuited *phenomena* (Kant 1990:156-167) and its understanding in the categories. Kant built on an inherited legacy of ontological detachment passed on to the Enlightenment by late Scholastic nominalism that sought to remove unnecessary metaphysical appendages. According to Kant, any supposed reasoning about the transcendent, substantial reality, or the noumenal cannot be ontological or real but merely the apprehension of one's own pure categories of the mind. When we think we know metaphysically, we merely are reflecting on the categories of pure reason (the transcendental aesthetic and transcendental logic). Our error is in thinking we have grasped metaphysical reality because we can reflect on our own transcendental capacities to shape sense experience.

Thus as for metaphysics or an ontology of transcendence, reason is limited and agnostic, which is a needed corrective to hard rationalism but a blow against divine revelation. Transcendence is limited to our own capacity as ego to reason and shape experience, the transcendental. The transcendental thinking ego gives form and meaning to the world as it perceives and intuits the experiential horizon of phenomena and processes it through the transcendental categories of logic and judgment (Kant 1990).

Like as in nominalism, Kant, did not hold to any version of participation in the universals or ideas of God through an *analogia entis* or in any purely analytic categories apart from experience. Rather our active mind participates in constructing phenomena through the stimuli of the senses creating knowledge without real transcendent grounds or reference beyond our own cognitive categories. For Kant, these transcendental Ideas[12] hold no ontic status or connect with any "object" of metaphysics, such as God. Kant would later turn to practical reason - the deontological, the categorical imperative to connect with God. Its impetus would not be found in Cartesian *thinking* but in moral *willing*. Such a move sets the stage for Nietzsche and Foucault, as they would soon uncover the power *motive* of "pure reason" or metaphysics.

Kant's impact on ontology and theology is seismic. We are trapped in a sense-based world with no access to revelation or even metaphysical realities except in delusion. The knowledge of God, the grasp of the supernatural, or contact with any transcendent ground beyond the Ego is nonsensical and without a basis in the senses in Kant's scheme and results in antinomies. The Transcendental Ego through the apperception of the unifying medium of consciousness holds all experience together, grounds it, and gives it form and meaning through its own categories. Anything beyond sense experience remains unknowable. We can see how the development of Descartes' *Cogito* and Kant's Transcendental Ego were formative to the Western construction of the modern, autonomous, free individual, and how these thinkers have practically deified "man" by empowering "him" with rational power to *create* the universe. The universe no longer is suspended from God and participates in his being, but is produced from *above* by the Transcendental Ego, looking down on its own experience of the world below.

I believe Kant's critical philosophy bore heavily on and incarnated through "classical" liberal theology, which sought a critically historico-rational ground as correlative to any theological endeavor. Post-Kantian liberalism is manifest in its ethical incarnation promulgated by Albrecht Ritschl (1822-1889) and Walter Rauschenbusch (1861-1918), in its existential incarnation by Rudolf Bultmann

(1884-1976) and Paul Tillich (1886-1965), and in its historical-critical incarnation as characterized by David Strauss (1808-1874) and later evolving in the twentieth century into two "Quests" for the "historical Jesus.[13] Liberal missiology would suffer from a crisis of identity and purpose as it no longer had a King for its kingdom, a cross for its salvation, or a unique Messiah or message.

Kantian dualism so inflated the critical task that the non-existent noumenal had to be acted on 'as if it were there'. Kant understood ontological claims as "transcendental illusions". The decline of theological liberalism and mainline denominationalism has at least revealed this very thing, the difficulty to save face and sustain an 'ontological superstition'. Of course, I am not saying Christianity is such, but I am saying that classic theological liberalism has sought to act as an authentic expression of the faith while thinking that there is nothing there beyond the practice of the moral imperative. Kantian transcendental Ideas became merely useful fictions in a phenomenal world. Classic theological liberalism still has to reckon with its DNA of Enlightenment rationalism that has produced both an epistemological ground for its theology and radical historical criticism and an epistemological ground for the colonial hegemonies and injustices that it has sought to combat. It would also have to reconcile its docetic, mystical tendencies of its Bultmannian existential theology, which actually came out of the hyper-rationalism of scientistic criticism, and its gravitation towards soteriological materialism found in its adaptation of Marx and social critical theory. It is not the focus of this study to continue along this line, but merely to trace the influence of Kant on his theological offspring and stepchildren.

Post-Kantian theology could not accommodate a historical and ontological Jesus as Christ. It also could not admit the Resurrection as physical or other seeming antinomies of traditional Christianity. Thus it relegated such "mythologies" to existential proclamations that correlate with and speak to our situation, *sitz em leben*[14], and require an ahistorical leap of faith from Jesus to Christ. Then another leap is required from our phenomenological context to a *noumena* of nothingness, where we are faced with our own universal obligation generated out of our own practical reason, which is predicated on moral autonomy and a will to power. Along with the *Cogito*, the categorical imperative became integral to the construction of the modern self, a modern self that became an ontological sphere for many later ideologies, including Freudian psychology, phenomenology, and existentialism that grounded all reality even the historical in the existential experience of the empirical ego.

In my not so graceful efforts, I have sought to trace a systemic ontological deflation that has correspondingly resulted in an epistemological inflation of rational constructs, ie. Kant's categories, that are designed to hold the center, a proposal of virtual epistemologies that are meant to reify being. In the case of Kant, reality is a product of sense perception shaped by transcendental rational categories of the ego. Yet, transcending these categories remains nothing that we can know. Pure reason leaves us with antinomies about metaphysical reality, and apart from the categorical imperative, metaphysics is abolished. With Kant, the process of ontological deflation takes a moral turn into practical reason, which is propped up to bear the heavy metaphysical weight. Under the load of the critical, metaphysical foundations begin to buckle, allowing for the weight of authority to shift to purely rational constructs, while at the same time the increase of authority becomes demanding on such constructs. Autonomous will and reason gain unprecedented authority and uphold the entire modern experiment of Western civilization, while at the same time under an unbearable metaphysical load they begin to deform and give and ultimately give way to nihilism and the despair and *angst* of being upheld by nothing, as is seen in existentialism.[15]

Thus in modernism one can trace a collapse of ontology into epistemology, and in turn, a crisis in epistemology, which helplessly seeks certainty in its own scientific constructions, while all along asserting its authority in the individual and its democratic based modern nation-state and its geo-politics of applied scientism and technology which would greatly impact mission. Existentialism would arise at the end of modernism to critique the privileged autonomy of reason and expose its humanity and subjectivity preparing the way for postmodernity.

An Existentialist Critique of Modernism

One of the major critiques of the Enlightenment came out of late modernism through Existentialism. Existentialism is a backlash of modernism. It is probably not fair to call Existentialism a "movement" or school, making it too intentional or unified. Walter Kaufmann says that "Existentialism is not a philosophy" but a label for several widely different revolts against traditional philosophy" (1975:11). Thus, it has no academic center, such as Paris, Vienna, Tubingen or Oxford. It has no official tenets or doctrine. It is more of an anti-philosophy, and the philosophy it was primarily against was the Enlightenment's version of the absolute and certain nature of reason and particularly determinism. Existentialism is an anti-rationalist posture that was probably first seen in figures like Dostoevsky and Kierkegaard as well as later in a type of phenomenology that finds its roots in Edmund Husserl and Husserl was influenced by the *Cogito* tradition of Descartes, Kant, Fichte, Hegel, Schelling, and Brentano.

Although it is almost impossible to catalogue and package Existentialism into any reducible definite form, one can attempt to characterize its many expressions. First, it is helpful to list some of the thinkers that have been frequently labeled as Existentialists. They include Fyodor Dostoevsky (1821-1881), Soren Kierkegaard (1813-1855), Friedrich Nietzsche (1844-1900), Karl Jaspers (1883-1969), Martin Heidegger (1889-1976), Jose Ortega y Gassett (1883-1955), Maurice Merleau-Ponty (1908-1961), Herni Bergson (1859-1941), Albert Camus (1913-1960), Samuel Beckett (1906-1989), and Jean-Paul Sartre (1905-1980) among others. Some of the characteristics of existential thinking include: a focus on the irrational (Dostoevsky, Nietzsche, Camus, and Beckett), the anxiety and dread of existing (Sartre), the absurdity and meaninglessness of existence (Beckett and Camus), human freedom and choice (Sartre and Heidegger), being in existence, despair, and death (Heidegger), commitment (Kierkegaard and Bergson), authenticity (Kierkegaard, Nietzsche, Ortega y Gassett and Sartre), and subjectivity (Kierkegaard, Nietzsche, Sartre).

Of the many critiques afforded by Existentialism, the most pronounced may be the *humanistic* critique. In one sense, the Enlightenment was humanistic. It certainly celebrated and even exaggerated the status and achievements of humanity, but many of the exponents of Existentialism in bringing the subjective, the experiential, the existential, and the volitional (freedom as opposed to determinism) dimensions of reality back into epistemology have allowed us to see the humanity, that is the limitations, of our epistemic context. Reason could not claim a privileged position of objective autonomy or claim its own ontological ground. Existentialism provided a corrective to a blind spot in rationalism, blindness to the human condition. Knowledge is contingent as are we.

The Enlightenment saw reality as ordered and connected by a great chain of being and each link ran like clockwork in respect to the other. All of nature ran smoothly by the watchmaker's preestablished harmony of laws, including humanity operating by the law of the categorical imperative and the laws of reason. On the other hand, Existentialism saw the world as an absurdity without meaning or purpose, and humanity was not only out of synchronicity with nature but with itself. Alienation is a common theme to describe an existentialist's view of humanity. Humanity just finds itself here as a happenstance without an essence or a direction, a nothingness that is forced to choose its own meaning from a world of meaninglessness. Existentialism exposed and explored this aspect of humanity beneath the façade of the fine-tuned rational machinery of Western civilization. Existential prophets discerned that our knowledge claims were "human, all too human."

As a whole the spirit of Existentialism sought to swing the pendulum of philosophy away from the mechanics of reason and back to "man's inner life, his moods, anxieties, and his decisions that are moved into the center" (Kaufmann 1975:13). Existentialism is clearly a form of humanism, not so much in a classical sense highlighting the grandeur of humanity, but more so the dark side of humanity in its weakness, fallibility, alienation, irrationality, and contradictions. Existentialism, as opposed to the Enlightenment, revealed human limitation, not progress, and it revealed human pain and suffering, not satisfaction. Existentialism put the *human* back in knowledge, something that every epistemology of theology needs to reconsider. While the Enlightenment allowed humanity to see outside of itself, often to a fault, Existentialism allowed humanity to see itself and its struggles in the process of knowing.

Just a cursory look at Existentialism provides one with a starkly contrasting perspective of human nature and the universe than that of the Age of Reason. The existentialist saw that humanity is not in control of nature. Humanity fails to understand itself and is impotent to control its own actions (Exemplified by the absurd characters in Camus' work, namely *The Stranger, the Plague, and the Myth of Sisyphus* and Beckett's work, specifically *Waiting for Godot, The Endgame*, and *The Unnamable*).

Reason is not absolute and exhaustive but struggles with its own inner absurdities and outer contradictions, its human situatedness. Humanity is not merely a thinking thing, a conscious mind that creates the world from its own innate ideas, but is a creature of passion and action, often instinctive, irrational, and inexplicable action. There can be no rational science of the universe for humanity that is at the center of the universe is irrational. Pure objectivity cannot be obtained because humanity always perceives from its own subjective conditions, which are often filled with anxiety and passion. Humanity is an absurdity (Camus), a nihilating nothingness (Sartre) or a useless passion (Sartre) primarily because humanity is free and not predetermined. Kierkegaard illustrates the connection between existential freedom and the irrational in *The Concept of Anxiety* in which he roots disorderd passion, temptation, human sin and the existential human condition of anxiety in the dread caused by the awareness of the infinite choices of our freewill as finite beings. The writing came as a response to his study of Hegel, Leibniz and Descartes and the tension of a rational existential system or science versus human freedom (Kierkegaard1980:vii-viii). Reason is not capable of systemizing the universe or the human condition into a science of determination. Reason itself is part of the human condition of freedom and its own dread has imprisoned it in anxious and irrational passion. The subjective has overtaken and captured the objective. The claims of neutral science are subjective instruments to will (Nietzsche) and to believe (Kierkegaard). The subjectivism highlighted in Existentialism is a precursor to an instrumental view of knowledge and science.

For an existentialist like Kierkegaard, there is no tension between fact and value. When "truth is subjectivity," everything is value (Kierkegaard 1941:170-224). Virtually every point featured by Bosch in an Enlightenment worldview is turned on its head by the existentialist. One of Kierkegaard's responses to Enlightenment claims is the human factor at the base of epistemology. We do not understand things as pure "knowers" who observe reality as an object within the subject-object scheme of the Enlightenment. We are a *part* of that reality. Kierkegaard's *Philosophical Fragments* and *Concluding Unscientific Postscript* are to some extent responses to Hegel's system of dialectical idealism, a crowning achievement of Enlightenment thinking.

Hegel's work is one of the last modern attempts at a purely rational ontology. Hegel's philosophical system of history sought objectively to systematize the concretization of the absolute spirit's movement in the world – the ultimate ontological connection between God and human reason. This system would seek not only to provide rational demonstration of the validity of the Christian faith, but also a historical demonstration of the reign of the spirit of reason (the absolute spirit) in the world (Hegel 1991 and Harris 1995). Hegel's philosophy captures the spirit of the Enlightenment with its focus on absolute reason, objectivity, the application of science to other fields (i.e. history and philosophy), the justification of Western supremacy, and the reign of ideas over the world.

Of course, Kierkegaard takes issue with the whole project, and in *Postscript,* he tackles the idea of objectivity and its impossibility, especially in a historical system due to its "approximate nature" (Kierkegaard 1941:25-47). Since any so-called objective historical system is an approximation, looking backward and is incomplete looking forward, then the nature of the task is impossible (1941: 75 and 98). For Kierkegaard, truth was not something objectively ascertained, but it was a subjective commitment and leap of faith that bore witness to veracity inwardly. He writes, "Truth is inwardness; there is no objective truth, but truth consists in personal appropriation" (1941:71). Kierkegaard echoes somewhat of the epistemological fiduciary tradition of Paul, Augustine and Luther, which we later see recovered in scientist turned philosopher, Michael Polanyi and yet anticipates scientific instrumentalism. I also concur that we are justified by faith and not justified by reason.

Kierkegaard identifies a subjective and human dimension to knowing which cannot create an absolute system, primarily because one is not philosophy in the abstract but an existing, thinking individual and a part of the reality sought to be systematized (1941:108-109). Humans are participants in the knowing process not apart from it. Humans are existential factors in existence. We cannot systemize about it, as if outside of it. Kierkegaard protests that Enlightenment speculative philosophy has abolished the individual human (1941:113). Kierkegaard lifts off the Cartesian blinders and reveals the contextual dimensions of autonomous, absolute reason and its assumed and privileged ontological position.

In a scene in the futuristic movie *The Matrix Reloaded (II)*, Neo, the protagonist, reaches the heart of the Matrix to find the Architect. The Architect wrote the program for the computerized world called the Matrix and sits in a fully white room filled with monitors viewing everything in the Matrix at one time. The Architect is almost an allegorical figure for God or pure reason. The Architect created all; is outside of all; above all; sees all; and knows all. He is able to enjoy a position outside of everything. All of life's happenings, even the thoughts of people are seen objectively before him on multiple screens. This is a kindred picture to the lofty image that Hegel and the Enlightenment had of the self. Hegel is the Architect of a system that rolls up all of history into one big ideological bundle. Yet, Kierkegaard is saying that there is no white room for any individual, except God. There is no privileged epistemic position of absolute certainty. There can be no epistemic or cognitive detachment from being.

The notion expressed by Kierkegaard anticipates Heidegger's understanding of *da sein* (being-there) (Heidegger 1961:8). We are already in existence and aware of it. We begin with this fact or revelation. We are not outside of it or attain to it. Sartre sums it up in his famous dictum "existence precedes essence," reversing the Platonic notion that the *essentia* precedes *existentia*.[16] This suggests that human existence comes before any assigned meaning, and thus that meaning is what humans choose to make it (Kaufman 1975:37). The condition of human freedom and its accompanying anxiety trump any ruse of science, system, order or preestablished meaning.

There is a human factor in knowing, which cannot be mechanized and reduced to pure reason or objectivity. For Existentialism, it begins with our existential location, which for Sartre begins with the phenomenology of human consciousness as a starting place, instead of pure reason or universal *essentia*. Existence is a non-derivative category, a prime datum, from which we begin. Sartre says our existence, our being here, is "*de trop*"- just there - or "gratuitous." For Sartre, existence trumps reason, as he owns what Descartes denies, that is, that an ontology detached from transcendence is an ontology of subjective consciousness and phenomenology and not pure reason (Sartre 1956:8-12; 17-24).

As Sartre evaluated Descartes' *Cogito*, he recognized the personal and existential nature of knowledge. The *Cogito* was not a divine revelation or an epiphany of pure reason that becomes the foundation of all reality or even the product of rational deduction. In *Being and Nothingness*, Sartre uncovers that Descartes' *Cogito* is a "pre-reflective" *cogito* stemming from consciousness itself and not a deduction made out of *reflective* consciousness (Sartre1966:13) The *Cogito* had emerged directly from consciousness, a human and existential context. Consciousness was conscious of the thinking subject. For Sartre, and originally Husserl, consciousness is not neutral or in vacuum but is always consciousness of *something, a* transcendent object, even itself (Sartre 1966:13). Thus in reflection Descartes constructs what he believes to be the analytic that existence is proven in thinking itself, that thinking gives birth to existence or somehow justifies or proves existence, but rather with Sartre it is existence which produces thinking.

After the *Cogito,* Descartes had to reify and infer the rest of the world and even God from the thinking self. For Sartre, the perceiving ego and the world arise in correlation, since consciousness is always *consciousness of something* (Copleston 1965: vol 3:347). Sartre's pre-reflective *Cogito* shifts the primacy of knowledge in Descartes to the primacy of existence, but he also reveals the ontological *locus* of modern and postmodern thought, the perceiving subject (Sartre 1966:17). Sartre recognized that the epistemological problem of modernism in Descartes was an ontological one.

Existentialism marks a movement from knowledge as scientific rational exactitude to knowledge as a product of human condition. In the case of Nietzsche, he understood the context of knowledge through the sensibility of existence as passion and exertion and hence knowledge as a "will to power." For Nietzsche, truth, knowledge, and morality are not something objectively to be found by human reason in nature or in God, but rather are a product of the will, and are used as a means of power (Nietzsche 1939:122-125). What the Enlightenment considered unbiased truths of reason and science, Nietzsche called the will to power, pointing out the human, subjective, self-serving and exerting dimensions of knowledge. With Nietzsche, all knowledge is suspect and value-laden. Nietzsche takes his critique of modern ontology deeper than Kierkegaard or Sartre. Not only does he recognize its human, contextual *locus,* but he also identifies its volitional potential as a super-actualization, *ubermensch,* power as *a priori*. Existentialists like Kierkegaard, Heidegger, Sartre, and Nietzsche sought to disclose the human dimension, and often the depraved human dimension, in philosophy, a dimension that was grossly ignored within the Age of Reason. Postmodern thinking would get much mileage out of Nietzsche.

An Ontological Evaluation of Existentialism

The existentialist or humanist critique unmasked the Enlightenment illusion that reason holds a privileged ontological position of God-like absoluteness and objectivity. Existentialism reveals the socio-existential location of knowledge in the human context. Consciousness of the phenomenological becomes central to the existential vision of reality. Phenomenology and its offspring Existentialism have more of an ontological preoccupation than did Descartes, Kant, or the Enlightenment as a whole. Consciousness becomes ontological.The shift is from knowing to existence or being. Conscious existence becomes transcendental and a starting point in Husserl, Heidegger, or Sartre rather than the *Cogito* or categories of knowledge. Husserl's ontology was located in the being of the individual, the ego, and its consciousness – the Transcendental ego. Heidegger, never considered himself an existentialist but is often classified as one, made it his prime directive to study being *qua* being, arriving at the *da-sein* of being as the true sense of being. Sartre's classic *Being and Nothingness* claims to be a "phenomenological essay on ontology." Existentialism marks a move back towards ontology, but its focus remains within the closed-system of the individual consciousness. The ego becomes the infinite boundary, the metaphysical limit. Although Heidegger claimed to examine being in the ontological difference, being's location in the consciousness of the ego or its location in the concretization in the human condition still remains an ontic study. Our field of examination is still the phenomenological, the visible. As a self-proclaimed science, phenomenology cannot admit the transcendent or the existence of God. Such inferences are to be bracketed and suspended. Of course, not all brands of Existentialism are included in this analysis, as Kierkegaard and Bergson and other religious existentialists embraced a radical commitment to a living God but maybe more in its fideist form than in any sort of traditional historical form, or realist or critical realist form.

Thus, when examining phenomenology and Existentialism in this section, I am alluding more to its atheistic or agnostic forms that take the phenomena of consciousness as the boundaries of a strict science and bracket out all other transcendent considerations. This brand of pure scientific phenomenology operates out of an imploded or deflated ontology that rests in the pure subjective experience or consciousness of the transcendental ego, and somehow manages to claim subjective existence as necessary existence. Such a foundation generates at least two major charges against the movements of phenomenology and Existentialism.Those charges are radical subjectivism and claims of being a pure presuppositionless science of consciousness (Moran 2000:126). The use of an ontological evaluation of phenomenology can easily elicit the classical indictment made by Heidegger that metaphysics and specifically ontology has posed itself as theology and the Logos or reason-truth of all Western thinking. What Heidegger calls onto-theology.

The argument against Heidegger's *Dasein* analytic as a response to the "heresy"of onto-theology and the ontological difference being itself the premiere Christian heresy in modern philosophy and other similar charges are not to be explored here within these parameters. I think in one way John Milbank has already overcome metaphysics with theology.[17]

Back to phenomenology and Existentialism, ontology within Existentialism is the experience of consciousness and the object-directed intentional acts of consciousness.[18] Husserl construed phenomenology as the presuppositionaless science of consciousness. Existence, as well as consciousness, although contingent, are treated as necessary and foundational to experience and the construction of our world. It is my contention that such a reduction and focus on the subjective can easily become ahistorical,[19] idealistic, fideistic[20], mystical or even solipsistic. Solipsism[21] seems to be an inevitable nemesis of the phenomenologist and the existentialist. In any case, being and knowledge lose any referential mooring outside of one's field of consciousness. This is the contention against Husserl's science of phenomenology.

Husserl

Edmund Husserl (1859-1938) sought to construct a science out of the phenomological study of consciousness. As mentioned above, such a "science" has a challenge to overcome the charges of radical subjectivism. Husserl worked diligently to counter charges of solipsism by proposing a theory of intersubjectivity based on analogical apperception[22] as a solution to the "other minds" problem. In my estimation, even with his work on intersubjectivity, the "objective world" is still somewhat of a projection and is based on the primordial world of the subject (Husserl 1999:146-160). "Other minds" do not find a basis in a universal *imago Dei* or some other participatory construct, but in the image of the ego. Like Kant, Husserl assumes objective categories like space and time that serve as a transcendental aesthetic and the condition for objective material, but these can never be known, only assumed. All we can know is phenomena (Husserl 1999:164-185). At best, such a view of other minds, externality, and matter is instrumental and not real. Husserl abandoned his own attempt at linking subjective knowledge with real naturalistic knowledge and opted for Transcendental Idealism.

Edmund Husserl, the founder of phenomenology, inherited Descartes and Kant's stress on the thinking subject and the phenomenal world. However, unlike Kant, Husserl's phenomenology of consciousness was actually transcendental in its claims. He thought he could locate the essence of things via the transcendental subject. Husserl did not relegate the transcendental to solely cognitive categories but sought to ground the objective and the noumenal in the subjective ego (Moran 2000:107 and 138). Thus he purports that one can actually access the essences of things and the transcendental domain of experience through the subjective, the transcendental pure ego (2007:106-107). Husserl claims contact with the transcendental and the noumenal by bracketing off (*epoche*) and suspending judgments and theories about metaphysics, causality, and the natural world and coming in contact with pure consciousness and the essential forms of objects that are rooted in the transcendental ego (Moran 2000:117). Husserl's bracketing, transcendental reductions and the experience of pure consciousness at times almost borders on mysticism or fantasy, which is frequently a critique leveled against him. At what point does such a theory of knowledge become pure revelation?

I believe that Husserl improves on Descartes and Kant in that he believes that through the intentionality of consciousness we perceive the object *itself* and not an idea, a representation, a sensation, some mediation, or merely natural phenomena, though I think his proof is insufficient for the claim (2000:122). There is somewhat of a claim to realism operating here but without any basis or justification. There is no mention of substance, universals or participation in being or any other standard metaphysical apparati. What prevents Husserl's phenomenology from being mere instrumentalism? For Husserl, conscious experience presents itself in an absolute sense. What is his reason for coming to this conclusion, while Kant did not? With Husserl, it is not because of any transcendent cause, structure, substance, rhetoric, or being that is outside of the subject. The problem with Husserl is that he roots essences and being ultimately in the transcendental ego, the intuitions of the transcendental ego (Husserl 1999:164 and Moran 2000:125). In some ways for Husserl, there is no difference between something in the external, real world and something in the internal imaginary world. The structure and essence of phenomena, real or imaginary, manifest similarly to consciousness (2000:132). Yet this is the radical conclusion that Husserl must arrive at under such radical subjectivism. Questions of the real, the external, objective reference, the quantifiable etc. beyond subjective consciousness and interpretation are ultimately indeterminable and irrelevant (2000:133, 152 and 153). To which Husserl would have responded that this is the very essence and orthodoxy of phenomenology.

The construction of a contingent world rests in the hands of contingent being, though Husserl relied on consciousness as an absolute and not as contingent, not merely in a social sense, as in the sociology of knowledge or in a social dimension of knowledge construction, but in a transcendental, *a priori* and absolute sense (2000:132 and 136). Husserl does not intend for this world-construction to be thought of as objective and external in any traditional realist sense but as subjective and yet essential, physical and real, the revelation of consciousness. The transcendental ego forcibly takes on the role of the absolute, a transcendence through immanence, an eidetic intuition of the universal in the individual (2000:125, 133 and 134). Yet he makes this inference without reference to God or being outside of the ego, which makes the inference exempt in Husserl's eyes from charges of Platonism, mysticism, or theology and qualifies it as a science (2000:135). Nonetheless, Husserl's phenomenology and much of Existentialism locate ontological transcendence in the subject (the ego), deifying the perceiving, autonomous individual as the measure of all things. Husserl's thought represents the classical Western emphasis on the inflated self as the locus of reality. Society becomes an atomistic collection of conscious egos each driven to actualize one's own intentions. The will-to-power charge may be valid in the case of phenomenology.

This is not a wholesale condemnation of Husserl, who is a significant bridge figure between modern and postmodern and Continental and Analytic traditions, but it is a cursory look at some of the inherent problems phenomenology carries with it into a conversation with ontology and theology. With his focus on experience and revelation, Husserl makes headway for theological discourse and unintentionally sets phenomenology up for further experimentation and a theological turn in phenomenology, which I believe is a more conducive framework for handling theological questions than analytical philosophy.

Radical Subjectivism, Kierkegaard and Fideism

Radical subjectivism, individualism and moral relativism are strong charges and arguments against both phenomenology and Existentialism. Yet phenomenology as a science of consciousness claims neutrality and purity as its vantage.[23] A subjectively shaped world somehow comes off as neutral and value free. How does one test and judge such claims effectively and accurately? The *aporia* in the inflated claims of Husserl's transcendental ego is that it claims to be a pure presuppositionless science of consciousness, a non-mathematical science of conscious perception that claims to bracket and suspend (*epoche*) all assumptions, values, beliefs and theories in its observations and descriptions in order to arrive at the pure structure of consciousness (2000:126, 131, and 146). How do we remove ourselves from all assumptions, values, beliefs and theories? How do we enter into vacuum? How do we remove ourselves from context and claim pure neutrality, objectivity or absoluteness in our experience? It seems like Husserl's *epoche* and transcendental reduction methodology for arriving at the pure starting point of consciousness is quite illusory. Created being and our consciousness of existence are not necessary but contingent. Yet Husserl's attempt to construct the knowledge of other minds and an external world are merely founded on the appresentation of all reality as it is assimilated to the conscious ego. The epistemic lens seems narrow and transcendence crammed into the horizon of consciousness' field of vision, a field of vision that is given pure value-free perception of all phenomena. How do we approach experience without value, theory or category? Is a pure leap possible?

Before evaluating the problem of subjectivism in Kierkegaard, it is important to affirm the great Danish theologian and philosopher as a believer in Christian theism and in Jesus Christ. Kierkegaard expressed a radical commitment to return to authentic discipleship over against the practices of the stale ecclesiastical institutionalism of his day. Kierkegaard stands as a stalwart of the Lutheran and even Anabaptist traditions with his stress on faith and radical commitment to the life of Christ as expressed in one's actions and service. Much more praise can be offered for this reformer and prophet elsewhere, but my object is to examine the Kierkegaardian notion that "truth is subjectivity." I am not arguing against the fact that truth's appropriation is at least in part personal and within one's subjective context. This is a given. The contention is more so with the dialectic that truth is attained by the absolute certainty of a scientific sort, or it must be attained by a leap of faith, which is subjectivity. Kierkegaard opted for the latter.

One can see a form of this problem in Kierkegaard's critique of historical knowledge, specifically a response to Hegel's historical system. In *Postscript,* Kierkegaard opens the book with a chapter that analyzes the "historical point of view" in terms of Christian faith. His thesis, borrowed from Gotthold Lessing and his famous ditch (1729-1781), is that "anything historical is merely an approximation. And an approximation, when viewed as a basis for an eternal happiness, is wholly inadequate, since the incommensurability makes a result impossible" (Kierkegaard 1941:25). I alluded to Kierkegaard's contention earlier.

With this thesis, he looks at the historicity of the Scriptures and the Church and finds that any scholarly inquiry for truth based on these sources is incomplete and inadequate and at best an approximation, and hence faith cannot rest in such an objective approach and hope to find secure knowledge. When looking to the historical to substantiate a truth claim, "the approximation-process begins; the parenthesis is launched, and no one can say when it will end; for it is and always remains only an approximation, and this has the remarkable property of being able to continue indefinitely" (Kierkegaard 1941:41). If the science of knowledge claims to give thorough explanations and formulas of objectivity, then when does the project end, and if it never ends, we cannot have scientific knowledge or scientific knowledge concerning issues of faith. We must then choose to leap over this ditch by faith, and in our inwardness that mediates revelation, we have found truth.[24]

The authenticity and commitment of the person is valued as truth over and to the exclusion of any transcendent, rational, referential, correspondent, coherent, propositional, or external values, not that *commitment* and these adjectives are necessarily incompatible, but can commitment or duty stand on its own. In essence, Kierkegaard is demanding that unless historical or objective knowledge is full, certain, and absolute, then one cannot employ it for religious knowledge. Since such certainty is not possible, then one must take a leap of faith across the infinite chasm in order to arrive at truth. A fideistic certainty becomes the only response to an unattainable scientific certainty. Since some qualifier or disclaimer has to be put on historical truth, then it must be rejected altogether, and an inward leap of faith must be made to secure knowledge, all or nothing. This fallacy signifies that partial knowledge is no knowledge at all. So often this is the legacy of both modern and postmodernism, that is, that once knowledge is *qualified* and *limited* in some way, as historical, phenomenal, textual, contextual, perceptual, subjective etc., it is thereby disqualified or reduced.[25] The truth is that knowledge can be properly qualified but not totalized. Yet this is the case of a collapsed ontology, which puts the full weight of justification on epistemology. The requirements are unbearable. For certain types of modernism and postmodernism, justification is all or nothing.

In the case of Kierkegaard, neither Hegelian logic nor history can yield full proof justification, and the only alternative is a fideism that tends towards radical subjectivity. We find the consequence of this type of existential fideism in some of Kierkegaard's successors, like Tillich and Bultmann, with whom the whole historical question is demythologized. The historical Christian faith as witnessed in the Scriptures and the Church is an existential analogue for personal experience that is outside of external critique. Truth, regardless of referent or content, is anything we experience and that gives us meaning.

This problem of subjectivity intensifies when brought to the realm of ethics, an arena in which Existentialism frequently prophesies. Existential anti-heroes, like Meursault in Camus' *The Stranger*, are often celebrated for their offbeat antics and even unethical acts under the greater virtue of authenticity or honesty. The novel opens with main character Meursault attending his own mother's funeral. He is cold without feeling or expression as he represents the honesty of being unconventional and even unnatural. The reader follows this carefree anti-hero through a life of casual sex, revenge, senseless murder, and incarceration without interpreting a hint of regret, sorrow, or guilt. Meursault even attempts to assault the chaplain who offers him God and repentance before his execution. He does not want to avoid the meaninglessness of death or escape the honesty of who he is. Meursault merely reflects a life without meaning and purpose and his authenticity to be in the midst of it is prized. Reality is too absurd that one is to be held to any conventions of behavior or justice. Authenticity trumps righteousness, virtue or responsibility.

Offbeat and even immoral existential characters are often not portrayed negatively but favorably due to their acts of authenticity admidst life's absurdity. Every act is self-justifiable because it is a personal honest expression of one's commitment or non-commitment. Even Sartre's borrowing of Kant's "act as if you are acting for everyone" type of categorical imperative, if not situated in a framework that finds meaning external to self, is deflated of any ethical import and can merely be a device for self-service. Without any external mooring, Existentialism has an inherent flaw of self-reference without need of sufficient reason to explain or justify itself. Self- authentication becomes its only means of validation or justification and *homo mensura*[26] its ethic, because there is no metaphysic or transcendent basis for our actions in Sartre's neo-Kantian ethic.

The positivism of modernism has failed to recognize the human and contextual dimensions of knowledge, creating the fallacy of pure reason, which had been the engine for the hegemonic drive of colonialism and Christian mission globally. Existentialism stands as a corrective to this problem with its recognition of the human location of knowledge. However, in its radical subjectivism, many types of Existentialism have lost any appeal to anything higher than self-will. Both the modernist category of reason and the existential categories of consciousness and the authentic self can become self-absorbing and self-serving, especially when understood as autonomous. There is little ontological space for anything transcendent within such a claustrophobic sphere of either pure reason or radical subjectivism. The center of epistemic gravity is located within an ontological autonomy that depends on nothing but its own interest, exertion and will to power. Yet within its own finitude and contingency, such an autonomy built on nothingness, not even

God, is imploding on itself leaving a wake of violence that draws everything in its path into the same fate of death. This leaves nihilism as a logical conclusion to modernism. Ahead, we will see that it is a logical conclusion for postmodernism as well.

A Postmodernist Critique of Modernism

Postmodernism is as elusive a term as Existentialism. Walter Truett Anderson calls it a "makeshift word we use until we have decided what to name the baby" (Anderson 1995:3). There is no official school or tenets of postmodernism. There is no originator of postmodern thinking, though a case can be made for Nietzsche fulfilling that role. The word "postmodern" is almost as elusive as the idea. The word may have been first used by English painter John Watkins Chapman in 1870, when he referred to the avant-garde painting of his time as "postmodern painting" (Best and Kellner 1991:5). David Harvey "defined postmodernity as the situation in which the world finds itself after the breakdown of the Enlightenment project, which lasted from the latter part of the eighteenth century until well into the twentieth" (Anderson 1995:4). The term first gained major expression in structural and post-structural linguistics and anthropology and later in art, architecture, semiotics, literary criticism, psychology, philosophy, and social and culture theory.

Since the term has been so broadly used, many simply use the term to denote "after" modernism (Best and Kellner 1991:4-5). Following modernism both chronologically and consequentially, postmodernism can be construed as hypermodernity or extreme modernism. Postmodernism has inherited much of the legacy of modernity's epistemological breakdown from Descartes to Nietzsche. One finds many similarities between the two, especially with late modernism, i.e. Existentialism. Some of the similarities between postmodernism and Existentialism include a rejection of metaphysics, metanarratives,[27] and rational foundationalism and an acceptance of truth as subjectivity, and a focus on experience.

Like Existentialism, postmodernism is more of a sensibility than an official school, so locking down its "beliefs" is difficult. However, the following could characterize a postmodern sensibility: plurality, locality, narrative, contextual knowledge, deconstruction of texts, multivalence, hermeneutics of suspicion, voicing marginalization, and a rejection of metanarratives, totalizing theories or texts, discursive hegemonies, unified field theories of knowledge, or logocentrism.[28] Much of the latter are constructs which flourished during the Enlightenment but postmodernism has rejected them.

One of the primary critiques of postmodernism leveled against the Enlightenment concerns its claim that reason is autonomous, neutral, and unbounded or context-free and is qualified to construct metanarratives about reality. Postmodernism does not look at reason as innocent, but with suspicion it applies discourse theory which:

analyzes culture and society in terms of sign systems and their codes and discourses. Discourse theory sees all social phenomena as structured semiotically by codes and rules, and therefore amenable to linguistic analysis, using the model of signification and signifying practices. Discourse theorists argue that meaning is not simply given, but is socially constructed across a number of institutional sites and practices...Discourse theory also interprets discourse as a site and object of struggle where different groups strive for hegemony and the production of meaning and ideology (Best and Kellner 1991:26).

Thus, according to Jean-Francois Lyotard (1924-1998), any belief in the ability of reason to construct a metanarrative that applies to all people is suspect. Postmodern thinking is not so much interested in "what" reason has to say, but "why" it says it. There is a "hermeneutics of suspicion," linked to a concern to expose hegemony and resist exertions of power. The voice of reason, that is all discourses, needs to be interpreted with an ear for motive. We see this clearly in Michel Foucault (power-knowledge), Jacques Derrida (reality as the text), and Jean Baudrillard (reality as the sign). Foucault, who studied modern institutions like hospitals and prisons (Foucault 1984:141-166) and through the genealogical and archeological tracing of social systems, saw knowledge as a product of power structures and coercive social and political forces (Foucault 1980:131-133). Reason in creating a culture's norms creates a socio-political hegemony and a power-play to marginalize, control and exploit.

What the Enlightenment may have understood of itself as an age of reason, in a Foucauldian sense was an age of power and control. Foucault sought to focus on discontinuities and irregularities in history and especially marginalization as a product of the Enlightenment institutions' definitions of "the self," "human nature," and "normalacy"and understood much of the metaphysical claims of the *Cogito*, the rational thinking self, as socially constructed for the purpose of institutional domination. Institutions employ knowledge as discourse for exercising their power over a domain that they claim to have knowledge on or mastery over. Power and knowledge institutionally sustain each other in their invention and perpetration of their own discourses or "regimes of truth." All of society's acts are acts of self-interested power, whether they come from communities of science, education, government etc, and any constructed positivist history of society is a ruse for these violent endeavors of self-exertion and control. Foucault's archeology and genealogy seek to unearth the real causes for the rise of institutions and the creation of regimes of truth. For Foucault power assumes almost a metaphysical role, and in my estimation he is correct in a sense because of the ever deflating structure of ontology due to an inflated epistemology, the ontological "excess" must appear *de facto* in some locale. Thus, the entities that wield knowledge become structures inflated with power. Hyper-rational norms and regimes of truth fill autonomous space with structures and bastions of power and control. Such space gives place for the creation of the modern nation-state and its modern institutions that are built not on their ontological participation in anything transcendent but on their own rational ground that often becomes grounds for propagation and domination under a system of technology and competition. This *a priori* analytic of power and violence takes on the role of a metaphysical field in which all relations are tempted to operate; hence a hermeneutic of suspicion concerning any claims.

For Derrida, the suspicion is also toward the nature of knowledge. Derrida sneers at the Western metaphysical enterprise as fallaciously based on the centrality of the *Logos* or overarching reason that attempts to hold all things together. The Enlightenment, and even most of Western civilization, has tried to propose a metaphysics of presence (a transcendental signified - the Ideal, the Logos, the Word, the Cogito, the Transcendental Ego etc.), a logocentric view of reality. Derrida understands this attempt at logocentricity as a cover for a metaphysical absence. For Derrida, since everything is in the text, words and writing are necessary not because of metaphysical presence but because of an absence. There is a need for mediation and representation due to absence. However, language itself is the clue to metaphysical absence because it is based not on presence but on *difference*. Language is a system that infinitely plays off a present absence and a deferral in meaning from one signifier to another, using Saussure's theory. Thus, any claim to meaning and presence can be deconstructed by the internal nature of language itself, where it is shown that outside of the text there is no signifier. The text is just one signifier deferring meaning to another, and no signifier is able signify any presence by itself or with another signifier. The text, mediation itself, as an epistemic structure becomes ontological. It is a closed ontological system as well, since there is nothing outside of it. There is nothing that "signifies" the text. It is pure mediation of nothing. The text has no transcendent and no internal stability, as it is merely flux supported by the void, the metaphysical absence. Derrida's ontology is a deflated ontology of text, a text in flux agitated by its own ground in absence.

Cunningham holds that Derrida is claiming that language and even textual reality do not have an *outside* (Cunningham 2002:155). Cunningham claims that "The Derridean text *is* without being" (Cunningham 2002:158). Due to the metaphysical absence in reality and language, there is no inherent meaning but an infinite deferral of meaning from sign to sign while an interminable play of difference/*differance* takes place[29] (Powell 1997:42). Derrida's method of deconstruction discovers the inherent *differance* found in a text that dismantles its intended meaning, as meaning is deferred and plays interminably with alternative and marginal readings. Thus, language is both a hermeneutic and an instrument of power.

Later, subaltern hermeneutics would use it as a method of textual subversion. This is very different from Cartesian rationalism which naively thought it had found the Archimedean point of certainty. The text plays a negative ontological role that is the text is flux and void, an apparition, in this form of reduction. In fact, most reductions in postmodern thinking take on transcendence. Yet the taking up of such a role is futile, since nothing is outside of the text referentially, spatially, temporally or in any other sense. There is no signification. The text is everything, and yet the text is nothing. Derrida echoes Kant as a significant ontologist of the transcendent nothing.[30] With Descartes, ontology fell to epistemology. With Derrida, epistemology is reduced to textualism as a meta-hermeneutic[31] and a deflated ontology, even an ontology of the void or nothingness.

For Jean Baudrillard, it is not the text of Derrida which sets the ontological boundary but the sign. Reality has not been a Hegelian evolution of the Idea, but an evolution of *simulacra*. In the Enlightenment, sign equals referent. In the Industrial Revolution sign is exchanged for referent. In postmodernity, sign is exchanged for sign (Baudrillard 1983:83). With simulacrum, the real is transferred and copied from medium to medium, so that meaning is destroyed ("implosion of meaning") and the real becomes the hyperreal (a type of fetish of the real). Simulation replaces reality in a hyperreality or reification through signs (Baudrillard1983: 138-152; Best and Kellner 1991:119-121; Appignanesi and Garratt 2003:54-55). The sign or the code becomes a deflationary ontology and replaces Enlightenment metaphysics and the real. Baudrillard prophetically discerns the eschatological deflation of the real throughout history until it has become pure *simulacra*. The sign becomes ontological in a way that transcends the real. The real is now the hyper-real comprising signs that makeup the capital and currency of the market's exchange.

Baudrillard combines semiotics with Marxist critical theory in his evaluation of the sign as a commodity with value consumption. The economy follows the ever-moving sign that produces consumption and capital. The code of production not the mode of production controls the economy and society (Lane 2000:69-76). Hyperreality is a product of advanced capitalism, where experience is commodified in signs and consumed. With Baudrillard, reality is not ratio-empirical but sign-driven capitalism that leads to nihilism (the implosion of meaning in the sign). Hyperreality is the transcendence of the sign to nothingness. The *simulacra* has swallowed the real and yields nothing but itself, leaving us in a universe of virtuality where digital ghosts of *simulacra* are disembodied from the real and are in competition one with another seeking a host server that will enable commodification, which is the incarnation of the sign, and consumption. For example, Las Vegas is the quintessence of the hyperreal. Its simulacra are "more real" than the real. The whole world is on one street. Its buildings are" more real" than the originals. Its porn is" more real" than sex. Its games are "more real" than life. I believe that Baudrillard has keenly detected the absence of ontological transcendence within hyper-real postmodernity.

Recent trends in postmodern phenomenology epitomize the deflation of ontology with its focus on the phenemona of revelation, the gift, and the event without recourse to being. [32] Phenomenology with its theological turn would attempt to make God a purely phenomenological category by deflating God of any ontological weight. In the spirit of Heidegger, Jean-Luc Marion's seminal text *God without Being* says it all, the existence of God without any reference to being or ontological categories, which Marion considers to be an idol. Marion, like Heidegger, operates out of a univocity of being[33], seeking to detach being from God. He rightfully claims that being and God are not identical and thus the need to separate them (Marion 1991:62). God is "liberated" of being and is located as distance and trace at the site of presenting or what is presented, the revelation, the gift, charity, or the event without any ontological reference. The problem is that neither Heidegger nor Marion considered being as analogical. Being is not a common predicate shared by God and creation and not synonymous. A thorough purging of ontological categories is not necessary. However, Marion, like Luther, Kierkegaard, Barth and Heidegger before him, cannot reconcile theology and philosophy or faith and reason on any level. Faith must occur within the realm of *Dasein* and not metaphysics as in an onto-theology (1991:69). Yet none of these fideists, who allowed Scripture to define their understanding of God, would admit a God without *ousia* or *hypostasis*, except Marion.

In the world of postmodern science a social instrumentalism drains being of any substance or reality. Thomas Kuhn recognized that scientific revolution and innovation come through paradigm shifts that are ultimately social products of the scientific community (Kuhn 1962). Peter Berger also introduced us formally to the social construction of reality, which has been influential in the social sciences and in missiology (Berger and Luckman 1966). Social and research traditions bear the ontological weight of their epistemological products. These postmodern thinkers have far removed us from the autonomous, neutral reason of Descartes, Spinoza, Leibniz, Locke or Hegel and have brought us to a place where the motive for knowledge is uncovered and qualified by its context, that is its power structures, social institutions, language and signs and other virtual epistemic devices and deflated ontologies.

An Ontological Evaluation of Modernism and Postmodernism

Throughout my critique of modernism and postmodernism, I have implicitly contended for a robust ontology that is transcendent and ultimately points to the existence of God as understood by Christian theism, as well as a creational ontology that participates in God and is a basic framework in which we experience reality and construct knowledge.[34] Without such an ontological vision, I find it difficult to account for anything except nothing. Two consequences, among many, of modernism seem to be atheism and nihilism, and that these are intricately involved. In an Enlightenment worldview, such an ontological vision is replaced by a self-evident foundationalism established along the lines of epistemological constructs. Knowledge theory takes on the primary task and function of justifiable authority. The Scientific Revolution and the use of new technology and the discovery of nature's laws gave knowledge a degree of empirical authority it did not have before. Rationalists like Rene Descartes (1596-1650), the *Cogito*, Gottfried Leibniz (1646-1716), the Monad, and Benedict Spinoza (1632-1677), the One, gave reason great authority to explain the philosophical universe with attempts at a grand theory of everything. John Locke (1632-1704), Thomas Hobbes (1588-1679), and Jean-Jacques Rousseau (1712-1778) laid the foundation for the modern-state relocating political authority in the laws of nature that reside in the rational individual. In a postmodern worldview, rather than finding new ways to legitimize authority, all authority is questioned and deconstructed for its internal contradictions, contextual biases and possibly self-serving assertions.

However like Existentialism, postmodernism leaves one with few alternatives but nihilism. The three postmodern thinkers that I have investigated have qualified or even reduced knowledge in terms of power, the text, and the sign and have sought transcendence in an evacuated ontology, evacuated of reference. For many within and without postmodernism, ontology is a myth or an imaginary field of reference. There is no escape from the field of text and signs and the interpretations we manufacture. Can all things truly hold together or fall apart under the power of the sign, without transcendence or is it another ontological implosion into nihilism?

Later we will be examining how Radical Orthodoxy provides an insightful analysis of postmodern ontology and epistemology. In preparation, though, it needs to be said that even though postmodern thinking has uncovered the ontological skeletons in modernity's closet, the problem is not solved but is exacerbated by a hyperrationalism that still shakes with Cartesian anxiety for certainty and finds it in closed system reductions, like the text, that float on ontologies of nothingness. Reality is reduced to text, signs or fields of power that hang from nothing. Nothing holds up meaning or meaning's deferral.

Nihilism with its imploding ontology of violence and closed hermeneutical systems of survival win the day, and their fruit of radical pluralism and relativism are given democratic and equal truth warrant by reason of their authentic voice as long as they play rightly by their own rules within the language games they have established from their respective traditions. These conclusions strike at the root of Christian claims to the revelation of God and creation as the true ontological vision. Epistemological genealogies that stem from a univocity of being and give expression to differential violence are not acceptable or congruent with a Christian revelation that recognizes a benevolent Creator of all things (including "difference") who redeems and sustains life from death through the person of Jesus Christ. In the next chapter, I will explore an option that seeks to reestablish a vision based on this theological revelation. Yet first, I will apply my examination of modernism to the theology and practice of mission.

The Impact of Modernism on Mission

Shifting to modern mission, I will illustrate some of the negative impact that modern thinking has had on mission theology and practice. First, it is important to point out that *all* of the work and sacrifice of those dedicated to spreading the gospel does not deserve the ensuing critique. Much of the work was done out of a pure heart and a sincere desire to fulfill Christ's command. Missionaries and mission societies were subject to their own times, at least in part. However, in many cases significant achievements were attained like the work for peace and justice ministered by Bartolome de Las Casas (1484-1566); the evangelical and exemplary work of Hudson Taylor (1832-1905) through the China Inland Mission, especially during the purges of the Boxer Movement; the ecumenical mission movement beginning with the World Missionary Conference at Edinburgh in 1910; the incredible rise of African Independent Churches; and the indigenous ministry among the Masai by Vincent Donovan (1924-) are *some* highlights of God's grace in mission. Often educational efforts, language studies, and medical and technological advancements throughout the two-thirds world have been helpful to ameliorating the quality of life. Modern mission has made a positive impact on the world, as well as advanced the Kingdom in the world.

Yet, modern mission has also had a negative impact on the status of many two-thirds world countries as well. One of the themes of this research is that some of the negative impact stems from the Enlightenment ideologies and epistemologies that were borrowed from this period and from the fact that modern mission was carried out in the context of political and economic oppression. Bosch comments "that the Enlightenment would profoundly influence mission thinking and practice, the more so since the entire modern missionary enterprise is, to a very real extent, a child of the Enlightenment" (Bosch 1991:274; see Stanley 2001). The two go together.

Rationalism applied to the scientific revolution, which advanced technology, in the process created national hegemonies in the West, which thought its manifest destiny to expand its territories into those of others and civilize and colonize those people with their culture and customs. This geo-political effort often went hand in hand with the missionary enterprise (Bosch 1991:275). The colonial efforts in Africa, Latin America, Asia and North America by the English, German, French, Dutch, and Spanish were coupled by a missionary thrust to Christianize those same people, exhibiting a symbiosis of church and state (1991:275).

Much of the confidence and sense of destiny of these endeavors came from a sense of cultural superiority based on the achievements of ratio-empiricism in a capitalist society, the scientific calculus of wealth, as mentioned above. Reason becomes architectonic in terms of building a base of power. Such exploitation of autonomous realms of power is a product, at least in part, of the development of the univocity of being in terms of rationalism, scientism, capitalism, and nationalism as a natural progression. The univocity of being provides space for autonomous realms outside of God to be birthed and to self actualize into destinies of control. In the humanism of the Renaissance and the advancement of the Enlightenment many of these realms were seized and exploited for power. As mentioned, these realms include rationality, scientism, capitalism and nationalism, including the national church. The univocity of being creates space for secular autonomous institutions like the nation-state and national churches to flourish.

Reason became its own basis of authority to validate these other realms. With the breakup of the empires and the spread of the Reformation, the spirit of individualism and autonomy was fostered and inspired the birth of nationalism and national churches, which were grounded in their own *raison d'etre*.[35] The contention for global control was birthed out of these national hegemonies striving for land and power. There was a race to conquer. In fact, Anders Stephanson identifies the westward and southern expansion of a young America as "geographical rationalism" (Stephanson 1995:43).

Missiologists Bevans and Schroeder remark "One of the consequences of the development of nationalism was the idea of *manifest destiny"* (Bevans and Schroeder 2004:207). The forging of America seems to best exemplify this phenomena. Historian Sydney Ahlstrom states that "manifest destiny as an American idea is probably as old as the 'sea to shining sea' charters of the earliest colonies" (Ahlstrom 1972:877). The church also fostered this vision early on with the Puritan's sense of divine mission in the new world (1972:877-878). Ahlstrom continues, "In the antebellum decades evangelical dreams of a vast Christian republic brought prophetic certainty to the idea. Manifest Destiny became the catchword of an epoch."(1972:878). Ahlstrom cites *The New Era; or, The Coming Kingdom* written in 1893 by the general secretary of the Evangelical Alliance Rev. Josiah Strong as a prime example of "manifest destiny" in which Christianity and the process of civilizing are tied together with imperialism and racism. In this work, Strong proclaims the superiority of the Anglo-Saxon race with its pure form of Christianity and its privileged destiny to dispossess the weaker races (Ahlstrom 1972:849-850). Stephanson confirms the strong ties between manifest destiny and Christianity:

> When "manifest destiny" was coined in 1840s, apocalyptic Protestantism and utopian mobilization had actually reached a level unmatched since early colonial times. So it is no surprise that the expression should have been heavily suffused with religious overtones. Its origins, in fact, lay directly in the old biblical notions, recharged through the Reformation, of the predestined, redemptive role of god's chosen people in the Promised Land: providential destiny revealed. (Stephanson 1995:5)

The church based its theologies on the same rational grounds as the forging nations had, and together "became agents of the Western imperialistic enterprise as the three "Cs" of colonialism, became Christianity, commerce and civilization" (2004:207). In implementing the three Cs, the national powers and Christianity had to wipe out the conquered cultures in order to build and civilize, i.e. the doctrine of *tabula rasa* emerged to serve the purpose and keep the argument rational. Again the justification for cultural extermination was architectonic reason – cultural superiority. Totalization and hegemony stem from an ontology of differential violence, in which difference cannot mean peace or unity but competition.

Bevans and Schroeder comment that the Enlightenment fostered a division in civilization based on ethnicity and race to determine superiority (2004:208). It became the white man's "responsibility" to civilize as the superior race. From the Enlightenment into the modern period, national powers raced throughout the globe to subjugate "inferior" peoples to their hegemonic brand of culture and civilization. From the conquistadors in Latin America to manifest destiny against the Indians in North America to British control of India, to the French, German, Belgian, British, and Dutch carving up of Africa and Central and Southeast Asia cultural imperialism spread out of a manifest destiny inherent in an ontology of violence.

In examining the impact of the Enlightenment on modern mission, I want to consider three cases that touch on three problems that in my estimation stem from a univocity of being and an imploding ontology. The problems are differential violence, rational hegemony, and closed systems. In *Asian Biblical Hermeneutics and Postcolonialism,* Indian theologian R.S. Sugirtharajah tells the story of how postcolonial India had to recapture its own hermeneutics from colonial influences. This is a case of differential violence. How does a culture encounter a different culture? The British had to decide how to remove the Indian identity from the people in order to re-identify them within the British Commonwealth. The hegemony of reason could not tolerate difference for it disrupted the power structure. Difference means opposition in a totalist scheme. India has a rich history and identity which actually encompasses diversity, including religion, ethnicity, and language. The goal in colonization is enculturation to the new culture, beginning with changing the identity of the people and how they see the world, their hermeneutic.

Sugirtharajah identifies three phases of hermeneutics that were applied to biblical interpretation and define mission postures: the Orientalist mode, the Anglicist mode, and the Nativist mode. The Orientalist mode, following Edward Said's work, sought to revive "the lost Golden Age of Indian civilization based on ancient Sanskrit texts and Sanskrit criticism" (Sugirtharajah 1998:5). This movement venerated Sanskrit and the Vedic texts and sought to make connections between the Vedic and biblical texts (1998:5). Sugirtharajah remarks "Orientalism provided educated and urbanized Indians a new sense of social and communal identity" (1998:7). The problem with this selective interpretation of the Indian people through textualization was that it reduced India to "Hindu-Aryan privileged Sanskrit texts over vernacular, and negated the Indian native and folk traditions" (1998:8).

The next attempt at creating a hermeneutical tradition for the Indian people was through the Anglicist mode. This mode sought to counter Orientalism by replacing indigenous texts and learning with Western science and modes of reason (1998:8). There is no need to expound on the results of this mode, for it characterizes much of what has been said. Foreign forms of reason and criticism were superimposed on a culture who had little orientation or identity in such traditions, creating a sense of inferiority and violation.

The third attempt came as a Nativisitic mode, which sought to revive vernacular traditions, especially Tamil culture, literature and philosophy (1998:12). This movement "promoted an awareness of neglected indigenous traditions," but it also created a particularism and isolationism that reduced the polyphonic culture of India (1998:14). Sugirtharajah's work in this book is a movement towards a postcolonial hermeneutic that seeks to unmask the power-play behind Western texts and to liberate texts to allow them to speak on behalf of the marginalized. Such liberation allows them to speak equally alongside other texts and not hegemonically (1998:17).The illustration in the case of Indian hermeneutics is that an ontology of differential violence could only perceive of difference as oppositional.

One tradition excluded the other. More important it was the colonizer who decided which hermeneutic would be applied to most benefit those in power.

There is a similar case in Kenya with the work of Ngugi wa Thiong'o in his *Decolonising the Mind*. This book exposes a case of rational hegemony. The book addresses the hegemony of the English language imposed on the people of Kenya which sought to wipe out the indigenous culture and replace it with a foreign one, what Ngugi calls an "imperialist tradition" (wa Thiong'o 1986:2). This tradition is made up of a neo-colonial bourgeoisie, which is multinational. This imperialist tradition exercises political and economic control over the restive population, which represents the resistance tradition, who is controlled by force and culture (wa Thiong'o 1986:2-3). Ngugi identifies the "cultural bomb" as the most lethal of all of the weapons wielded against the resistant population (1986:3). Ngugi claims that the "effect of the cultural bomb is to annihilate a people's belief in their names, in their languages, in their environment, in their heritage of struggle, in their unity, in their capacities and ultimately in themselves" (1986:3). Ngugi locates the origin of this imperialist tradition with those European powers which originally came to Africa to colonize with "bible and sword" (1986:4). One of the main weapons within culture that has been used against the people has been language.

Ngugi believes that language is "central to a people's definition of themselves in relation to their natural and social environment, indeed in relation to the entire universe" (1986:4). Similarly, to the case in India, a colonizing culture seeks to purge the "inferior" culture in order to control it, and it uses language or text to do it. In both cases, the language and textual tradition defined the people and their worldview. Control over these areas was imperative to controlling the people. English ideas and language created a rational hegemony over the people. Again, these are some of the cultural consequences of a hegemony of reason within a univocity of being. Difference is seen as competition and opposition that must be eliminated to fulfill the destiny of hegemonic control. The eschatological future of univocal being can be nihilistic and destructive.

Ngugi and the resistance tradition sought to recapture the culture by recapturing the language and ideas of the African people expressed in their own oral and literary traditions. For Ngugi language is a primary carrier of culture (1986:13). The liberation of language would liberate the mind and begin to liberate the culture. He calls this process "decolonizing the mind" (1986:13-18). After recapturing the language, specifically the written language, then the language can be applied to other art forms like theater and fiction. In this way, the resistance tradition is using the same weapon of culture and language to liberate the mind from colonizing affects. In the last chapter of this work, I will discuss critical contextualization, which is a tool that fosters the expression of the gospel in indigenous forms. The reason is that an ontology of participation that understands all of creation as rooted in God can inherently facilitate diverse cultural forms, whereas an ontology of differential violence cannot.

A final example of the impact of the Enlightenment on modern mission comes from a much different source. Charles Kraft is a professor, missionary and cultural anthropologist who resides in the West. His story goes back to 1982 when he was sitting in on a class at Fuller Seminary entitled *Signs, Wonders, and Church Growth*. There in the class he saw people get healed. He was taken back, as an Enlightenment-oriented evangelical, who had his mind made up about such practices. In that class, he observed not only healing but deliverances and manifestations of the gifts of the Holy Spirit (Kraft 1989:2). This class was an eye-opener for this former missionary.

Kraft tells of his experiences in Nigeria where he and other missionaries were ill-equipped to assist the Nigerian church leaders who had strategized to conquer the evil spirits that were in that area through the authority of Jesus Christ (1989:4). None of Kraft's training in Bible, theology or anthropology prepared him for such encounters. He felt powerless. However, the Nigerian leaders and the people knew about spiritual power but not from Christianity. They were convinced that "whatever power Christianity brought it wasn't adequate to deal with such things as tragedy, infertility, relational breakdowns, and troublesome weather" (1989:4). Kraft and the other missionaries did not know the power of God, and thus could not call on God to deliver from the influences of evil spirits.

After Kraft returned from Nigeria, he often remembered his inability to help the Nigerian people in the area of spiritual power and evil. At times God would nudge him through contacts with Pentecostal and charismatic churches. He began to believe that the reason why these churches grew was that they satisfied a need people had for spiritual power (1989:6). All of this prepared Kraft for the class he would sit in on under John Wimber in 1982. This class would forever change his perspective on Christianity beginning with a change in his own worldview. Kraft attributes his lack of understanding of the spiritual world to the fact that he was educated within an Enlightenment worldview, which was a closed natural system that did not allow for supernatural phenomena. Kraft claims that this worldview is dominant in the entire West (1989:26-35)

The case of Kraft is common in Protestant Christian circles that have inherited a ratio-empirical worldview that is closed. It does not need transcendence to explain anything or to operate sufficiently. It contains observable and quantifiable laws of nature that regulate and control all of reality. Reality is reduced to the natural or sensible-intelligible realm, and reason is able to comprehend fully its processes. There is no room or need for the supernatural. Hence, many Western missionaries when confronted with spiritual issues and problems in cultures that operate out of a more spirit-based worldview are confounded and powerless.

The case of Kraft's early theory of mission fits into our analysis as a missiological case of a closed hermeneutical system. Closed hermeneutical systems are in part the result of an ontological structure that is deflated of reality and meaning and is collapsing on itself. The reason it is deflated is because it is filled with nothing. It is "resting" on non-being and cannot sustain itself without the assistance of transcendental being. It is a closed system seeking to operate on the myth of pure reason. Within Kraft's particular closed system, which is symptomatic of many modernist missionaries, there is no interaction with a transcendent spiritual realm.

Kraft believed in a transcendent God, but in his worldview, God does not interact in supernatural ways such as healings or deliverances. Kraft operated as many Christians still do, as dualist deists.

In the last chapter, I will discuss the work of the Spirit in an ontology of participation. Such an ontology allows for an openness to God. God's grace regularly infuses life and power into the created order and especially in his church. A worldview that accounts for the spiritual dimension of reality will recognize both demonic powers and the power of God and their influences in creation. A holistic theology of mission will have a comprehensive vision for the cosmos and a fully-orbed pneumatology that understands the person and work of the Spirit in the church to minister salvation, healing, deliverance, and blessing to the world

Critical Realism Considered

Through the preceding critiques one can see that modernism and postmodernism are in one sense at odds with each other, and in another sense they represent a continuum of hyperrationalism that continues to reduce reality, ontologize nothingness, and justify a violent hermeneutic of difference as the only epistemic possibilities. As mentioned earlier, one of the difficulties that give rise to these issues is the collapse or implosion of ontology on top of epistemology, leaving epistemology in the center with the entire weight of reality, truth and meaning bearing down on it. As a result, modern thinking must rest on ratio-empiricism within a closed system of nature, while postmodernism rests on hermeneutics within a closed system of semiotics.[36]

A viable solution must examine and address the ontological problem in these systems, as well as affirm and salvage their insightful contributions. One attempt is a critical realism found in some circles of the philosophy of science, initiated by the American pragmatist Charles Peirce (1839-1914) who gave voice to several philosophers of science, including Ian Barbour (1923 -), Arthur Peacocke (1924-2006), and John Polkinghorne (1930 -). Missiologist Paul Hiebert (1932-2007) has built on their work and has addressed the problem of epistemology in modernism and postmodernism as it applies to missiology. He seeks a solution in a critical realism that acknowledges a real external world (modernism) that is apprehended and known contextually and symbolically (postmodernism).

Hiebert points out the epistemological extremes in both the Enlightenment and postmodernism cases. In *Missional Implications of Epistemological Shifts*, Hiebert critiques three existing epistemological systems:

- Positivism from an Enlightenment-modernist worldview
- Instrumentalism from a postmodern worldview
- Idealism from a postmodern worldview

Hiebert notes that positivism acknowledges a real, external world, and that the mind is able to know that world as it is objectively, objective realism (Hiebert

1999:4). The way of knowing is found in the rational, empirical method of Western science. Through skepticism put to empirical observation and hypothesis, factual, certain and positive knowledge would be attained about the natural world. Anything outside of the empirical realm, such as metaphysics, religious transcendence, revelation or purpose, would be dismissed as inaccessible, irrelevant or enthusiasm. Ontological and metaphysical concerns are assumed by scientism.

In the modernist paradigm, true knowledge would be value-free, neutral facts that were empirically verifiable. Also, a shift of epistemic authority moved from tradition to the autonomous individual, who was seen as the foundation of reality in Descartes (Hiebert 1999:8). And finally the establishment of positive objective knowledge as the only true form of knowledge was a rejection of any form of "traditional" knowledge, and thus such cultures were seen as primitive, inferior, and uncivilized and fit to be colonized and exploited (Hiebert 1999:8,16).

Within postmodern worldviews, Hiebert examines instrumentalism and idealism. Instrumentalism is a weak form of realism that posits a real, external world but concedes to the fact that it cannot be known in-itself (Hiebert 1999:38-39). All of our knowledge is a socio-cultural creation that functions pragmatically at solving problems. There are no facts or objective knowledge about reality, though reality does exist. Our understanding is theory and value-laden. Knowledge of the external world is not available and no truth claims can be made about the models that we construct concerning reality, and so we have no way of discerning between theories that reflect external reality and mere creations out of our own contextual paradigms. Instrumentalism is highly aware of the subjective and contextual nature of knowledge and abandons any traditional concept of truth (Hiebert 1999:40).

Idealism, on the other hand, posits that reality only exists in the mind. There is no external world. One can only know ideas in terms of one's particular system of knowledge (Hiebert 1999:47). Like instrumentalism, there is no objective knowledge. Ideas are historically and contextually shaped. Language itself is the only thing real, language without a referent (Hiebert 1999:48). All of reality is within the text, and nothing is outside of the text and meaning is interpretation, which is found in the mind of the individual. This type of idealism is reflected in the deconstruction of Derrida or in the knowledge-power hermeneutic of Foucault. The problem with radical idealism is that there is no way to discern if the paradigm has any objective referent or which conflicting paradigms are incongruent with empirical observations (Hiebert 1999:48-49).

Hiebert identifies the strengths that can be gained from postmodernism as a response to the Enlightenment. Postmodernism seeks to dismantle the hegemonies of reason, metanarrative, scientism, rational government, and cultural imperialism by understanding the contextual nature of knowledge. However, the common problem that both idealism and instrumentalism share is the danger of pluralism to the point of relativism (Hiebert 1999:53-54). From the instrumentalist perspective, when all knowledge, including theology, is shaped solely by cultural and historical contexts, "the result is a theological relativism that denies any claim to the truth" (Hiebert 1999:58).

The implications for missions is that since "all religions are seen as autonomous, incommensurable paradigms, and because we have no privileged position from which to judge them, we must affirm them as subjectively true," a claim which undermines mission itself (Hiebert 1999:60). Instrumentalism seeks a pluralistic theology of religions that puts all religions on equal truth grounds (Hiebert 1999:62). Likewise from the idealist perspective, if the nature of truth is in the mind and apart from contextual factors, including theology, then there is no way of objectively testing truth claims. Any theological claim is as valid as the next. There are no ways to test competing paradigms. In regards to instrumentalism and idealism, Hiebert claims that they employ reason selectively. The two systems "collapse under the weight of their own internal contradictions. Both use reason to discredit rationality. Both absolutize relativism" (Hiebert 1999:66).

Another problem with idealism is that it claims knowledge in pure forms apart from cultural forms, rendering the Gospel as an abstraction. Thus, the Gospel can never be received contextually but must be received only in its ideal original form. This can lead to cultural imperialism, dogmatism, and split-level Christianity. People groups that hear the gospel will always hear it in a specific context. A gospel that is left in the context of the missionary and not contextualized for the hearer, leaves the receptor people group with the *form* of the gospel wrapped in *meaning* that is alien to their worldview. If the gospel does not penetrate the worldview, it will not penetrate the culture and will not bring lasting change.

Critical realism, proposed by Hiebert, offers ballast to these two contrasting views by acknowledging a real, knowable, external world (positivism), but that world is known contextually and in part (instrumentalism). Critical realism as an epistemological system is sympathetic to both a real world and to the personal and social dimensions of knowing. As a system it is comprehensive, descriptive and flexible and so is being employed across a variety of disciplines, including missions, theology, science, and the social sciences. Critical realism also embrace epistemic humility (we do not know as God knows); as well as being compatible with Scripture. We see through a glass darkly.

Hiebert feels that critical realism strikes a balance between positivism's emphasis on objective truth and postmodernism's stress on the subjective nature of knowledge (1999:69). It recognizes that knowledge is both subjective and objective. This claim stems from the fact that critical realism sees the connection between epistemology and ontology, although it does not specify the nature of that connection. There is a real, external knowable world (ontological reality), and one can know that world in part through subjective and contextual means (epistemological reality). Van Huyssteen, a critical realist theologian, says it this way:

> Without losing the validity of the facts that all our knowledge us always socially contextualized, critical realists – with good reasons, but not on compelling grounds – claim reference for their tentative proposals. A critical realist viewpoint is indeed realist because, in the process of theological theorizing, this model enables us to recognize the cognitive and referential nature of analogical language as a form of indirect speech. (Van Huyssteen 1997: 43).

Critical realism does not claim to know the world exactly as it represents itself but in terms of maps or models that correlate and approximate the world. Approximation means that the knowledge is not complete, exhaustive or at times even exact, but it is real and true and not relative. Van Huyssteen describes knowledge as a metaphysical *and* an empirical claim that is experientially adequate (Van Huyssteen 1997:41-42). Critical realism is similar in some ways to instrumentalism in that it distinguishes between reality and our knowledge (1999:71). Like positivism, it recognizes that the world can be known and knowledge can be true, as well as evaluated (1999:71). The assertions made in critical realism are subject to critique and change (1999:70). Such critical reflection is often done in hermeneutical communities that "set the standards, define proofs, and integrate one or more theories into a comprehensive system of knowledge (Hiebert 1999:94). Members of the community hold each other accountable by examining each other's research and claims in search of agreement on theories (1999:95). Even though critical realism asserts that knowledge can be real, it is also limited, subject to critique and provisional.

Van Huyssteen recognizes that critical realism "makes a proposal about the *provisionality*, but also the reliability, of theological knowledge (Van Huyssteen1997:43; see also Pannenberg 1991). In its provisionality, knowledge reveals its human constraints and limitations. However, in critical realism this is not a detriment but the impetus for creativity and exploration. Van Huyssteen notes that critical realism acknowledges "both the creativity of human thought and the existence of structures in reality not created by the human mind" (1997:134). This personal creative factor in the knowing process is located clearly in Polanyi with his fiduciary program of knowledge – "The personal participation of the knower in the knowledge he believes himself to possess takes place within a flow of passion... we recognize intellectual beauty as a guide to discovery and as a mark of truth" (Polanyi 1958:300). Other philosophers of science, such as Roy Bhaskar, Arthur Peacocke, Ian Barbour and John Polkinghorne, have also found the system of critical realism to an effective working epistemological model to take on the challenges of the Enlightenment and postmodernism.

Hiebert's critical application of critical realism offers epistemology a real external world and a place for contextual and semiotic apprehension of knowledge, which are vital components of an ontology and an analogical epistemology. In fact, much of the conclusions of critical realism can be adopted to solve the dilemma between modern and postmodern epistemology. All that said critical realism, at least this brand, lacks development in a few important areas. First, the critique posits solutions to the problems of positivism, idealism, and instrumentalism without really engaging the struggles and challenges that are inherent in movements that seek epistemic certainty under an imploding ontology. For example, in the Hiebert text there is no wrestling with Derrida or Foucault and the intricacies of their postmodern claims. A world outside of the text is simply *assumed*. He merely posits an external real world that is expressed scientifically in symbols and models.

What is his basis for an external, real world? Hiebert's work implicitly draws from Charles Peirce. Hiebert was not a philosopher, but an anthropologist and a missiologist, so I will not examine his philosophical position or claims concerning ontology. Hiebert and other scientists from the critical realism school draw heavily on Peirce who laid the philosophical foundation for many critical realists. Thus, in keeping with the methodology of philosophical genealogies as I employed earlier, I will briefly examine Peirce's ontology, which is the root ontology for critical realism.

Peirce was clearly a realist and not a nominalist (Copleston 1967 vol.viii:313). However, Peirce ontologically did not tie his realism to God as a realist such as Aquinas would, not that Peirce did not believe in God. Peirce held the "humble argument" or the "neglected argument" for God which was based more along the lines of pragmatic religious experience rather than on an ontological vision (Anderson 2004:177). Peirce's argument was based on "instinctive or commonsensical belief," which was a type of direct experience or perception (Anderson 2004:177). Impulses and perceptions of God were subordinated, as are all beliefs, to empirical verification. The *practice* of religion is tested by its conformity to the good life and love.

For Peirce, the purpose of religion is to conduct ourselves according to such common sense beliefs for the amelioration of human life (Anderson 2004:179). The practice of religion was an open experiment in the good life, beginning with an internal religious impulse that is carried out in conduct and developed and perfected as an experimental science (Anderson 2004:178-181). Peirce was opposed to theology which he felt sought to stifle this process because it did not allow for the experimental nature of the spirit of religion, which in Peirce's mind should function as a science always under experimentation, critique and adjustment, while theology was rigid and dogmatic (Anderson 2004:181-185). Thus, Peirce avoided a vision of reality that was theologically constructed, including a theistic ontology. Religion was to be subordinate to science and experience serve a pragmatic function.

John Boler makes the argument that Peirce's scientific realism was influenced at some level by scholastic-Scotistic realism. Scotus, who held to the universals or "real generals," gave ontological priority to being as first substances within things (Boler 2004:66 and 72). Peirce worked with Scotus' notions of "common nature" or "first substances" and *haecceity* (individual differentiation) and modified them into three modes of being (Boler 2004:65-77). Peirce's realism combines "firstness," (pure possibility),"secondness," (actuality), and "thirdness," (mediation, potentiality) into a "three-categoried ontology" (Boler 2004:66 and 71-72)[37]. Peirce, influenced by Aristotle and Kant, reduced all reality and predication to these three categories. Peirce, like Scotus, understood intellectual concepts as universals that have a counterpart in reality, understood as laws (Copleston1967:313). The laws of reality reflecting the universals are derived from the essence or common nature as described by Duns Scotus, which stems from a univocity of being (Scotus 1987:2-4 and Copleston1967:313). In both Scotus' version of realism and

Peirce's version of realism, universals are rooted in a univocal experience of being. In Chapter 3, we will look at Scotus' problematic ontology. It is sufficient to say in the case of Scotus, and seemingly in Peirce, being is a natural object of the intellect and that the same being is shared by God, thus the univocity of being, which means an ontological foundation rooted in created being not dependent on transcendent being. This becomes the primary critique of the history of philosophy beginning with Scotus up until today made by Radical Orthodoxy. In Scotus, ontology is detached from God and is rooted in a concept of being that hangs on nothing, which results in its nihilistic implosion. Univocal being that is attributed to God and the created order equally is no being at all. The created order cannot rest in its own being apart from God. Ultimately, ontology detached from a transcendent God is standing on its own, another deflationary ontology.

Peirce's ontology may be too connected to an independent evolutionary creation so that, like Hegel, he assumes a world process, an objective idealism that he mistakes for God. Such radical panentheism is in part a product of the univocity of being and may have a tendency to diminish the transcendence of God, which can be noted in some of the critical realist philosophers of science and religion (Peacocke 1984:55, 64 and 79). Critical realism needs to draw a clear connection between the human context, the external world, *and* an ontological mooring in the eternal, not in the univocal being of the cosmos. For an epistemology that will serve a theology of mission, a clear ontological connection needs to be made with the scriptural God of creation. What I will propose incorporates an analogical epistemology compatible with critical realism but within a larger ontological framework.

In the next chapter, Radical Orthodoxy offers a stinging *theological* critique of modernism and postmodernism and provides a post-secular solution to the problems of a detached ontology of violence[38] and closed hermeneutical systems. Radical Orthodoxy attempts to go to the root of the problem with a revelational understanding of the cosmos and its participation in God. Through this framework, the created order can be "reconnected" to God in an ontology that may be fitting for a theology of mission. As we will find out in the last chapter, transforming mission is not the project of human enlightenment or progress, nor is it the work of the church, but it is the work of God (*missio Dei*)[39].

Notes

[1] The third "order" of the sign is when it replaces the original. The original or the real has no more meaning. The meaning has imploded into the sign. It is now pure simulacra. The simulacra has transcended reality and is *more* "real" than reality, hence "hyperreal." For example, Baudrillard talks about Las Vegas as hyperreal. Its representational and pseudo-reality provides more sensation for people than reality. Las Vegas, as a sign-polis, is "more real" than reality.

[2] Latin for "I think; therefore, I am."

[3] One example is indicated in the title of Antonio Damascio's enlightening book *Descartes' Error.*

⁴ Greater voices than mine, like Wolfhart Pannenberg's, have been more sympathetic toward Descartes. Pannenberg's reading of Descartes in the first volume of his *Systematic Theology* chapter six is that Descartes is a fairly orthodox Christian in the line of Augustine and Anselm with his pursuit of the ontologistic nature of innate ideas, especially as they relate to the existence of God. Descartes constructed his own version of the ontological argument. Pannenberg understood Descartes' philosophy and program to be based on the innate idea of God as infinite, and that our innate ideas, including the *Cogito*, are finite and based on our intuition of God's existence. Descartes' *Cogito* is an adaptation of Augustine's proof against skepticism. The reason his proof of God comes after his proof of his own existence in the *Meditations* is not due to priority but more to style or structure in the *Meditations*. Pannenberg feels that Descartes' idea of the infinite is already in the back of his mind when he undergoes his famous methodological doubt. According to Pannenberg, the *Cogito* does not support or prove God's existence, but Descartes' innate intuition of the infinite is already there to support the *Cogito*. Thus, the charges of radical subjectivism and the like are not warranted. It's a good argument and attempt at saving Descartes, but I don't think it holds. The *Meditations* as sort of series of journal entries of Descartes creative and methodological process in the art of first philosophy are quite psychologically revealing in terms of what some have called a Cartesian anxiety that do not reflect certainty but more a quest for stability. He finds stability in the *Cogito* as consolation not in a revelation or epiphany about the Divine. The *Cogito* is clearly the epiphany not his ontological argument that came later. It is not to say that he did not have faith. The *Cogito* was an attempt at faith seeking understanding, but its radical nature was revealing and indicates a modern shift in authority from the church or institution to reason and the individual, which is probably the reason why Descartes' works were often condemned by the church. Descartes had ontological concerns, but I believe he had a difficult time connecting them to the material world and his scientific interests and endeavors, hence his mind-body dualism. I believe this dualism can be seen in his ontological argument and his *Cogito* epiphany, the latter gave him psychological certainty in this secular world.

⁵ *Telos* is Greek for "purpose," "goal," or "end."

⁶ Francis Bacon wrote the novel *New Atlantis* in 1626. It depicts a utopian society where scientific methodology (Baconianism) governs society, technology brings betterment to human life and science replaces Christianity as the belief system of the people.

⁷ *Christian Missions and the Enlightenmnent* is a collection of essays edited by Brian Stanley that identify and address many these dynamics.

⁸ For Locke, all knowledge is the perception of simple and complex ideas, which *represent* things – a representational epistemology.

⁹ Hume believed that objective events like cause and effect could not be proven but were constructs of the mind created to bring order to the two events.

¹⁰ Kant understood knowledge as a marriage between sense perception and rational structures in the mind. Kant divided the rational categories of the understanding into four groups of three. The four major groups are quantity, quality, relation and modality.

¹¹ Many analytic philosophers, including those in the physicalist (i.e. Quine) and linguistic essentialist (i.e. Plantinga) camps have abandoned strong foundationalism, finding it to be an impossible project. In postmodernism, we find the deconstructing of the self in thinkers, such as Nietzsche, Gilles Deleuze, and Robert Jay Lifton in *The Protean Self* (1999).

¹²Kant held that we cannot know things in themselves (*ding an sich*), only their phenomena. The transcendental ego, or our sense of a unity of our consciousness, is the condition for our knowing. This transcendental ego of apperception precedes the content of our

perceptions and gives them order and meaning through the categories of our understanding and our intuition of space and time. Our knowledge is not of the objects themselves. These transcendental Ideas are all that we know.

[13] The Jesus Seminar reflects a revival of the second quest. Conservatives, like N.T. Wright and Ben Witherington, represent a "third quest" for the historical Jesus.

[14] German for "setting in life" or "context."

[15] Wolfhart Pannenberg offers a thorough critique of the development of self consciousness and subjectivity from Descartes to Heidegger in the light of metaphysics in *Metaphysics and the Idea of God* (Pannenberg 1990).

[16] Latin for "essence" precedes "existence." Sartre claimed that existence precedes essence.

[17] See Milbank's *The Word Made Strange*.

[18] Sartre was heavily influenced by Edmund Husserl's form of phenomenology.

[19] For existential theologians such as Tillich and Bultmann, it meant demythologizing, de-historicizing and reinterpreting the Christian faith through existential experience.

[20] In the case of Kierkegaard

[21] Solipsism is the philosophical position that only the self exists (metaphysical solipsism), and that knowledge cannot transcend one's own conscious mind. All one knows is the content of one's own mind (epistemological solipsism).

[22] Apperception is the direct intuition of one's own consciousness that unifies experience as of one subject, and one relates and understands the experience of others as analogical to their own apperception.

[23] Gadmer saw this twofold problem within hermeneutics, the need to over subjectivism as well as objective methodology. In the case of phenomenology, Gadamer recognized a pre-understanding that comes with the empirical ego as it confronts the horizon of consciousness.

[24] This is Kierkegaard's rereading of Lessing's famous "ditch".

[25] Reductionism

[26] Latin for "man is the measure" (of all things) as applied to ethics.

[27] Jean-Francois Lyotard defined postmodernism as the incredulity towards metanarratives or grand narratives - that is narratives that totalize.

[28] That is the "ism" formulated by Jacques Derrida that describes the Western predilection towards speech and metaphysical systems of presence, such as "the Logos" in Scripture, "the Idea" in Plato, "the *Cogito*" in Descartes and "the System" in Hegel. At the center of Western thinking is the metaphysical presence of the word, according to Derrida.

[29] Derrida was heavily influenced by the French structuralist Ferdinand Saussure. Saussure derived that signifiers are based on difference not on identity. I.e. A is not B, as opposed to A is A. Although a significant figure in postmodern thinking, Derrida operates heavily out of a modernist framework. His deconstruction methodlodgy relies on Saussure and structural anthropology's construal of binary oppositions, in which reality is bifurcated into digital opposites in which deconstruction proceeds to decentralize and relocate the conventional locus within a binary opposition.

[30] What is meant here is that both Kant's critical philosophy, and Derrida's pan-textualism leave "nothingness" as transcendent. Being in terms of the transcendent is unknowable and left outside of what is known, the text.

[31] When everything is said to be the text and in the text, and there is no transcendental signified or a meaning or referent above everything or outside of the text, then such a view can be called textualism (Rorty's term). Some use the term "pantextualism." I do not believe that this result was Derrida's intent, but I do believe it is a consequence of his hermeneutics.

Derrida's hermeneutics are twofold. First, he supplants writing over logocentric language or speech. Derrida uses Saussure to show that language is merely a play of differences in the symbols used for language, and so is speech. Meaning is all text with an interminable interplay of difference. I believe this is his recognition of text as "metaphysical" (my assessment), though it is a metaphysics of absence and not presence, a type of negative theology. Second, in this metaphysics of absence and deferral of meaning via the vacuum of "differance" in the text, Derrida seeks the "other" in the text, the other that is marginalized from the center of interpretation. Alternative readings and justice are the goals of his hermeneutic of deconstruction not necessarily "destruction" or nihilism. However, the result can be the same. The end that Derrida has in mind is admirable, but the means do not justify the end here. The presupposition in deconstruction is no "being" outside of the text; no transcendental signified of reference to our text. We, the text, stand alone in binary opposition wrestling and warring for the power of meaning – an *apiori* warfare, nihilism.

[32] Alain Badiou's philosophy of the event would also characterize this type of phenomenology. Badiou does not fully deflate ontology. He simply denies its unity or oneness in God or in anything and moves from any version of ontological singularity to pure ontological multiplicity, multiples based on multiplicity. Based on set theory, Badiou's claim is that existence is based on being an element of a set and not on its own substance, nature, or individual properties or definition. Nothing is atomic or in and of itself. Everything is a multiple. With existence as belonging, there is a type of participation in Badiou, but for him it cannot be theological because there is no being *in se* or expressed as a monad. However one could ask if the Trinity could be conceived as a multiplicity? For Badious, mathematics is ontology, in which multiples are consistent and found in sets only, but sets are multiplicities that are inconsistent, even anarchical. Badiou's ontology, however, is what he calls "generic," and does not admit a transcendent orientation to ontology. Based on his view of set theory, the nature of mathematics is not founded on continuity or a continuum or even a transcendent, governing, external order but on an unpredictable numerical anarchy that has no mastery but is inconsistent multiplicity. Ultimately, multiplicity is founded on the void, which is neither unit nor multiple and not presentable in a set. In my estimation, Badiou is positing the usual transcendent ontology of non-being that is typical of postmodern aficionados of the void (Hallward 2003).

[33] Being when spoken has one voice. Being for God and being for creation refer to the same thing and not something different or analogous.

[34] I have not attempted to construct any formal argument concerning the existence of God or any particular ontology or epistemology. I am simply contending for the need for God's existence and an ontology of creational participation in God that informs epistemology. I do not hold this as a formal argument but as an informed conviction. I have arrived at this conviction based on God's revelation in creation, Scripture, and in Jesus Christ and the theological transmission and witness of the truth of that revelation to the church and to my own heart. I would not consider this a formal transcendental argument that is that I am arguing transcendentally for theism and participation as a necessary condition for all things. In terms of transcendental arguments, formal transcendental arguments have been used since Kant and probably before. These arguments begin with accepted common experience, knowledge, or belief, and posit a necessary *a priori* condition, category that allows for such an experience, knowledge, or belief. Kant posited subjective, rational categories that were *a priori* synthetic knowledge of experience. Others, such as P.F. Strawson and Kenneth Westphal have offered variants of the transcendental argument, while philosophers, such as Barry Stroud have sought to refute it. While Kant by his transcendental dialectic rejected ontology, I presuppose it as a condition for existence. My attempt is not so much a "formal"

argument but a presuppositional vision of faith that has its confirming reasons concerning the ontological framework of creation as a moderate transcendental realism that conditions the construction of our knowledge.

[35] French for "reason of being" or "reason for being"

[36] A closed-system of semiotics would involve any interpretation of reality that is totalized in sign systems, a type of sign, linguistic or textual reductionism.

[37] Peirce's philosophy is often quite complex. It seems his understanding of being draws primarily from both Aristotle and Scotus and secondarily from Kant. Like Scotus he recognizes being in its modal or possible sense as real, and in this case as the first order of being.

[38] A "detached ontology" is one in which created being is separated from uncreated being. Since being is univocal, created being can be construed to stand on its own apart from God. An "ontology of violence" is an ontology of sameness where difference is not permitted. All knowledge is part of a power-play. There can be nothing outside of the realm of violence. The Radical Orthodox critique holds that this is the logical conclusion to a univocity of being.

[39] Latin for "mission of God"

Chapter Three

Ontology of Participation:
A Radical Orthodox Proposal

Thus he has given us, through these things, his precious and very great promises, so that through them you may escape from the corruption that is in the world because of lust, and may become participants of the divine nature (2 Peter 1:4).

Radical Orthodoxy and the Secular

Postmodernism has received criticism from a variety of camps within Christian circles, some of which have not done the rigorous homework necessary to deal with the complex issues that Postmodernism has placed on the table. However, some of the more serious critiques have come out of the Radical Orthodoxy movement, a theological sensibility that draws from Postmodernism and speaks its language in order to dialogue with it and respond to it theologically. In employing Radical Orthodox analyses and using the term "Radical Orthodoxy," I realize that the movement, though generally speaking is voicing the same concerns, does not speak univocally. There is difference, variation, and nuance within its discourse. The tern Radical Orthodoxy does not always mean the same thing for all its proponents.

My use of Radical Orthodoxy is limited to three interrelated functions, as a Christian apologetic against nihilism, as a critical methodology towards modernism and postmodernism, and as an insightful "philosophical theology" that joins the two disciplines of theology and philosophy together to cast a vision of participation between God and the world. Radical Orthodox thinkers still need to wrestle with some basic theological disciplines, such as scripturally grounded dogmatic, systematic, constructive and biblical theologies. Also, its methodology of genealogical critique can be criticized at times for making sweeping, big brush stroke interpretations of often nuanced and detailed contours within the history of philosophy and pronouncing them as canonical or the only interpretation. In this light, it is said by Laurence Paul Hemming that the Radical Orthodox hermeneutic is implicitly proclaimed as "inerrant" and refuses to be "apologetic," often leaving its theology with a lack of "self-reflexivity" (Hemming 2000:4,12).

The use of one of the Radical Orthodox critiques is not an endorsement of the project as a whole, nor is my use of one of their critiques a statement that that critique is the *only* way to understand modernism and postmodernism. The use of Radical Orthodoxy is primarily theoretical as a critical apparatus and a prelude to an ontologically based epistemology. Radical Orthodoxy, as a young movement, can be accused of making sweeping ideological generalizations of history, philosophy and various movements. However, I find its specific analysis of the ontological problem in modernism and postmodernism to be insightful and possibly revolutionary. Again my use of the term, "Radical Orthodoxy" does not mean that all of those who use that title say or mean the same thing, though it sometimes may look like it. I will attempt to echo what I hear to be a common call.

Radical Orthodoxy is attempting to be a prophetic movement that is calling the church to repent and change its mind from a secular orientation to a theological one. The way that the church is to do this is to return to the point of lapse, in this case in the history of philosophy, and take an alternative route. I also envision it as potentially a renewal or revitalization movement within theology at the confluence where philosophy and other fields overlap theology in this postmodern time. At this place, there is a state of anxiety and disorder seeking a new "steady state" (Wallace 2003:14). Which direction will Christendom turn, back to theology or to the sciences and continue to relegate theology to a ghetto or even an obsolete status?

Radical Orthodoxy in all of its philosophical intricacies accomplishes something very fundamentally theological. It attempts to bring us back to Genesis 1:1 and reestablish its significance as the fundamental ontological reality - God revealed in and through creation. Philosophically and theologically we need to simply return to this place, this revelation in which we now stand existentially. Such a movement may seem radical, but it has been done before and fairly recently in von Balthasar, as he posited a theological *a priori* that identifies us as primarily spiritual beings with an inner capacity and sense of God's divine revelation. A theological *a priori* is an inner instruction or illumination that by faith is receptive to and understands revelation. We are God-compatible. In terms of a universal witness, or as some call it a general revelation, I see it serving as a non-salvific, obscured by sin, but a universal sense of the revelation of God.[1] It is our first and nascent point of contact with the divine in an incipient form that is being called out to receive greater grace and light.

Radical Orthodoxy is attempting to point us back to the theological and our theological senses. It points out where we have deviated from this revelation and built our own revelation of the *nihil*. In applying Radical Orthodoxy and later St. Maximus, my desire is to return to the theological basics and begin with the beginning. The Radical Orthodox move is primarily theological and a return to God first. Maximus is a return primarily to Christology, Jesus Christ first, which is where I think our theology ought to stand. The doctrines of the Triune God and the Incarnation are the most important and bearing in the Christian faith. The faith and practice of the church begin with the Trinity and the Incarnation. Though we employ apologetics and contextualization, at times, *chronologically* prior, these doctrines are always first theology and have preeminence and serve analytically as the beginning without anything prior or prerequisite. They are the revelation of God, which are eternal and preeminent.

However, although Radical Orthodoxy claims for itself this position of pure theological analysis devoid of cultural correlation, this writer does not believe such a claim is possible. All theology and all revelation are embodied in some cultural clothing and expression, and in fact need to be. The Word will always become flesh. I will try to make a distinction between the Radical Orthodox charge of correlation (syncretism), as a form of heterodoxy, or missiologically speaking a syncretism, and proper critical contextualization of revelation, which is necessary in an analogical model of ontology. Radical Orthodoxy claims an analogy of being rather than a univocal being, but at times it is not coordinate with its theology of revelation, which comes off as univocal and monolithic when applied socio-culturally.

This research seeks to meet various missiological and philosophical problems head on in their context and works at that point of contact, but ultimately, it is not a matter of working from philosophy to theology or from mission *praxis* to theology. Whichever problem is addressed and road taken, the diagnostic reveals an underlying theological problem in need of a theological solution. Thus concerning the faith and mission of the church, we begin with the Triune God, the eternal personal community of holy love, and God's creation and mission through his Logos, Jesus Christ. Hence, even as I work from philosophy to theology in the first chapters of this book in order to 'become flesh,' the issue is always theological and is resolved and begins with the Triune God as revealed economically in the Incarnation.

The critical methodology of Radical Orthodoxy, and the one adopted for this work, is employing "genealogical" analysis to the history of philosophy in the vein of Nietzsche and some postmodernists in order to discover points of discontinuity, breaks, and alternative readings in the narrative of a history of philosophy. Radical Orthodoxy looks at a strand of history of philosophy and uncovers the genealogy of postmodernism and discovers its roots in the univocity of being proposed by Duns Scotus (1266-1308) in late medieval Scholastic philosophical theology. The Scotus error of the univocity of being is a fundamental tenet or canon in the critical Radical Orthodoxy genealogy and is part of a heated debate among Radical Orthodoxy critics. With the univocal expression of being, Scotus left the world in its own autonomy, creating the secular.[2] The essence of original sin is when humanity seeks its own autonomous domain apart from God, grounding its existence in its own being and forsaking trust and dependence in God. The shift to a univocity of being is a reoccurrence of the original sin. Late Scholastic philosophy sought to give the created order its own independent autonomous ground.

The primary problem uncovered by Radical Orthodoxy in the genealogy of modernism and postmodernism is this bad gene, the univocity of being. The secular realm possessing its own being apart from God is ultimately rooted in nothingness, since apart from God there is no univocal category of being. Conor Cunningham makes the radical claim that any attempt at a univocity of being is truly the univocity of non-being (Cunningham 2002). When attempting to do non-theologically based philosophy or even philosophy without ontological transcendence, such a pull can draw ontology into a number of closed epistemic systems, whose signs cannot point beyond themselves and in the end collapse, diminish, and vanish. Radical Orthodoxy proposes an ontology of participation as a solution to this problem.

Radical Orthodoxy is a movement that came originally out of Cambridge a decade ago with the publication of *Radical Orthodoxy: A New Theology*. However, the movement had been brewing nearly a decade prior, ignited by Milbank's *Theology and Social Theory: Beyond Secular Reason* (Milbank1990). At first, the movement was fueled among Anglicans but since has become a "concrete ecumenical proposal" crossing many denominations (Smith 2004:65). Among the leading exponents are John Milbank (1952 -), who is Professor of Religion, Politics, and Ethics at the University of Nottingham, Catherine Pickstock, who is Director of Studies in Philosophy and Joint Director of Studies in Theology and Religious Studies at Emmanuel College Cambridge, and Graham Ward (1955 -), who is Professor of Contextual Theology and Ethics at the University of Manchester.

Milbank and the movements other scholars are well-versed in French post-structuralism and Continental postmodern philosophy in general, and are strongly influenced by Catholic thinkers of the *nouvelle theologie*,[3] such as Henri de Lubac (1896-1991) and Hans Urs von Balthasar (1905-1988), as well as ancient thinkers, such as Augustine (354-430 A.D.), Gregory of Nyssa (ca.334-395 A.D.), and Thomas Aquinas (1225-1274). As its name indicates, Radical Orthodoxy seeks to critique the secular and bring theology front and center by returning it to its roots in revelation and by critically adopting premodern sources and early Christian tradition (2004:66). Radical Orthodoxy is orthodox in that "it seeks to be unapologetically confessional and Christian" (2004:65).

In subverting the hegemony of the secular and going back to Scripture and the early traditions of the church, Radical Orthodoxy shares a "catholic vision of the Patristic period through to the high middle ages" (Milbank 2000:36, cited in Smith 2004:66). However, in going back to premodern sources, Radical Orthodoxy does not become shortsighted primitivism or remnant fundamentalism. In seeking to avoid the correlationist, projects of modern and postmodernism, which it does not always do effectively, Radical Orthodoxy critically remixes and adopts premodern sources that share a common ontology in creation and the God of creation. The thinking is that an epistemology that is not dependent on an ontology that is "suspended" from the transcendent God is a secular autonomous construction. When theology adopts such an epistemology, it resorts to the method of correlation.

One of Radical Orthodoxy's major polemics is against the program of correlation. Correlation is what occurs when Christian theology feels it can best communicate its message through secular voices rather than through revelation. James

K.A.Smith, Reformed philosopher and professor and Radical Orthodox contributor, defines the correlationist project as "formulating the claims of Christian revelation in terms of given cultural frameworks (sometimes masking as the human condition) aims at ultimately making sense of revelation in terms that are (supposed to be) universally accessible" (Smith 2004:35). According to Radical Orthodoxy, there is no neutral universally accessible reason or autonomous science that speaks the whole truth and nothing but the truth. No field of knowledge holds a position of privilege that is untouched by theory or uncommitted to belief. Thus, theology speaks best on theological issues and not social theory. Too often theology has believed that revelation can be best spoken in terms of a universally accepted language, like Newtonian physics, Cartesian foundationalism, Kantian critical philosophy, Marxist social theory, Freudian psychology, or Wittgensteinian lingustics, as seen in liberal, post-liberal and fundamentalist theologies that have uncritically accepted such frameworks (2004:148-150). The results have been bifurcations such as reason and revelation, secular and sacred, fact and value, and science and faith.

Radical Orthodoxy attributes these bifurcations and correlations to the creation of modern secularity. Milbank's *Theology and Social Theory* demythologizes the metanarrative of scientism, specifically social science, as it describes Christianity in terms of social theory, rather than on its own terms. Christianity has often seen itself through such a social correlation. While such a metannarrative has claimed neutrality, the fact is that no discourse is uncommitted. Such metannarratives have a genealogy in secularism. Secularism is a sphere that has claimed objective reality but in essence always assumes a standpoint. Milbank declares, "Once, there was no secular" under the domain of Christendom (Milbank 1993:9). However with the coming of Scholastic nominalism through to the Protestant Reformation, and to seventeenth century Augustinianism, Christianity had "completely privatized, spiritualized, and transcendentalized the sacred, and concurrently reimagined nature, human action and society as a sphere of autonomous, sheerly formal power" (Milbank 1993:9). Modern secularity is an illegitimate birth from the womb of Christian theology.

Smith also believes that the secular, "as neutral, objective, and universally rational, is a modern invention intended to secure a universal reason that could ground a public politics" (Smith 2004:50). In light of the fact that Radical Orthodoxy considers modern secularity as a Christian heresy, Radical Orthodoxy traces the modern state as well to its secular origins as a simulacrum or false copy of the church, offering an alternative soteriology to that of the church, i.e. Hobbes' Leviathan (Cavanaugh 1999:182,186-188). Thus as the Christian faith is a theology embodied and lived out in the polis of the church, so secularity is a heretical theology lived out in the polis of the modern state.

Radical Orthodoxy understands all discourses as essentially theological, even political ones, and when theology commits idolatry, it syncretizes with secular reason and

connects knowledge of God with some particular immanent field of knowledge –
'ultimate' cosmological causes or 'ultimate' psychological and subjective needs.
Or else it is confined to intimations of a sublimity
beyond representation, so functioning to confirm negatively the questionable idea
of an autonomous secular realm, completely transparent to rational understanding. (Milbank 1993:1).

Secularity in relation to orthodox Christianity is a heresy (1993:3). When secular reason speaks metadiscursively, it speaks as a "secular theology" (Smith 2004:144-147). Ultimately, Radical Orthodoxy traces the institution of modern secularity back to Duns Scotus and the univocity of being and the privatized space it affords creation outside of God.

I affirm Radical Orthodoxy's commitment to the priority and primacy of theology in informing our understanding of God and his mission and even his creation. I also concur with Radical Orthodoxy's condemnation of the correlationist project. There is no universal language of reason through which revelation can speak that does not carry cultural baggage, especially as secularity has understood such a language. However, I do not hold that such a commitment needs to exclude the critical and subordinate use of science, cultural anthropology, or other theories. It is impossible to express theology without a context. There is always going to be revelation and contextual analogy. Only the Triune God is his own theological context. A commitment to theological *priority* means that other theories are subjected to theological scrutiny and are evaluated by God's revelation to see if such theories contradict or are compatible with theology. If theories are adopted to the detriment and damage of theology and its task, then such syncretism is correlation and is to be avoided, or if non-theological theories are to be given primacy in theological matters, such actions are to be avoided.

It is a contention of this study that theology or knowledge is not to be reduced to context (contextualism) but at some lower level, it is surely contextual in its indigenous forms of socio-cultural expression. Contextualization is not an option. It happens whether we want it to or not. Knowledge has a socio-cultural contextual dimension to it. Pure revelation without analogical human context can never be apprehended. It is always embodied and incarnated though its truth does not change. For revelation to reach people, it must take on context, for we are contextual creatures. Radical Orthodox claims an analogical participation in being. Yet, such an ontology is in accord or compatible with contextualization. Univocity of being is more compatible with monoculturalism and ethnocentrism, allowing one voice of communication and strict, literal formal equivalence in translation or the impossibility of translation itself (Quine).

Critical contextualization is not the question. The question is if theology is unlawfully wedded to an *incongruent* corollary in culture, i.e. syncretism. Ultimately, even Radical Orthodoxy's adoption of an ontology of participation is adopting a corollary from neoPlatonism, possibly exhibiting the method of correlation. Critical contextualization seeks a type of congruence or dynamic equivalence between revelation and its cultural forms. Thus, later I seek to modify Radical Orthodoxy's version of Platonic participation into a more Christological form, as exemplified in Maximus the Confessor. At this point, let us examine the Radical Orthodoxy's critique of Western ontology.

Radical Orthodoxy, The Univocity of Being and Nihilism

Radical Orthodox thinker and University of Nottingham Lecturer, Conor Cunningham identifies the Western ontological crisis and its descent to nihilism in his work *Genealogy of Nihilism*. In the descent to nihilism, there have been two strands of ontology, one that answers every question with an infinite regress of *somethings*, that is ontotheology, and another that does not seek to regress back to a something but a *nothing,* which is construed as *something*, meontotheology, grounding being in non-being (Cunningham 2002:xiii). This is Cunningham's primary critique in his *Genealogy of Nihilism*. Ontotheology grounds all being in prior being. Meontotheology grounds all being in nothing. Cunningham says that the first leads to nihilism, and the second is the realized logic of nihilism (Cunningham 2002:xiii). In his book, he traces the latter, the "nothing as something philosophies" which he calls "philosophies of nothing," or meontotheology, from Plotinus to the Medievalists (Henry of Ghent, Duns Scotus and William of Ockham) to the Enlightenment (Spinoza, Kant and Hegel) to Existentialism and Postmodernism (Nietzsche, Heidegger, Sartre, Deleuze and Derrida). These meontotheologies or expressions of univocal non-being represent an attempt at hypostasizing nothingness. Cunningham notes that each construal contains a dualism of an ontic assertion and a negation, which form a nihilistic monism (Cunningham 2002:250). For example:

> Heidegger grounds Being in *das nicht*; Deleuze, sense in nonsense, thought in nonthought; Hegel, the finite in the infinite; Fichte, the I in Non-I; Schpenhauer, representation in will; Kant, the phenomenal in the noumenal; Spinoza grounds Nature in God, and God in Nature. Each of these dualisms collapses into a Monism as each dualism resides within a symbiotic unicity... (Cunningham 2002:236).

Cunningham identifies the primary dynamic in these dualistic monisms[4] as attempts at creation out of nothing, *creation ex nihilo* (2002:254). Yet what is created is *nothing*. Systems with univocal non-being in their genealogy are ultimately philosophies of death, specifically death to differences and particulars, in Cunningham's estimation (2002:254). Univocity is non-differentiation from pantheism to nihilism and everything in between. Both pantheism and nihilism are systems of non-differentiation. Pantheism says all is God. Nihilism says all is nothing. Univocity as an ontological descriptor is ultimately unified in voice and results in totalization. Theology, however, finds unity in a primal triadic difference from which is suspended a creation of particulars, a differential unity made possible and driven by love (2002:264-265). Theology can do what nihilism cannot, and that is give space to difference.

In my opinion, Cunningham, wittingly or unwittingly, employs transcendental reasoning to this problem of meontotheology (nothing as something). Something is affirmed as the condition for our experience. The nihilist would give ultimate validity to nothingness, while operating out of a position of "something," that is a positing nihilist employs arguments that use language and reason. Nihilism is always an annihilation of "something." Nihilism presupposes something, and thus admits some justification for being. Cunningham recognizes that nihilism seeks to establish nothing as something, and hence again justifies being. It seems that nihilism, and all of the modern and postmodern epistemological constructs and closed-systems cannot help but presuppose some ontological structure, even in their own self-reference. Can anything hold together without an ontological and transcendent vision?

Along with Cunningham, it is also the common assertion of Radical Orthodox theologians that Western philosophy has taken the train of univocal non-being to its nihilistic destination. Radical Orthodox genealogical accounts usually begin with Duns Scotus. As mentioned prior, he posited a univocality to being in that being becomes something predicated to and thus transcendent over both God *and* creation, and something which they both share. Being becomes a common predicate for God and creation. Creation exists *as* God exists, in the same way. The problem is that, apart from God, being has no ground and thus is rooted in nothing. Scotus' univocity of being is ultimately a univocity of non-being. The created world, a hypostatic nothingness, is now an autonomous realm hanging from an ontology of non-being. The univocity of being makes room for the creation of the secular. The world no longer participates in God but has its being apart from him. Thus, the secular is born, and its authority is found in autonomous reason and expressed through the modern state both of which lead to the nihilism and ontological violence found in Nietzsche (Cunningham 2002; Milbank 1993:278-32; Smith 2004:87-103).

Concerning the univocity of being, in Radical Orthodox genealogical studies there is a noticeable break in metaphysics between Aquinas and Scotus and William of Ockham. This break marks a major transition in the history of philosophy and initiates an epistemological crisis. Radical Orthodoxy locates the origins of nihilism and postmodernism at this break. Aquinas metaphysical vision was analogical, in what later developed in philosophical theology into the *analogia entis,* which describes more of a "participatory metaphysics" in which creation "participates in the being of the Creator" (Smith 2004: 96). In an ontology of participation and its corollary analogy of being, creation cannot be uprooted from its grounding in the Creator and given separate status. Everything is seen through and defined by its relation with the Creator. Only as things participate in God, do they have meaning, and do we gain knowledge of them.

Smith also locates a break with Thomist metaphysics beginning with Scotus, who "asserts that *to be* is predicated univocally. Both the Creator and the creature exist in the same way or in the same sense," placing the concept of being higher than God and creation and providing a metaphysically grounding for creation apart from God, which opens the door to a fully secular realm suspended by nothing (Smith 2004:97). "A univocal ontology that denies the depth of things, shutting us up in a suffocating immanence" ends up resulting in nihilism and the closed hermeneutical systems of Postmodernism (Smith 2004:103). A similar case within Radical Orthodoxy can be made against the nominalist William of Ockham (1287-1347). Ockham, who disregarded the notion of eternal ideas, believed that universals are in name or in terms only, *termini concepti* (Cunningham 2002:17-20). There are only particulars or individual things for which the terms signify and represent in propositions (Ockham 1990:33 and Copleston 1962 vol. 3:56). Universals are not to be posited to explain particulars, which stand on their own without mediation (Ockham's razor). Ockham's razor cut away all apparent ontological excess that was not necessary. The real is contained within the particular existent without further reference. Because being is not a universal, existing and being (existence and essence) become synonymous which was not the case with Aquinas. For Aquinas, creation did not have being in itself, but it participated in being analogically. For, Scotus and Ockham, being is univocal (Copleston 1962 vol 3:78). It is predicable to both God and creation. Creation then has its own reference in being which is in its *own* particulars. Thus like the Radical Orthodox Scotus, the Radical Orthodox Ockham offers a secular world with its own internal grounding, opening the door to nihilism, a groundless world, a nothing purported as a something.

Scotus and Ockham bifurcate ontology from theology setting the stage for a further ontological breakdown that would collapse the detached, univocal being into a deflated view of reality that can no longer accommodate for the remaining void without reducing and nihilating. The implications of the Radical Orthodox critique of univocal being and its impact on the modern period is a serious charge. I will now integrate their ontological analysis with my own cursory analysis of deflationary ontology from the previous chapter concerning modernism.

As the sun set on nominal Scholasticism, the humanists began to look inward to human achievement rather than to the Divine, and they began to look toward a more tangible, empirical grasp of reality. The Scientific Revolution and the Enlightenment squeezed out the remnants of Thomistic ontology, deflating its substantial claims and increasing the weight of warrant and proof on ratio-empirical science. During its development over the last four centuries, scientific philosophy as a whole would seek to create a unified field theory of knowledge that would explain everything by the universe's own internal causes and religion in like fashion would resort to deism to allow science such space.

In philosophy, Descartes is forced to prove the universe and God *vis 'a vis* proving his own existence through methodological doubt, which would have been foreign to Aquinas. With Descartes, being is reduced to a cognitive act, birthing the secular foundation of autonomous reason and also creating an unnecessary mind-body dualism with priority given to the former, which is no longer contingent on God or universals but upon itself. With Spinoza and his strong proclamation of univocal being, theology is collapsed into ontology by a panentheistic Unity, which would provide inspiration to Hegel's absolute Idealism, all attempts by pure reason to totalize.

The ontological breakdown and epistemic inflation ensuing from the separation of ontology from theology through a univocity of being occurs also in the empirical philosophies of Locke (sense-based representational knowledge) (Locke 1964:89 and 320), Bishop George Berkeley (*esse est percipi* – to be is to be perceived) (Berkeley 1929:124-126), and David Hume (causality as a cognitive ordering principle that does not exist in the nature of things) (Copleston on Hume's *Treatise* 1963:3:269-271). The British empiricists inherited the nomimalist tradition, and thinkers like Locke struggled as to where to locate anything real and substantial and so constructed a dichotomy of *real* and *nominal* essences. In order to uphold the empirical world and our ideas of it, Locke assumed the notion of a *substratum*, a useful construction, which he admitted could not be known or proven, that supports or upholds our ideas of the reality of our sensible perceptions. The mind constructs a complex idea or a nominal essence of a particular that logically reflects the nature of a particular's real, sensible, and material essence, which ultimately, in itself, is unknowable. Nominal essences or the naming of a complex idea is a product of scientific inquiry, experimentation and classification. The knowledge of substances are not in any way "real" but are empirically gathered and nominally attribute, an immanent substratum "supporting" the assertion of a nominal essence. The scientific construction of nominal essences begins to suggest the Kantian categorical constructions of the phenomenal world.

Locke offers us an experience-based world that immanently supports itself. Though he clearly held to a faith in God, Locke is tilting our mind towards more of a deistic and natural understanding of its operations. We are left in a self-contained world of pure experience and left to what our senses can gather and our ideas can construct, truly the Enlightenmnet dream. The draw and pull of the immanent and the empirical begins to take the air out of any ontological atmosphere. An empirically based, closed-system ontology begins to implode on itself and will attempt to totalize through subjective modes of apprehension – representational ideas, perception, and cognition. The more being deflates the more the ratio-empirical structures inflate and given importance. The later radical empiricism of William James, John Dewey and neo-pragmatists like W.V. Quine and Hilary Putnam would relativize ontology, as experience itself becomes its own ontology, or ontology is dismissed altogether in post-critical philosophy.

For Descartes, being is reduced to thinking. With the British empiricists, reality is reduced to impressions or perceptual based ideas. Disconnected from a metaphysical backing in God, Locke's understanding of reality as sense-based ideas has no way of offering assurance that it is delivering what it claims by representation. In the end, he resorted to a fideistic explanation that God would not create a world that is not the way that it appears (Gilles 1987:129). For George Berkeley (1685-1753) things exist only as they are perceived. He goes further than Locke. Ideas are not representative of reality but are reality. Like Berkeley, David Hume

(1711-1776) felt that our perceptions of the world are reality, and these perceptions are impressions that become ideas, including causality. There is no metaphysical reality behind any of these perceptual smoke and mirrors.

Ultimately, "there is neither matter nor mind in the universe; nothing but impressions and ideas" (Copleston 1963 3:366). The skepticism that began with Continental rationalism and British empirical philosophy was taken to its logical conclusion with Kant. Again, Immanuel Kant (1724-1804) somewhat synthesized his predecessor movements by uniting the innate ideas of rationalism with the sense formed ideas of empiricism. Knowledge becomes a product of the wedding of sense perception in experience to pre-existing categories and structures in the mind. However, that which is known is the phenomenal world. The noumenal world, the transcendent – the thing in-itself, is unknowable (Kant 1990:158).

Copleston, who is not a Radical Orthodoxy thinker but a Jesuit historian of philosophy, posits that "if the thing in-itself is eliminated, it follows that the subject creates the object in its entirety" (Copleston 1963 3:431). Epistemology creates a virtual reality. Kant bifurcates the transcendental from the empirical, where the former is inaccessible. All we have are phenomena that are shaped by the creative intellect via transcendental Ideas which are not connected to the objects themselves but the mind. Internal cognition is totally disconnected from ontology within a realm of phenomena that intimates the contextual construction of knowledge that we have come to see in postmodernism. It was an advance in thinking to identify creativity in scientific knowledge, but such a discovery would become too difficult to bear in such heavily hermeneutical based methods as Derrida's deconstruction.

Autonomous reason (the transcendental ego) and morality (categorical imperative) are the results of a Kantian collapse of ontology found in his dualism of noumena and phenomena. These notions would later influence idealist totalizations in thinkers like Fichte and Hegel. These systems would be the last attempts at a totalizing of reason before the arrival of Nietzschean nihilism to put all of the theological and ontological import back into a univocal being of nothing. As noted earlier in Kierkegaard, a totally rational system is not possible, and in fact such tyranny elicits the radical backlash of a Nietzsche and his brand of nihilism which would be one of the biggest influences in postmodernism.

Moving forward to postmodernism, Milbank "treats the writings of Nietzsche, Heidegger, Deleuze, Lyotard, Foucault, and Derrida as elaborations of a single nihilistic philosophy" that demonstrate an "absolute historicism,"[5] a nihilistic genealogy which claims an objective and positivist account of its predecessors will to power (Milbank 1993:279-82), an "ontology of difference," an ontology of opposition or violence stemming from the will to power, (Milbank 1993:279), and an "ethical nihilism" as a consequence of an ontology of violence (Milbank 1993:278-82). For Milbank, postmodernism posits a positivistic metanarrative of nihilism that precludes any narrative from claiming outside status as a narrative or ontology of peace, i.e. like the Christian faith. Yet, due to a selective account of facts within its historical genealogy and its pretension to objectivity rather than interpretation, this metanarrative of nihilism is more of a myth for Milbank (Milbank 1990:280-281). For Radical Orthodoxy, nihilism stands as an illegitimate possibility or choice (Cunningham 2002: 169-170).

According to James Smith, nihilism is the logical consequence of Scotist ontology which leads to a closed- system world without divine reference.

> Nihilism is a consequence of the ontological flattening of the cosmos by the univocity; in other words, once immanence was unhooked from its suspension from transcendence and granted an autonomous self-sufficiency, it also enclosed itself within a closed system. We can think of it this way: Nihilism is obviously linked to the *nihil* of nothingness. According to a Christian theological understanding, creation in itself is nothing; that is, created things depend so radically on God for their existence that "without God, created things can only be perceived as *nothing* since they are, indeed, in themselves nothing." With the advent of Scotist ontology, created things were unhooked from their participation in God, such that they are now taken to be independent realities. (Smith 2004:102).

Nietzsche's nihilistic critical suspicion has been adopted as a hermeneutic by many postmodernists. Nihilism has become the DNA of much of postmodernism's deconstruction, hermeneutical suspicion, and power-knowledge critiques, which see difference as violence.

Eastern Orthodox theologian and former student of John Milbank, David Bentley Hart has some sharp insights into the problem of postmodernism's predilection toward an ontology of violence which is in direct opposition to Christianity's ontology of peace:

> A certain current within contemporary philosophy, however, asserts that violence Is – simply enough – inescapable; wherever Nietzsche's narrative of the will to power has been absorbed into the grammar of philosophical reflection, and given rise to a particular practice of critical suspicion, a profound prejudice has taken root to the effect that every discourse is reducible to a strategy of power, and every rhetorical transaction to an instance of an original violence. From this vantage a rhetoric of peace is, by definition, duplicity; subjected to a thorough critique, genealogy, or deconstruction, evangelical rhetoric can undoubtedly be shown to conceal within itself the most insatiable appetite for control; the gesture by which the church offers Christ to the world, and bears witness to God's love for creation, is in reality an aggression, the ingratiating embassy of an omnivorous empire…the difference between two narratives: one that finds the grammar of violence inscribed upon the foundation stone of every institution and hidden within the syntax of every rhetoric, and another that claims within history a way of reconciliation has been opened up that leads beyond, and ultimately overcomes, all violence. (Hart 2003:2).

Scotus' move to a univocity of being detached reality from its participation in the transcendent (God) and has given reality it its own shadowy reference, a vapor of what was. Nietzsche uncovered the roots of Western thinking, and his followers have grown their philosophies from this bed of nihilism, whether it is Derrida's deconstruction of the text based on metaphysical absence and the "*differance*" played out in the inherent absence of meaning, or in Foucault's reduction of knowledge to power games.

Whether reality is located *strictly* in the text, the power play, the sign, or in social construction, a closed hermeneutical system is created apart from external or transcendent references, such as the *Logos*. Such a closed hermeneutical system seeks to stand on its own without a sufficient internal description, explanation, warrant or substantiation for its own claim about itself or the ultimate reality to which it claims to reduce. Closed hermeneutical systems are liable to reductionism and the fallacy of self- reference. Postmodernism's reductions are characteristic of the breakdown of the univocity of being as it exists in reality apart from God, who holds all things together. Being begins to shatter into textual or semiotic pieces that mean nothing ultimately apart from God. Almost every epistemological reduction of reality takes on ontological proportion and form, claiming transcendence, though in actuality being nothing and hanging from nothing, meontotheologies to use Cunningham's term. These reductions are all features of a univocal foundationalism that have been foundational to Western epistemology. What is proposed here, and I affirm, is not foundationalism but "suspension." Everything is suspended from nothing and both are suspended from God.

Postmodernism's critique of the age of reason holds only when it holds to a God who holds all things together. Radical Orthodoxy recognizes this need for the transcendent, an ontology of participation. Without the transcendent to suspend[6] a creational ontology, the ontological structure of univocal being collapses within its own self-referenced closed hermeneutical systems into a nihilistic plunge. A heavy charge is that the genealogy of nihilism and all of its ancestors and offspring represent a philosophy of death, which is not compatible with a narrative of life as expressed in the warp and woof of the Christian message of good news.

Unfortunately, theologies of correlation are also trapped in this endgame as they seek to express scriptural truth in a postmodern world through ontologies that nihilistically bottom out under the guise of radical pluralism, relativism, or scientism. Yet another problem that is created by the ontology of nihilism is the issue that every discourse, regardless of its claims, is a ruse for violence, as mentioned in the first chapter. Violence is the assumption of every discourse of difference in a power-knowledge hermeneutic.

Radical Orthodoxy and an Ontology of Violence

Nietzsche's "will to power" analysis of Western metaphysics surely is descriptive and warranted at some level, and at best penultimate, but Milbank notes that this analysis is proposed as a genealogy claiming absolute historicism (Milbank 1990:280). The implications are that it absolutely describes *all* knowledge claims excluding its own. It becomes its own "discourse of universal reason," a new positivism" (Milbank 1990:264).

Within the nihilist's genealogy of knowledge, there is one thought – power is knowledge. Everything else is difference, and that "difference is defined as oppositional difference, a difference which enters the existing common cultural space to compete, displace, or repel" (Milbank 1990:289). In a univocity of non-being, difference cannot be understood in any harmonious composition, as in an analogy of being, but has to be understood as oppositional. Warfare becomes a universal *a priori* (Milbank 1990:289).[7] Conflict and violence become primordial categories that describe the *actus*, human action in general, and depict reality.

Although postmodernism speaks frequently of difference, within a collapsed ontology on a flattened monistic plane of immanence, philosophies of difference become either philosophies of sameness or philosophies of opposition (Smith 2004:195). Sameness here takes on total and fascist forms, and opposition means warfare within an ontology that speaks a non-analogical language. Discourses from this perspective are the same in that they all exude violence in their difference. Discourses are also all the same in that they are all only interpretation. With Nietzsche and Foucault all knowledge is interpretation and not fact, excluding their own genealogical history (Milbank 1990:281). Milbank grants that the will to power can be one possible interpretation but not the only one (Milbank 1990:281). As we have noted, when theology correlates with pure reason and scientism, Nietzsche's charge is valid, but as we shall observe it is not the only possibility for theology.

Is then Nietzsche ultimately correct about Christianity itself being a power regime? Milbank says that for Nietzsche "every denial of power is a ruse of power" (Milbank 1990:286). If that is the case, then Christianity as an absolute denial of power through self- renunciation and a renunciation of ultimate allegiance to earthly rule must be the final ruse of absolute power (Milbank 1990:286). However, Milbank does not grant Nietzsche's claim metaphysical status but calls it another *mythos* (Milbank 1990:279). In turn, Milbank offers a counter-ontology, an ontology of peace (Milbank 1990:279). As will be explored later, an ontology of peace stems from an *analogia entis* which "conceives differences as analogically related, rather than equivocally at variance" (Milbank 1990:279). Here, Milbank is employing Scholastic thinking about predication, or how to say something *about* God or *about* something. Equivocal predication is pure difference. With Nietzsche, such difference is oppositional. However, with analogical predication difference and similarity work together. Analogy harmonizes likeness and difference. For Milbank an ontology of peace or affirmative difference is just as valid as an alternative narrative as an ontology of violence (Milbank 1990:289). Since for Radical Orthodoxy all claims are theological, an ontology of peace is a more just alternative. Analogy provides a more just framework for difference, and a creational ontology of peace and goodness reveals the ultimate intentions for the cosmos discursively and eschatologically.

In theology proper, we find differential unity and goodness best expressed in the three different *hypostases* united relationally in love in the same *ousia*. The Trinity and creation express a differentiation and particularity that is whole, at peace, and good (Hart 2003: 179-183; 250-259). In Christian revelation, we do not have an original violence that is to be ontologized, creating an eschatology of cosmic death. Likewise, Milbank sees Augustine (*Civitas Dei*)[8] as offering a counter-history "which reads war as an absolute intrusion, an ontological anomaly" (Milbank 1990:294). Such a reading has not always been the story for the church, Orthodox, Catholic, and Protestant, as it has divided and excommunicated its fragments into anathema. Such a reading has not always been the story for mission, as a crusader model of evangelism has been frequently implemented out of an ontology of violence. Many crusaders and conquistadors have executed holy war, *jihad*, as a political and religious solution to difference. Yet the only thing religious war proves is not who is right but who is left. People like Las Casas are often the anomaly in mission. In the next section, an onto-epistemological solution from the Radical Orthodox critique will be presented as a basis for the development of an epistemology for a theology of mission.

Radical Orthodoxy, Participation, and *Analogia Entis*

At this point I will summarize where I have been in my implementation of Radical Orthodoxy. In examining modern and postmodern thinking, Radical Orthodoxy traces the problem with these systems to Scotus' univocity of being. With the univocity of being, the created order became a detached and separated order from the Creator, the transcendent. Being became an equal predicate for both God and the world. The world became its own autonomous reality grounded in being in itself. Radical Orthodoxy understands this autonomy as the making of the secular. With the univocity of being and the making of the secular, the ontological structure of reality, which was once suspended from the transcendent, is now collapsing on itself.

As the world is unhooked from the transcendent and being is given univocal status, being no longer is suspended from God. Being is grounded in nothingness, a univocity of non-being. We have a deflated immanent ontology that now relies on pure epistemic structures for meaning and certainty. These epistemic structures in a closed univocal ontology become closed systems themselves. Taking on ontological roles, these epistemic structures become reductionistic in their attempt to totalize. Also stemming from a univocity of non-being, they are nihilistic in nature. Finally, being nihilistic in nature they operate out of an *a priori* of violence, in which all knowledge is forged to eliminate opposition.

The Christian revelation seeks to offer a counter ontology, an ontology of peace. The harmonious differentiated structure of the Trinity and creation, whose motion is relationality in unity, provides a model and a basis for difference that is non-violent and analogical. Radical Orthodoxy describes its counter ontology as an ontology of participation (*methexis*) (Milbank, Pickstock, and Ward 1999:3-4). Humanity cannot detach itself from its participatory origin, which is an act of violence itself, and declare independence. With *methexis*, participation, creation assumes no autonomous order of its own but is suspended from the transcendent, and the nature of the relationship of being is analogical. The univocity of being becomes an analogy of being which understands difference in non-violent terms.

Also, the nihilistic vortex that collapses a detached ontology is replaced in an ontology of participation in God by an eschatological hope of *pleroma,* fulfillment or fullness, as the cosmos fulfills its *telos* in the divine Logos. Hence, epistemology is then reconnected to ontology through the analogical-participatory *logos* structure of the cosmos.

Radical Orthodoxy recovers this creational ontology by invoking Plato. Radical Orthodoxy frequently calls upon classical sources and remixes them in a new context. Catherine Pickstock's *After Writing: On the Liturgical Consummation of Philosophy* takes an alternative look at Plato, especially in the *Phaedrus.* While Plato is often seen as a dualist, Pickstock's claim is that "Plato does not wish to drive a wedge between form and appearance, the strongly positive view of *methexis* (participation) in the *Phaedrus* frees him from the charge of otherworldliness and total withdrawal from physicality" (Pickstock 1998:14). Her reading of Plato detects a celebration of physicality in its suspension from the transcendence.

In Pickstock's *After Writing,* Plato is seen as a theurgical philosopher in the Neoplatonic light of Iamblichus and Proclus. In Pickstock's estimation, Plato values the body, beauty and materiality, as opposed to a dualist as he is often interpreted as in *Phaedo* (Pickstock 1998:12 and Smith 2004:104-105). Theurgy, which literally means "divine-working," often is used to describe the NeoPlatonic rituals and operations whereby the soul ascends various emanations to reach the transcendent God. Pickstock is using theurgy in a general sense in that there is a participatory connection between God and creation, thus bringing value to creation as opposed to disregard. Pickstock's Plato as theurgical philosopher becomes a philosopher of embodiment valuing materiality in a sacramental or liturgical fashion, restoring a doxological, liturgical worldview to creation, which had been removed following Scotus (Pickstock 1998:135-157).

Where Scotus' politics, through univocity of being, legitimized spatialization that created autonomous and totalitarian regimes, an ontology of participation reconnects the *polis* to the transcendent. A positive valuation of the body in an ontology of suspended materiality has an impact on our politics and our social construction of reality that prohibits a dualistic and reductionistic devaluation of the body (Smith 2004:104). Hence, a Radical Orthodox ontology of participation claims a creation that is not secular but that is sacramental, incarnational, liturgical and doxological, embracing the theological import of all things.

Below, I will examine how this positively affects a theology of mission. However, in anticipation, we look to James K.A. Smith, an unofficial Radical Orthodox theologian by association, who highlights the importance of an ontology of participation according to Radical Orthodoxy (Smith 2004:189-204). First, it respects both materiality and transcendence. Extreme views of docetism, Gnosticism, or *ex opera operato* that rely on a false dualism have no place in a true analogical ontology. Since creation participates in the transcendent, it is given value. However, this embodiment is non-reductive since it is suspended from the transcendent. A valuation of the material is not a reduction to materialism. Matter is more than itself and finds its reality and significance in the immaterial and transcendent.

Methexis[9] stresses the dependent nature of creation upon the Divine (*metousia Theou*)[10]. Thus, all of creation is graced nature, revelatory and a gift (Smith 2004:192).

Second, as mentioned above, an ontology of participation, specifically in the Trinity, is an ontology of peace even in difference. Differential ontology or an ontology of violence is the consequence of a nihilistic ontology. In an ontology of participation difference is not necessarily oppositional within an analogical framework. With both the Trinity and creation as models of differential unity such harmony can be an eschatological realization in the *polis* (the church and the world).

Third, creation is good. It is good because it is incarnational and participates in the Divine analogically (Smith 2004:199). This does not mean that creation is incarnational in the same way and to the same degree, that God was incarnate in Jesus Christ. Creation embodies or is an "embodiment" of the creational Word of God and reflects the nature of God analogically. Creation is a physical expression of God's creative Word. Since incarnation in its various usages is descriptive of creation, Jesus Christ, and even *theosis* or new creation, incarnation in general becomes central to the shape of our epistemology and our theology. The creative *Logos* gives life and meaning to all things. All of creation is sacramental as God manifests his will in and through it, especially in the Incarnation of the *Logos*. Later, it will be observed in Maximus how God fulfills his liturgical purpose for the cosmos as doxological space for *theosis*. The goodness of creation and physicality reaffirmed in the Incarnation and Resurrection anticipates an eschatological hope for an embodied existence in the new creation (Smith 2004:202).

I have added a fourth benefit to Smith's list. An ontology of analogical participation provides a framework for epistemology which transcends the modern and postmodern tendencies towards nihilism, totalization, reduction, and closed-systems, which are all characteristic of a univocity of non-being. Analogical reasoning avoids the nihilism of univocal reasoning because of its relation to being. A univocal ontology seeks greater and greater certainty in its epistemological expression only to find greater reduction and more discursive or textual "slippage" into non-being. Nothing sustains. Eschatologically, an ontology of participation does not anticipate a nihilistic collapse into the void, but being purposefully suspended from the Divine, it finds the *pleroma* of God in the new creation through the resurrected Christ. A full ontology suspended from the transcendent does not find nihilism a necessity, but makes a choice to participate in God (*metousia Theou*) and fulfill God's purpose. Heidegger's onto-theological critique of philosophy and theology failed to consider being in terms of analogy but only as univocity and thus saw it as an idolatrous correlation to take "being" from Western metaphysics and deify it and pray to it. God is totalized in the metaphysical being of philosophy when being is univocal but not in an analogical construal of being.

Hart who recognized Heidegger's oversight also recognized the language of analogy knows no totalization, as it experiences ceaseless intervals of likeness and difference. It is an infinite striving or *epektasis;*

language, drawn on by the beauty of the Word who is the distance containing all the words of creation, traverses the analogical interval between God and creation (of which God himself is the distance), between creation's proportions and the proportions of peace that belongs to God's infinity; and so there can be no end to the progress of language toward God. (Hart 2003:301).

David Bentley Hart describes Gregory of Nyssa's understanding of the *analogia entis* in its infinite expression of both likeness and difference as:

> the actual movement of analogization of our likeness to God within an always greater unlikeness is the event of our existence as endless becoming ...However even though becoming is thus a kind of crisis, especially for sinful creatures, it is more originally peace, birth and life...Thus our likeness to God, which is all that makes us to be (to share in the Logos's eternal standing forth, in the light of the Spirit, as the likeness of the Father's being) is, in the difference between finite and infinite, always embraced in a greater unlikeness – and this is the difference that lets us be...The doctrine of creation, however, in saying that all things live, move, and are in God not because they add to God or can in any way determine his essence, but as gracious expressions of the plentitude of his his being, knowledge, and love, frees metaphysics from any nihilistic destiny: the *maior dissimilitudo* of the ontological analogy means that the *similitudo* between God and creatures, rather than dwelling in a thing's flawed likeness to some higher essence, distorted in space and time, subsists rather in that synthesis of transcendental moments and particular event that constitutes each things in its being. Each actuality, in its difference, shows forth God's actuality in its fullness. Indeed, the "greater unlikeness" in proportion of the analogy means that the "likeness" in the analogy is ever greater the more fully anything is what it is, the more it grows into the measure of its difference , the more profoundly it drinks from the transcendent moments that compose it and allows all its modes of disclosure to speak of God's infinite goodness. (Hart 2003:243-246)

In describing the inability to totalize within the *analogia entis*, David Bentley Hart continues that the "Christian narrative fixes analogy's proportions within an infinite (not a total) hierarchy of mediations, which can never become a taxonomic index of the world or an economy of epistemic correspondences" (Hart 2003:307). An *epektasis* of analogical transcendence in ecstatic desire is continuously fulfilled but never consumed and is left wanting and desiring in the apophasis. The flight is both cataphatic and apophatic. Analogy as a proportion always has an

> analogical interval that separates and unites its "objects;" and this is its peculiar beauty and elusiveness. A proportion is neither an essence nor a negation; analogy is that form of discourse that is apophatic and cataphatic at once... (Hart 2003:306)

Analogical reasoning not only does not totalize, but it also does not reduce. Its apophatic dimension of unknowing will not permit reductionism. The analogical interval or *diastema* of likeness and difference allows for cataphatic *and* apophatic dimensions of knowing.[11] Thus, no discourse is ever complete. God himself, who is beyond the infinite of the created order, is the boundary. Hart again complements the balance of apophasis and cataphasis:

> Analogy saves apophasis from assuming the form of a mere systematic privation of attributes, a mystical ascent toward annihilation in the divine silence, and saves cataphasis from becoming an absolute pronouncement that attempts to reduce God to a principle or object; analogy is that lambent interval between the two dreamt-of poles of totalizing metaphysics. (Hart 2003:310-311)

An analogical epistemology stemming from an ontology of participation in the *Logos* is also not a closed system but open-ended in two ways. It is open-ended ontologically because there is an utter and infinite dependence on the eternal God. God is the boundary. It is open-ended in infinite signification and analogical expression of both God and creation. As for the mode of knowledge apprehension in participation, since there are no secular or autonomous domains in an ontology of analogical participation, faith and reason are not bifurcated. All of creation is graced and revelational. In the Radical Orthodox remix of Aquinas, Milbank and Pickstock note that "reason and faith in Aquinas represent only different degrees of intensity of participation in the divine light of illumination and different measures of absolute vision" (Milbank and Pickstock 2001:xiii). *Fides et ratio*[12] in Milbank and Pickstock's Aquinas are not mutually exclusive but "faith involves an intensification of participation in divine intellectual intuition" (2001:23). Reason and faith are "construed by Aquinas as successive phases of a single extension always qualitatively the same" (2001:24). Thus an onto-epistemology of participation is compatible with a faith that seeks to understand (*fides quarens intellectum*) a universe that purposefully participates in God in a way that is understood and expressed through the semiotics of analogies (Holcomb 2005:248; Hart 2003:307).

Similarly, contemporary types of critical realism seek to depict the truth about reality in terms of analogies, models, metaphors and maps, as we noted earlier in our discussion about Paul Hiebert. Much of these sorts of discourses revolve around the nature of truth and theories of truth. Critical realism recognizes the symbolic nature of truth specifically in models. Critical realism, as well as other recent epistemologies, seeks to distance itself from modern *correspondence*[13] theories of truth within naïve realism. Milbank and Pickstock recognize that "modern theories of correspondence are grounded in epistemology rather than ontology" and thus their failure (Milbank and Pickstock 2001:5).

Both modern and postmodern ontologies have frequently been collapsed and flattened into epistemic systems that have had to take the transcendent role left behind by ontology but cannot transcend their own self- reference. Thus, epistemological attempts to correspond textual or discursive reality to anything external have been futile. Radical Orthodoxy revisits and remixes Aquinas to "show that the notion of truth as correspondence is in crisis only because it is taken in an epistemological rather than ontological sense (2001:xiii). Aquinas' theory of truth is correspondent only in the sense that it "depends entirely upon the metaphysical notion of participation in the divine Being" (2001:4). Truth has to do with analogization and participation in the *Logos*. Thus "to be in the truth is 'to correspond' to God in whom we participate" (2001:4). For Aquinas correspondence (*adequatio;* adequation) is relational and ontological, as it joins being and knowing. It is not a passive and objective mirroring of the external world in epistemic terms, but it is an "event which realizes or fulfills the being of things known, just as much as it fulfills truth in the knower's mind" (2001:5). This onto-epistemic process does involve sensory information, ideas and judgment concerning that information, but the knowledge of a thing also relates to its becoming what it is meant to be in its existence, unity, truth, goodness, and beauty.

In this sense, truth is a mode of existence and is convertible with being (2001:6). Truth is a transcendental and an attribute of being. Truth is not tested by the exact, representation and connection of a perception, idea, or sign to the thing itself, but it is evaluated according to how it fulfills its purpose in being, and how it is known in fulfilling that purpose. Milbank and Pickstock understand truth according to Aquinas as neither epistemological nor analytical (propositional) but that it is ontological and convertible with being, a mode of existence that corresponds to its *telos* in God (2001:9). Linking truth with being is a strategic Radical Orthodox move, echoing the one made by von Balthasar and others from the Catholic Ressourcement (i.e. Przywara), who revive the use of the classical and scholastic transcendentals (being, unity, truth, goodness, and beauty) as part of a coherent and comprehensive ontology that informs epistemology, teleology and ethics. Truth along with goodness, beauty, and the one are necessary attributes and adjectives of being. Balthasar noted in his colossal triology of aesthetics, dramatics, and logic,[14] truth and logic must be ontological.

In other words, truth is not reduced to a modernist notion of correspondence to empirical data and rational constructs. As opposed to being subsumed within strict epistemological categories, truth primarily belongs to existential and ontological categories, as well as to moral and aesthetic categories, and then to epistemological ones. Truth relates to things as they participate in God, according to their intended design. Truth is ontological and teleological in its analogization in that "the truth of a thing is taken as that thing fulfilling the way it ought to be" (2001:5). Participation replaces correspondance, as "a thing is fulfilling its telos when it is *copying God in its own manner,* and tending to existence as knowledge in the divine Mind" (2001:9). Truth is first in the mind of God and second as things copy the mind of God in analogical proportion (2001:10).

Thus, truth is primarily related to the Divine, and then secondarily related to things, and *then* to our knowledge of them. Unlike modern construals of truth, Aquinas' understanding of truth is theological, relational, analogical, ontological, teleological and thus eschatological. Truth in terms of being is analogical, or what would later be called the *analogia entis,* the analogy of being.[15] Being between God and creation is analogical. The predicates of being are transcendental, such as truth, unity, goodness, and beauty, and these are analogical as well. Truth is a function of being and being participating in God, *metousia Theou*, and thus ultimately Christological, for Christ is true in his embodiment of the life and being of the Trinity. Truth is Christological and has a Christological mode of correspondence for us through our imitation of Christ as we participate in him (2001:2). As Milbank and Pickstock put it, *analogia entis* becomes *analogia Christi* (2001:61). Things are true as they participate in God and specifically as they participate in the incarnate *Logos*.

Later it will be explored in Maximus and Wesley how this analogical participation in God, *metousia Theou*, becomes not only an epistemological framework but also a soteriological and missiological one as well. The *analogia entis* is a participation of the *logoi* of created things in the *Logos* with ultimate participation in the incarnate *Logos* (Hart 2003:303,305). *Metousia Theou* in Christ is to bring humanity into *theosis* and to transform the entire cosmos. This is the mission of God.

FIGURE 1
A Map of Some Contemporary Western Theologies and Philosophies

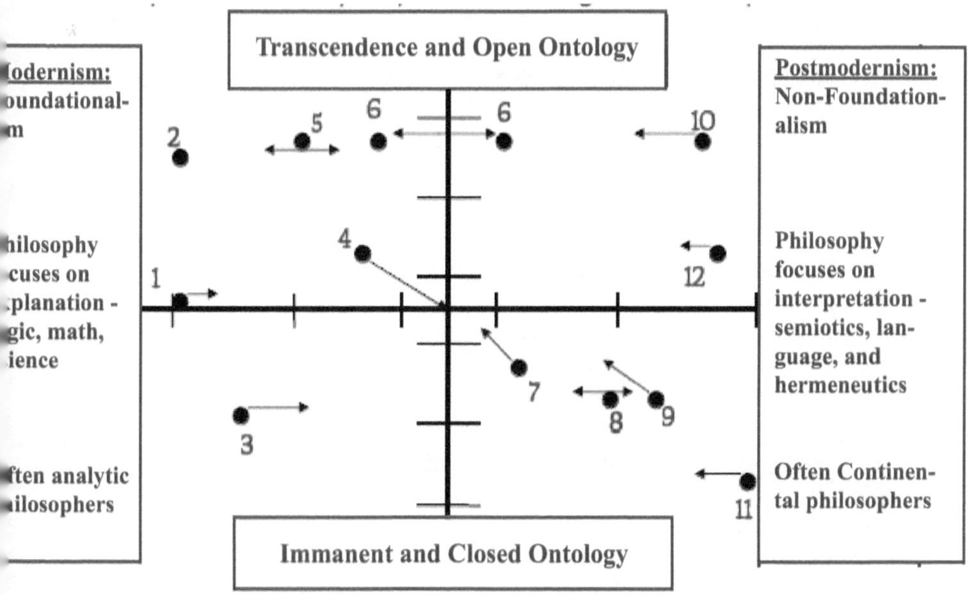

[Figure: A two-dimensional map with vertical axis labeled "Transcendence and Open Ontology" (top) and "Immanent and Closed Ontology" (bottom); horizontal axis with "Modernism: Foundationalism" / "Philosophy focuses on explanation - logic, math, science" / "Often analytic philosophers" on the left, and "Postmodernism: Non-Foundationalism" / "Philosophy focuses on interpretation - semiotics, language, and hermeneutics" / "Often Continental philosophers" on the right. Numbered points 1–12 plotted with arrows indicating tendencies.]

Note the arrows indicate that the movement has diversity and points to other tendencies within the movement. Also "closed" here is based on my usage of the term "closed-system." Participation is an open-system that allows for the transcendent, specifically in God. Closed-systems are more restrictive and immanent and often reductive.

Key to the Graph

1. **Scientific Realism** – It states that the world described by science is real. Ontologically, it holds to an external, objective world that can be known mathematically and experientially through the senses and technology. Scientific realism has a high view of reason similar to modernism. Often adhered to by foundationalists. E.g. Jarrett Leplin, Richard Boyd, and Philip Gasper (philosophers of science).

2. **Theological Fundamentalism** – holds to a literalist view of scripture and interpretation, and a rational foundationalist view of reality and knowledge. Ontologically, fundamentalists acknowledge a transcendent God and a real, external creation. E.g. B.B. Warfield, J. Gresham Machen, John McArthur, Bob Jones University.

3. **Theological Liberalism** – does not hold to a literalist view of scripture and interpretation. Like a positivistic science, it only holds on to that which can sustain historical, cultural, and scientific critique. Theological liberalism is more apt to have an immanent view of God, rather than a transcendent one. Yet it holds to a real, external world in the way that modernism does. E.g. Schleiermacher, Union Theological Seminary, Harry Emerson Fosdick, Rudolf Bultmann, Paul Tillich, John Shelby Spong, the Jesus Seminar.

4. **Critical Realism** – Critical realism holds to a real, external world that is apprehended critically and contextually. Knowledge is contextual. Claims are made from a socio-cultural context, as well as from a hermeneutical community. Also knowledge is qualified. Knowledge involves a fiduciary commitment. Critical realism is an epistemology that is prominent in both science and theology. E.g Michael Polanyi, John Polkinghorne, Ian Barbour, Arthur Peacocke, Alistair McGrath, N.T. Wright, Roy Bhaskar.

5. **Evangelicalism** – Often difficult to define, evangelicalism, according to one formula, usually holds to the authority of scripture, crucicentrism (faith exclusively in Christ and his death and Resurrection), conversionism (the call to born-again salvation), and activism (the mission of evangelism and transformation). Evangelicalism believes in a transcendent God and a real, external creation. Some evangelicals hold to a moderate view of reason that tends more towards critical realism and even postmodernism than would fundamentalism. E.g. Billy Graham, Carl F.H. Henry, Fuller Theological Seminary, Trinity Evangelical Divinity School, D.A. Carson, J.I. Packer, Millard Erickson, John Stott, and post-conservatives like Roger Olson and Clark Pinnock.

6. **Post-Secular Ressourcement** – The pronouncements of postmodernism have helped to usher in a post-secularity in which the modern wall separating fact and value and reason and religion have been torn down, and doors have been opened up to religion and spirituality. There have been attempts to reclaim a Christian or theological vision for the whole of reality. Also, there has been a return to "classical" or "consensual" Christianity to reclaim an authentic and orthodox faith and vision amidst postmodern pluralism. It is often conservative in theology but goes beyond the epistemological questions of foundationalism or modernist inerrancy. It presents an ancient-future cosmic vision of the faith according to Scripture as lived out in the early tradition of the church. It is a return to the transcendence and mystery of God, the doxo-liturgical, the tradition of the church, and the ancient consensus of faith and practice. It comprises a diverse group, e.g. Hans Urs Von Balthasar, this author, David Bentley Hart, some tendencies within Radical Orthodoxy, Thomas Oden, Richard Foster, Thomas Torrance, Alasdair Macintyre, John Zizioulas, and Robert Webber.

7. **Neo-Pragmatism** – A diverse camp of thinkers following the pragmatism of William James, John Dewey and at times Charles Peirce. Usually they are non-foundationalists, and hold to some form of instrumentalism in science and naturalism in epistemology. W.E. Quine. Hilary Putnam, Donald Davidson, Susan Haack (neo-classical pragmatism).

8. **Socio-Political Pragmatism** – It is difficult to find a category for these two unique thinkers, Jurgen Habermas and Richard Rorty. It seems even more difficult to put them together, but I have. They are both pragmatists and non-foundational, though Habermas desires to revisit and revise Enlightenment reason. They both seem to focus their work towards the transformation of the socio-political realm. They also both seek to use communication or communicative rationality to arrive at a more just and progressive society. The difference is that Jurgen Habermas, a neo-Marxist originally from the Frankfurt school, tends more towards revisiting and revising modern values and institutions and rebuilding them around rational-critical communication. Richard Rorty, on the other hand a proponent of liberal democracy, tends more towards postmodernism in his dismissal of analytic philosophy and any sort of foundationalism or modernist notion of knowledge. Rorty considers himself a pragmatist in the vein of John Dewey.

9. **Post-Liberalism** – Seeking to replace the cognitive-propositional and experiential-expressive models of religion, George Lindbeck, Hans Frei, and others from the "Yale school," offer a cultural-linguistic model influenced by the work of Karl Rahner, Bernard Lonergan, Neo-Orthodoxy, Wittgenstein and sociology of knowledge and religion. Post-Liberalism rejects foundationalism and is more of a bottom-up framework then a top-down ontological framework. Other post-liberals whose theologies somewhat reflect the Yale tradition are Stanley

Hauerwas, R.R. Reno, David Ford, James William McClendon Jr., William Willimon, and William Placher.

10. **Radical Orthodoxy** – Radical Orthodoxy is a movement that responds to both modernism and postmodernism, as it seeks to place theology and revelation at the center of academic study. It holds to a transcendent view of God and more of a postmodern view of reason. E.g. John Milbank, Catherine Pickstock, and Graham Ward.

11. **Postmodernism**, specifically semiosis, textualism, and hermeneutics. Postmodernism is a diverse and ambiguous movement crossing many disciplines. Ontologically, it often locates ultimate reality in language, i.e. the sign, the text, or hermeneutics. In terms of epistemology, it is anti-foundational. E.g. Jacques Derrida, Michel Foucault, Jean Baudrillard, Jean Lyotard, and Gilles Deleuze.

12. **Emerging/Missional Church** – The Emerging Church and the Missional Church movement, though not synonymous are interrelated. Both are movements that are heavily influenced by postmodernism. In this sense I incorporate them as one movement though they have difference. The movement is often "post" everything, i.e. post-conservative, post-evangelical and runs countercurrent to fundamentalism, evangelicalism and liberalism, as it seeks to express the gospel in postmodern terms, i.e. narrative. Although, it may uses both ancient (candles, prayer labyrinths) and future forms (multi-media) in its worship, it fundamentally sees the church as missional. It seeks to be non-dogmatic and prefers to express faith in community, conversation, and social action. In the diagram above, it is closer to postdmodernism than it is to most other forms of Christianity. E.g. Brian McClaren, Dan Kimball, and Stanley Grenz. I did not place post-conservatism (evangelical left) on this graph, but it shares some characteristics with the Emerging Church movement. Though I would place it to the left of the Emerging Church. E.g. Roger Olson.

Notes

[1] Hans Urs Von Balthasar identified a theological *a priori* in the first volume *The Glory of the Lord* of his triology. We are hard-wired to sense, know and receive God. We are primarily spiritual beings. The theological *a priori* is a first order point of contact that God has placed within us and is activated by God through his revelation of grace that enlightens the spirit. See pp. 156-171 of *The Glory of the Lord*, Volume One. I concur with von Balthasar in saying that we are fundamentally religious and even theological creatures. Every culture possesses a religious and even theological *a priori* that informs not only its sense of God but its sense of life and culture. We are beings of belief, and it is imbedded and expressed in who we are as people and as culture-builders.Theories within neurology, neuropsychology, sociology and anthropology of religion and other disciplinary fields reflect

that such thinking is on the rise, that is that we are hardwired for God. However I am putting an emphasis on the negative effects of sin against this *a priori* more than I find in von Balthasar, who would attribute much more to its salvific impact.

[2] The Radical Orthodox remix of Scotus is at times heavily criticized as an inaccurate and wrong-headed interpretation of Scotus' univocity of being. The whole Scotus debate is a significant one that cannot be taken up here, though it is needless to say that I concur with RO.

[3] This movement, that occurred in certain Catholic circles, was an attempt to correct the popular neo-Thomist position that radically bifurcated grace and nature, reason and revelation and philosophy and theology by returning to the early sources ("ressourcement") of Christianity, for example Augustine, Gregory of Nyssa, Maximus the Confessor, and Thomas Aquinas in order to situate the whole of Christian thinking in revelation.

[4] Basically a oneness made of a dichotomy

[5] Milbank accuses Nietzsche of "absolute historicism," meaning that Nietzsche thought that only his reading of history was the right one.

[6] James K.A. Smith's frequently used metaphor

[7] Milbank means that if all claims of knowledge are acts of power and violence, then violence or warfare is presupposed by post-Nietzscheans in every knowledge claim.

[8] Latin for "City of God"

[9] Greek for "participation"

[10] Greek for "participation in God"

[11] Cataphatic and apophatic knowledge of God is a designation commonly found among Eastern Orthodox theologians. In simple terms, cataphatic knowledge is that which can be known and stated about God. Apophatic knowledge, or negative theology, is what cannot be known or is unknown about God. Often in Eastern Orthodoxy God is defined by what God is not. Gregory Palamas made the distinction between God's essence and his energies. We know God through God's energies, God's working in human history. God's essence, or often called God's hyper or super essence, is how God knows God's self. God's hyper-essence remains apophatic. It is a mystery. Apophasis is also a safeguard against reducing God and even theology to what only human reason can grasp and express.

[12] Latin for "faith and reason."

[13] The correspondence theory of truth is basically that a certain belief is true if it mirrors or "corresponds" to the facts or reality.

[14] Hans Urs Von Balthasar penned his famous triology, *The Glory of the Lord, Theo-Drama, Theo-Logic* and *Epilogue* in sixteen volumes. His theological aesthetic attempts to approach the study of God phenomenologically and analogically through the transcendentals of beauty, goodness, and truth with Christ being their ultimate fulfillment and consummation.

[15] Surely the *analogia entis* is not without controversy and debate. Scotus, as opposed to Aquinas, held that analogy is ultimately based on univocity in that in order for something to be like and different, it must have univocal predication on both counts to begin with. Analogy stems from univocity. Yet, univocity cannot ultimately and absolutely be declared of anything because of the nature of language and meaning as deferred (Derrida) or "shared" in my interpretation. There is a relational nature to language and meaning within itself. Even a seemingly uivocal concept is analogical in meaning and language.No univocal predication in terms of meaning stands alone but is connected to other relations of meaning into an infinite regress, unless posting the notion of God, as the transcendental nominative who begins the process of nominating and predication . In this case, God is univocal in being (analogical within Triune relations) and speaks univocally to God's self, but is know to us

and speaks to us by analogy of being, for nothing is ultimately univocal but God. The debate continues with the most famous being between Barth and his Swiss contemporaries, the Protestant Emil Brunner and the Roman Catholic Hans Urs Von Balthasar. Barth felt that the *analogia entis* was the antichrist and kept him from being Catholic. He held to an *analogia relationis*. Barth refused to ground revelation upon any natural connection between a wholly other God and creation that can be apprehended by reason. Barth's radical renouncing of the analogy of being was probably based on his strong reaction to the theological liberalism of his predecessors who virtually were able to construct an entire rational Christian theological system without the need of supernatural revelation. This work is not intended to explore the depths of this rich discussion involving the nature of God, revelation, and the human context.However, unlike classical Protestant Liberalism, the adherents of an analogy of being within the Catholic Ressourcement and Radical Orthodoxy, the former strongly influenced by Barth, understand all revelation, including creation, as being of grace. The old grace-nature bifurcation of the Neo-Thomists (i.e. Maritain) is not made by these theologians. They would agree with Barth, that only by grace and revelation can humanity make contact with the Divine, but grace is revealed through creation as Word as well as through the written Word and the incarnate Word.

Chapter Four

Participation in the Logos (Metousia Logo) in the Theology of St. Maximus the Confessor

We declare to you what was from the beginning, what we have heard, what we have seen with our eyes, what we have looked at and touched with our hands, concerning the Word of life (1 John 1:1).

In James Smith's essay "Will the Real Plato Please Stand Up? Participation versus Incarnation," he challenges Pickstock's and Radical Orthodoxy's version of Plato as a sacramental philosopher. He agrees with Pickstock's reading of several passages within the *Phaedrus* but has doubt as to whether such a theurgical reading can be carried out through the entire corpus of Plato. Within the corpus, Smith cites references that exemplify the more *traditional* reading of Plato as dualist (Smith 2005:71). Smith's critique questions the whole project of remixing Plato into a "Christian" ontology of participation. Smith suggests the use of more "Christian" metaphors such as incarnation or covenant rather than Platonic participation.

I agree with responses from John Milbank and Justin Holcomb that participation does *not exclude* ideas like covenant as if one had to pick and choose between two mutually exclusive ideas (Smith and Olthuis 2005:30,244). Radical Orthodoxy claims a philosophy of participation *and* a theology of incarnation (Milbank, Pickstock, and Ward 1999:3). Although the creation accounts in Genesis chapter one and John chapter one and the *en Christo* ontology in Paul do not use the particular word "participation," or *koinonos,* the idea and dynamic is clearly in the Incarnation. In responding to Smith's critique, I will turn to an ancient theologian-monk named Maximus the Confessor (580-662). Maximus could be the link between the Platonic or Neoplatonic concept of participation as *methexis* and participation within Christian revelation, the incarnate Logos.

Life of Maximus the Confessor

Maximus was born in Constantinople in AD 580 during a time of dramatic transition. Early Christianity was shifting to what would be its medieval period. The

Western Roman Empire was falling, and the Eastern Byzantine Empire was peaking, while Islam in the background was soon to be on the rise. Most of the Christological heresies had been settled by this time except for the Monothelite controversy,[1] which would eventually find Maximus in the middle.

Much of Maximus' life originally comes to us from the Greek *Life of St. Maximus* which was composed by the Studite monk Michael Exaboulites in the tenth century (Louth 1996:4 and 6). A Syriac version of the *Life,* which gives some conflicting accounts, was discovered this past century. Maximus came from a noble family and received a classical education (Louth 1996:4) (Sherwood 1955:6). His studies in philosophy were primarily based in Plato and Aristotle along with various commentators including Neoplatonists like Iamblichus and Proclus (Sherwood 1955:6). Following his education, Maximus was appointed first secretary to the Emperor Heraclius. Later, Maximus left his post and became a monk at Chrysopolis across from Constantinople.

After ten or eleven years, Maximus moved to the monastery of St. George at Cyzicus (around 624-625), where he composed his earliest writings, including the *Ambigua, The Ascetic Life,* and *Centuries on Love* (Louth 1996:5). In 626 Constantinople was seized by the Persians, and Maximus fled to Carthage in North Africa (630) with stopovers in Cyprus and Crete. While in North Africa, Maximus was under the mentorship of Sophronius, the head of the monastery called Eucratas and who was later patriarch of Jerusalem (Sherwood 1955:10-11). In his first years in Africa, Maximus wrote the larger *Ambigua* and his *Questions to Thalassius* (Sherwood 1955:11).

It was at Carthage in 645 that Maximus publicly debated and defeated the Monothelite ex-patriarch Pyrrhus, who, following the debate, accepted orthodoxy (Louth 1996:16). This debate inspired a constituency of African bishops along with the Byzantine exarch Gregory to seek a bid for African independence from Constantinople, which failed (Blowers and Wilken 2003:15). Maximus participated in the Lateran Council (649) in Rome and allied himself with the papacy and the African bishops, concerning the Monothelite controversy.

When he returned to Constantinople, Maximus and Pope Martin I were arrested by imperial forces as enemies of the state (Blowers and Wilken 2003:15). Prior to this event, in 638, the imperial edict, the *Ecthesis,* which adopted the doctrine of Monothelitism and later the *Typos* which forbade further debate on the issue, set the Patriarchs of Constantinople and the Emperors Heraclius and Constans against the papacy and other sympathizers (Louth 1996:15-17).

Maximus was put on trial in 655 and was later exiled. His right hand was cut off and his tongue was cut out. Maximus died on August 13th 662 at Lazica off the southeast coast of the Black Sea (Louth 1996:18).

Theological Influences of Maximus

Earlier I stated that James Smith made a claim that Radical Orthodoxy's Plato is really Neoplatonism. I will not debate this claim either way in this research, but assuming that it is I will seek to locate the concept of participation in a more "Christian" source, i.e., Maximus. Maximus is useful in this research because he modifies the Neoplatonic and early Christian understanding of participation along incarnational lines and employs it onto-epistemologically in his cosmic theology.

In addressing the problem posed by Smith concerning the Radical Orthodox identification of Plato as a "sacramental" philosopher and its adoption of Plato as a proponent of participation, it is important that we identify the connection between Neoplatonism and Maximus, on the one hand, and between Origen and Pseudo-Dionysius, who mediated the Neoplatonic tradition to Maximus. Smith questions Radical Orthodoxy's interpretation of Plato, and the appropriateness of applying a Platonic concept to a Christian ontology. Smith attributes the Radical Orthodox Plato to Neoplatonism rather than to the actual corpus of Plato's writing. If that be the case, Maximus the Confessor of orthodoxy may stand as a corrective to the Neoplatonic elements inherited by Origen (ca. 185- ca. 254 A.D.) and Pseudo-Dionysius the Areopagite (an anonymous theologian of the 5th century).

Maximus was a receptor of tradition, but he did not receive it uncritically. In many cases, he rejected aspects of it, for example, in his reading of Origen. In other cases, he synthesized elements from many sources including Alexandrian Christology, the Cappadocians, and Neoplatonism via Pseudo-Dionysius. Maximus was fundamentally a champion of orthodoxy locating the heart of his theology in the Incarnation and basing it in firm Chalcedonian logic. He critically analyzed and received tradition upon these bases. His correction of Origen, specifically his cosmology, and his correction of Pseudo-Dionysius and his vision of cosmic emanations and hierarchies fall in line with this thinking (Louth 1996:66-68; Balthasar 2003:115-136). Let us briefly look at the traditions critiqued and adopted by Maximus.

Andrew Louth identifies three traditions found in Maximus' theology, the ascetic, the dogmatic and the cosmic traditions (Louth 1996:23-32). As a monk, Maximus traced his lineage back to John the Baptist, the prophets Elijah and Elisha and even further back to Moses and the Patriarchs who often wandered in the desert as they followed God. Near his own time, Maximus was influenced by the spiritual life of Evagrius, a monk from the 4th century who dwelt in the Egyptian desert. Evagrius interpreted the Christian life through Clement of Alexandria and Origen. Origenism was condemned by the Emperor Justinian (543) and again at the fifth Ecumenical Council (553). Origen's thinking still had its influence in monastic circles as the metaphysical background for the ascetical wisdom of Evagrius (Louth 1996:24).

Maximus critically incorporated Evagrius' ascetical wisdom while removing the Origenist metaphysical elements with its myth of the cosmic fall and reversing Origen's cosmic triad of *stasis, kinesis,* and *genesis* to *genesis, kinesis,* and *stasis.*[2] Maximus' correction of much of Origenism, specifically the nature of his cosmic vision, ended up as a correction of Neoplatonism. (Louth 1996:67) and (Von Balthsar 2003:127-131) both make the case for Maximus' correction of Origenism. Along with Evagrius, Maximus was influenced by the ascetic traditions in the

Macarian Homilies and in the writings of the Carthaginian bishop Diadochus, who represents a synthesis of Evagrius' analysis of human nature and *apatheia*[3] and the Macarian focus on the experience of sanctification (Louth 1996:26).

From the dogmatic tradition, Maximus inherited his Christology from the Alexandrians, Athanasius and Cyril, and the Cappadocians. As a defender of orthodoxy, Maximus fought against the prevailing Monothelitism of his day. He did so out of the Christological tradition that he adopted from Cyrilline Chalcedonianism (Louth 1996:28). Gregory of Nazianzus provided Maximus with the ontological framework and language to work out his own understanding of perichoretic dynamics within the logic of Chalcedon (Thunberg 1995:26 and Louth 1996:27).

Even though Gregory of Nyssa's speculative metaphysics and cosmic anthropology attracted Maximus (Louth 1996:27), he also critically examined the Cappadocians dogmatic tradition. Maximus' *Ambigua*[4] look at the writings of Gregory of Nazianzus, dealing with problematic passages that were interpreted by Origenists in monastic circles as supporting Origenism (Blowers and Wilken 2003:22). Maximus' *Ambigua* serve as a clarification to the reader of Gregory's work by bringing orthodox interpretations to Gregory's more difficult passages.

The third influence is the tradition of cosmic theology that came to Maximus through the writings attributed to Dionysius the Areopagite which where transmitted through the editing of John of Scythopolis. It was through Pseudo-Dionysius that many of the concepts and language of Neoplatonism were introduced and developed in Byzantine theology, including the apophatic and cataphatic dichotomy in theology (Louth 1996:29-30). Pseudo-Dionysius' cosmic hierarchy is a vision that depicts the glory of God descending to the entire created order and returning back to him in liturgical praise. This vision echoes the theurgy of Neoplatonism (Iamblichus and Proclus) and offers the cosmic framework for Maximus' theology (Louth 1996:30-31 and Luibheid 1987:145).

However as mentioned above, Maximus often provides a corrective to certain Neoplatonic elements in the traditions he receives. In this case, Maximus alters the ontological status of Platonic "ideas" in Pseudo-Dionysius' cosmic, scheme. Pseudo-Dionysius works the Neoplatonic emanations from the One into "principles of being and life" and then into a "graduated hierarchy of personal beings" (Balthasar 2003:115). John Scythopolis, the primary editor of the Areopagite's corpus, identifies these principles and hierarchy of beings as "ideas" or "God's thoughts" (Balthasar 2003:115). Balthasar notes that in doing this John is identifying these ideas ontologically with God's essence, being itself (Balthasar 2003:115).

In the process of adapting Pseudo-Dionysius and his somewhat Neoplatonic brand of participation in God to a more Christian scheme, Maximus corrects this sort of emanationism that identifies the general principles of created being with the ideas of God which are identified as God's essence. Maximus did not want to identify the general principles of created being with God's ideas. Instead, Maximus understood these general principles not in a Platonic sense of ideas but more in an Aristotelian sense of universals which he held in tension with particular being

(Balthasar 2003:116). Maximus still held to a view of ideas (*logoi*), but they were not created universals or even God's essence but God's "energies" expressing his will and plan for the cosmos.

Maximus would develop his doctrine of participation around the *logoi* in the *Logos* according to God's plan of cosmic *theosis*.[5] As opposed to Pseudo-Dionysius, Maximus did not understand the general principles of participation in terms of basic principles within created being but in terms of a supernatural participation in the redemption offered by God through grace (Balthasar 2003:124). Balthasar recognizes that "Maximus happily transposes the Platonic notion of participation, which Pseudo-Dionysius applied to created being as such, to the sphere of the supernatural – of grace" (Balthasar 2003:124).

This shift from a Platonic notion of participation to a Christian Logos notion of participation is anticipated in earlier Christian tradition. Thunberg in his bibliographic notes traces the Logos doctrine in the Stoic *logos spermatikos*,[6] Philo, Origen, Athanasius, Pseudo-Dionysisus and Evagrius and finally Maximus (Thunberg 1995:73). Maximus incorporates Alexandrian constructs of the Logos as the locus of the divine ideas and ultimately the unitary divine Idea that unfolds in the world and brings the world back to its original Idea in God (Balthasar 2003:117). For Thunberg, Maximus develops the doctrine in a more "deeper" and "systematic" way as the incarnate Logos takes center stage in his whole theological vision (1995:73-74).

According to Balthasar, Maximus "represents the Incarnation of the Logos and the whole historical course of the world's salvation as both a primeval idea of God and as the underlying structure of his overall plan for the world. He also designates the mystery of the Cross, grave and Resurrection (of Christ) as the basis and goal of all creation" (Balthasar 2003:120). Thus the cosmic theologies of Origen and Pseudo-Dionysius are critiqued and transformed into a cosmic liturgy where all of creation moves according to its own *logoi* and finds its purpose and destiny in the incarnate *Logos* in an ascent to *theosis*. In the case of humanity that purpose is fulfilled by the grace of God in the soul that chooses freely (gnomic will) such grace.

Participation and the Theology of the *Logoi*

James Smith was concerned about the Radical Orthodox evaluation of Plato as a sacramental philosopher, one that values materiality. Smith felt that Pickstock's version of Plato was derived more from a Neoplatonic interpretation. Also Smith was concerned about the movement's employment of a *Neoplatonic* form of participation. Without challenging Smith's claims one way or another, this writer sought another locus for the doctrine of participation beyond its alleged Neoplatonic form.

Although early patristic theology could never transcend the contextual structure of its own time and its ideas (Can any period?), Maximus brought Christological meaning to re-worked Neoplatonic forms, where the reigning ideas were purged and/or reshaped by Christian revelation. Maximus the Confessor purged the traditions he received of unnecessary Neoplatonism and other error as they diverged from orthodoxy (Balthasar 2003:60-61). Smith has a fundamental concern that an ontology of participation based on Plato may not affirm materiality and the goodness of creation in the way that the Christian faith should. However, Von Balthasar champions Maximus as "the most world-affirming thinker of all the Greek Fathers; in his basically positive attitude toward nature he goes even beyond Gregory of Nyssa" (Balthasar 2003:61). Maximus' notion of participation as an ontological structure is given specific meaning in his doctrine of the *Logos* and the *logoi*. For all created being participates in the divine through its *logoi* which are grounded in Christ the incarnate Logos. Maximus' ontology of participation is a *metousia Logo*, which is centered on the Incarnation.

At this point, we will go into further detail concerning the doctrine of the *logoi* and its relationship with participation. From Von Balthasar, we learn that the *logoi* are not universals within the created order nor are they the essence of God. Maximus will not allow for Neoplatonic emanationism or pantheism. Eastern Orthodox theologian Vladimir Lossky (1903-1958) identified the *logoi* in Maximus' work as "divine willings," "the creative ideas of things" (Lossky 1998:98). The *logoi* are God's pre-existent *ideas* concerning all created being. As God's ideas or divine principles, the *logoi* pre-exist in God as his will, plans and providence and are expressed best as his *energies* or workings rather than his *essence*, noting later the Palamite distinction between the two. Gregory Palamas (1296-1359) made dogmatic what had been taught in the Eastern Church for some time that God's *energies* are what can be known about God as opposed to his *essence* which is apophatic.

Patristic scholar Andrew Louth defines the *logoi* in Maximus as the principles that lie behind the natural created order as established by the Word of God, the *Logos* (Louth 1996:37). Blowers and Wilken define the *logoi* in Maximus as "the providential principles of creation and Scripture" (Blowers and Wilkens 2003:17). The *logoi* are ultimately rooted in Christ the *Logos* in that the *logoi* of creation and the *logoi* of scripture are in a sense "incarnations" of the Logos and point to Jesus Christ, who is the full and true Incarnation of the Logos (2003:21). The Logos is the Divine Mediator through creation, scripture and the Incarnation, and the created order participates in God through this mediation (2003:21).

God's ultimate purpose in the mediation of the Logos is to deify creation through the Incarnation. This is a universal and rational principle of created being within the *logoi* of creation (2003:23). The *logoi* serve as the *raison d'etre* for things as they exist in the Logos. Blowers and Wilken continue that "all created things are defined, in their essence and in their way of developing, by their own *logoi* and by the *logoi* of the beings that provide their external context" (2003:57). As well, all created things are purposed to move according to their own *logoi*, their divine purpose, towards each created being's own end *(telos)* (Maximus 2003: 92). Thus, the *logoi* of creation express God's will for cosmic deification through the incarnate Logos.

The *logoi* become the point of contact and means of participation for creation in the divine Logos. Maximus believed that "every created thing has its point of contact with the Godhead; and this point of contact is its idea, reason or *logos* that is at the same time the end towards which it tends" (Lossky 1998:98). The Word is the causal principle and end of all things, and thus it is participation in the Logos which brings the realization of God's will for the creation. In contemplating (*theoria*) the *logoi* of things, one finds its causal and teleological reason in the one Logos.

Maximus explains that one discovers this truth of the differential unity of all things in the Logos through contemplating creation (i.e. Romans 1:19-20). Upon contemplating the differences in creation as they exist by nature, one is drawn to the *logoi* or eternal purpose of things. In the *logoi* one finds the model or archetype, the *Logos*, which contains and holds together all of the *logoi*. It is the Logos in creation that intends the purpose of each created thing in its *logoi*. Each *logoi* in expressing the purpose of God implicates motion (*kinesis*) and direction (*skopos*) in accordance with that being's *logoi* or divine purpose (Meyendorff 1987:135; Maximus 2003:57). In this sense, the Logos serves as a divine nexus or threshold from which the *logoi* flow into creation, and it serves as the center toward which all created beings tend in recapitulation according to their *logoi* (Lossky 1998:99). Thus, through participation, the "Logos is (in) many *logoi*, and the many *logoi* are (in) the one Logos" (parenthesis are mine) (Maximus 2003:54, 57). Participation flows from creation to Incarnation to *theosis* via the *logoi* and the Logos. Of course, the participatory relationship is analogical. Meyendorff quotes Maximus from *Ambiguum* 7, "all things participate in God by analogy, insofar as they come from God" (Meyendorff 1987:135). There is no danger of pantheism with Maximus. Transcendence or God's hyper-essence[7] and apophaticism play too significantly in Maximus religious epistemology to allow for any total immanence of God or full transcendence of creation (Thunberg 1995:76-77). Also Maximus' strict Chalcedonian logic will not permit the nature of the Logos to be mixed or confused in participation or union. Participation is a *hypostatic* union that maintains distinction in natures.

Maximus, as he does in all of this theology, allows his understanding of participation ultimately to be shaped by the Incarnation. The union of God with creation is central to his thinking, not just hypostatically with humanity but also with the entire cosmos (Blowers and Wilken 2003:21 and Maximus 2003:100,124). Maximus understood man as both microcosm of the universe and mediator to the universe (Thunberg 1995:137). Yet humanity fell, but Christ supremely assumes both roles of microcosm and mediator in the incarnate Logos according to the plan of God. Through the microcosmic mediation of the Logos, the entire universe is enabled to participate in God and be transfigured (Thunberg 1995:142). A primary role of the Incarnation in Maximus is mediation, cosmic mediation of all division. The *telos* of the Incarnation is the recapitulation of all things, as adapted from Irenaeus. Maximus' is a cosmic theology, a cosmic theology of participation and *theosis* through the Logos. For Maximus Incarnation and deification are teleologically connected (Thunberg 1995:430). The hypostatic union in Christ enables us to be joined to God similarly. Maximus' ontology of participation is for cosmic deification through the incarnate Logos.

Thus, Maximus' *metousia Theou* is truly a *metousia Logo* in which all things participate by grace and love in the incarnate Logos. Participation occurs through the *logoi* that serve as the rational and teleological mediators for the Logos. The *logoi* serve as the providential "willings" of God in creation (*logoi* of creation) and into the *logoi* of revelation or Scripture, and the Logos of grace and salvation in Christ. The Logos is hid in the first two and revealed hypostatically in the latter (Christ) (Thunberg 1995:78). Even in the *logoi* of commandments, whether by the natural or written law, the Logos is present in them and revealed in obedience. Maximus stated "it is evident that every person who participates in virtue as a matter of habit unquestionably participates in God, the substance of the virtues" (Maximus 2003:58).

The incarnate Logos is at the center of the cosmos and Maximus' theology. All things visible and invisible are made by the Logos and are in the Logos. Through the Logos all of creation participates in God through its individual and differentiated *logoi* (the intelligible principles of being) which are united hypostatically (without confusion) in the Logos. The motion of the *logoi* in all creation is purposed in the incarnate Logos, meaning that the reason of being for all things is to be joined in Christ through the Incarnation. The *metousia Logo* offers an ontology which holds all things together in the Logos, through creation, the Incarnation and *theosis*. All of creation participates in God by grace through the *logoi*. Out of love, God initiates motion towards himself through his purposes revealed in the *logoi*, and humanity out of its gnomic will (freewill) responds to God's grace on behalf of itself and microcosmically on behalf of the cosmos. God's purposes are revealed to all in creation, Scripture and in the Incarnation.

This 'theo-ontology'[8] has all of creation participating in God, specifically in the Logos, at some level, even though the *tropos* (mode of existence) of humanity has turned away in the fall from its original nature and purpose in the Logos. The movement of God's grace through the Logos following creation initiates human synergy from the gnomic will. Maximus' system is not one of predestination or determinism. Choice allows humanity to fulfill its purpose in participation. Participation in God through a creational ontology is merely the initial motion in a cosmological process of deification, which requires choosing union with Christ. Maximus' ontology of participation has a very specific purpose that is relational and incarnational and is carried out epistemologically in Christ, *metousia Logo*.

The *metousia Logo* represents an epistemology in which things are known as they participate in the Logos. An epistemology of participation has to do with participating in the Logos and his eternal purpose for all things, as revealed in their *logoi* that ultimately are in the one Logos. Knowledge in Maximus' participatory scheme has to do with knowing the purpose or reason of being of a thing according to its creation and its recapitulation (*anakephalaiosis*) in Christ.

In his *Ad Thalassium 60*, Maximus references two types of knowledge. The first is relative knowledge based on reason and ideas (Maximus 2003:126). The mind moves in relative knowledge from the sensible realm to the intelligible realm of ideas (Maximus 1985:48). Often in modern thinking this is where we stop. Knowledge is abstract understanding. However for Maximus the goal is direct experiential knowledge which is through a participation by grace (Maximus 2003:126). Participation in a known object brings one into direct experiential perception which "suspends rational knowledge," going beyond mere conceptualization (2003:126-127). The ascent to true knowledge begins with ascetic practice (*praxis*) and then to contemplation (*theoria*) of the *logoi* leading finally to mystical insight and union with God (*theologia*), *vita practica, vita contemplativa,* and *vita mystica*.[9] This contemplation is not the "same as either empirical perception or mental comprehension" (Nesteruk 2003:26). Contemplation or *theoria* is a type of spiritual vision which sees beyond the sensible world and into the ontological roots of things which are grounded outside of the empirical world (Nesteruk 2003:26). In an ontology of participation the nature of things are not fully revealed in what is seen or known. Things are more than what they appear. There can be no reduction or totalization in such a scheme.

Science takes from the empirical realm and expresses its findings in symbols. We understand and communicate the empirical realm in terms of symbolic language and sign systems. However, this data does not reveal the meaning and purpose of created things. These are revealed in the *logoi* of created beings which are apprehended by the human hypostasis because it is fashioned in the *imago Dei* and is capable of *theoria* of God's divine intentions in the cosmos (Nesteruk 2003:26). Ultimately, God's intention is revealed in the incarnate Logos, in whom God desires that the whole universe inheres or participates in his hypostasis (the hypostatic inherence in the Logos of God) (Nesteruk 2003:114-116). From the spiritual contemplation of the differentiated sensible and intelligible creation, one arrives at the oneness of creation. The many *logoi* of sensible and intelligible things are united in their origin and purpose in the one Logos. The *Logos* is revealed in the contemplation of the *logoi* of creation (the "moral law") and the written law in Scripture, which inspire ascetic *praxis* and virtue and deeper participation in the grace of Christ (Thunberg 1995:394). For Maximus, the revelation of the Logos in creation through contemplation and in the understanding of the Scriptures is a work of the Spirit by God's grace. (Maximus 1996:109). This motion (*kinesis*) of the Spirit ultimately leads the universe mystagogically[10] into a process of *theosis* which Von Balthasar calls a "cosmic Liturgy" (Balthasar 2003).

At this point, it is noteworthy to make a distinction and clarify a subtlety in Maximus concerning two senses of participation. In one sense, all creation by its nature or essence participates in being, and being comes from the energies or works of God (Maximus 1981:123-124). Participation in this sense pertains to the created order which begins its participation in being at its incipience. Creation in this sense is called "participant being" (1981:123-124). (Participant) being also comes to participate in the virtues of God which are *infused by grace*. These energies or works of God do not begin at the incipience of creation, for God's goodness, blessedness and holiness do not begin with time but are eternal (1981:123). By grace, we participate and receive the energies of God. There is a participation by way of creation and a participation by way of salvation or deification through grace implanted in creation. This is not to dichotomize grace and nature which is foreign to Maximus and Eastern Christianity. It merely depicts a continuum or growth in grace from creation to new creation. Yet that growth is not a natural growth. It occurs through the Eternal Word and specifically his death and Resurrection.

Similarly in epistemology for Maximus, participation at times refers to direct, experiential knowledge that is beyond mere conceptualization, but it also signifies that all things "participate proportionally in God, whether by intellect, by reason, by sense-perception, by vital motion, or by some habitual "fitness" (Maximus 2003:55,126). As in the Radical Orthodox Aquinas, in Maximus' epistemology the truth of a thing is as it ascends in participation with the Logos. By grace, participation begins with creation and moves on to the Incarnation and on to *theosis* through the incarnate Logos (Meyendorff 1987:136).

Epistemology and truth become ontological functions involving relationality. Knowledge is not simply a matter of facts or objectivity. The project of scientism fails on faulty ontological premises. The knower is not outside of the sphere of participation to understand objectively without commitment, and that which is to be known does not enjoy such a status either that it can be known outside of participation. In an ontology of participation, everything (all creation) is in relationship, and nothing is in isolation, in a vacuum, or enjoys the ontological status of pure reason.

Within a relational structure, things are known as they are purposed in the *Logos*, giving knowledge a teleological dimension as well. Science has sought to know interior causes and effects but has often considered metaphysical questions as irrelevant or irrational, purpose being one of them. Yet in an epistemology that is closely connected with ontology, questions of ultimate purpose go hand in hand with issues of causality, as questions of eschatology go hand in hand with effect. Teleology brings an eschatological aspect to bear on knowledge. Until God's purpose is fulfilled knowledge is provisional, yet true knowledge nonetheless – "we know in part."

Implications of Maximus' *Metousia Logo*

In concluding this section on St. Maximus the Confessor and his doctrine of the *logoi,* it is important to recap a few points. Smith's problem with the Radical Orthodox use of Plato or Neoplatonism in its borrowing of the ontology of participation is answered by Maximus. Although the elimination of a Neoplatonic context at some level may not be possible, Maximus intentionally attempted to purge his theology of Neoplatonic vestiges that could not fit into his Christian ontology of participation, a *metousia Logo* (participation in the Logos). Maximus' Logos ontology supports the participation of all creation according to their *logoi.* Creation participates in the Logos for the purpose of cosmic transfiguration as a teleological and eschatological goal. This occurs through the Incarnation of the Logos. The hypostatic union between God and man is the foundation for the teleological and eschatological work of the Spirit in creation, which is primarily in *theosis*.

Like many of the early Greek fathers, Maximus did not separate his philosophy from his theology. Thus, the Incarnation is central to Maximus' theology and is also central to his ontology of participation. Participation is not merely a participation in being or in God but specifically in the incarnate Logos, in Christ. Creational participation through the *logoi* indicates God's will and direction for creation, with its purpose fulfilled in a Logos-participation *in Christ*. In this scheme, creation is connected with Incarnation and salvation. The Logos of creation is the Logos of salvation through Incarnation, and the *logoi* of creation are realized in the incarnate Logos. In Maximus then, ontology is shaped by creation and the new creation, specifically through the ontological framework of the Incarnation and its relation to *theosis*. Thus, Maximus' notion of participation is clearly theological, poignantly Christocentric, and in its orthodoxy overturns the charges of James Smith.

I believe Maximus' ontology of participation has epistemological implications as well. The two are inseparable for Maximus. Things are ultimately known as they are known in their original intention in the *logoi* and their participation in that intention. True knowledge is apprehending things as they are in God according to their participation, *metousia Logo*. Similar to Thomas' *adequatio*, Maximus understands that we know things as they ontologically participate in the Logos, and the nature of that participation is predicated analogically. Maximus' notion of knowledge is at first empirically situated within a larger framework of transcendence, which is then apprehended spiritually, an epistemic ascent. The knower moves from the sensible realm of things to the intelligible realm of concepts and, even further, by ascetic practice and deeper contemplation begins to understand the nature of things as they participate in the Logos. One comes to know that the *logoi* are one Logos and begins the experiential ascent of *theologia* until culminating in the unknowing of *theosis*.

Knowledge is in a sense an ascetic or sanctifying and experiential process towards the ultimate nature and *telos* of things. We know in part, but we do indeed know, and what we know is creation as it eschatologically participates in its *logoi*, until the day comes when we will know completely as we are know in our completion through the *Logos*. In participation, we see, know, and share through a glass darkly what God intends, sees and knows of his creation through the *logoi*. The knowledge of things is analogical and relational, as it relates to its purpose in Christ. Our knowledge is always *mediated* by the Logos through the *logoi* on an eschatological continuum of both vertical and horizontal transcendence. Knowledge is transcendent, immanent, provisional, teleological, and eschatological as the created order is lead more and more towards its original purpose in its *logos*. Knowledge is "on the way" but is not yet fulfilled. Maximus' triad of *genesis, kinesis,* and *stasis* identify causality and motion as having Christological direction and purpose and the increase and ascent of sanctifying knowledge as a product of the kinetic program of the Spirit, who leads the cosmos into *theosis*.

With the fundamental nexus between the *logoi* of creation and the *Logos* of salvation, Maximus' theology proposes a high view of creation, as does most Eastern Christian theology. Creation becomes a universal context, starting point or point of contact for the witness of God. All of creation is a revelatory expression of grace. There is no strictly "natural" realm, no pure nature. The cosmos is a gift of God's grace and is redeemed and sustained by God's power to reveal God's purposes. Creation becomes doxo-liturgical and sacramental, housing the mystery of God. Materiality embraces the divine glory of God's splendor. Creation then is a furnished, incarnational tabernacle of God's holy presence and the apprehension of its revelational knowledge an incarnational process as well. Knowledge within the created order is knowledge of the liturgical participation of all things in God's purpose and glory.

Maximus' *metousia Logo* stretches to cosmic proportions. Its scope extends over all of creation, and its depth is deification, and it provides the grand structure of God's mission in the universe. Maximus' version of the *apokatastasis*[11] is a restoration of all things as God had originally intended, a recapitulation in Christ. Our knowledge of God is then vitally connected knowledge with the ascetical and the transformational, the cosmic process of sanctification or *theosis*. In Maximus' "cosmic liturgy," ontology, epistemology, theology, doxology, soteriology and missiology all conjoin in the crescendo of *theosis*. The breadth of Maximus' "Christocentric cosmology"[12] serves as a framework for a theology of mission.

A Christocentric cosmology is set in motion by the *logoi* that intend that all things be gathered or summed up in Christ. Jesus Christ is the center of all creation, and deification in his image is creation's *telos*. The *logoi* reveal the will of God in this cosmic liturgy and are seen in creation, the Old Testament, the moral law in humanity, in God's providence and judgment in the earth, and ultimately in the incarnate Logos. From the beginning of creation, God has revealed God's purposes in the cosmos, which culminate and are fulfilled in Christ.

The Word is expressed first in creating, and then eschatologically as flesh, and is the culminating embodiment of God's purpose and his kingdom. The church, which is his body and a sacrament to the world, witnesses of Christ. He is to be the *logos* and measure of all things. Jesus is the form of God to which all things must conform eschatologically. Of course, the deification of the cosmos does not entail a changing or confusing of the differential or analogical nature of things or the changing of the hyperessence or ultimate nature of God, which is unchangeable. Things are transformed according to their own nature and according to God's purpose or *logoi* for each thing. Thus, the cosmos and all of its differentiation are to become analogs[13] of Christ. Each thing has its *logoi* and thus its reason and purpose for being. The purpose is that they conform to the image of Christ according to the *logoi* of their nature. Applying this sort of analogical participation to mission, I propose that a human construct such as culture becomes an analogue to Jesus Christ and his establishment of the Kingdom. Christ and Kingdom are the analogates, and culture and its society become the analogands. A culture's beliefs and practices are identified, measured, corrected, judged, atoned for, and fulfilled according to their purpose in Christ – to conform to his image. This is the work of the Holy Spirit.

Analogy by nature conjoins both similarity and dissimilarity. As an analogue, culture is similar (points of contact) to and different from the Kingdom of God. The goal is for a culture or a people to become citizens of the Kingdom of God and to become more and more like Christ through its baptism and transformation in Christ, reflecting the life and fruit of his Kingdom. Since all of creation has a universal witness, each culture has a point of similarity and contact, however vague, wounded, or fallen.[14] An *analogical-participation model* of Christocentric critical contextualization analyzes the similarity and continuity of a culture with the universal witness of God and his kingdom through the manifestation of the *logoi* in a culture's knowledge and application of righteousness, i.e. moral law, and in God's trail of providence and holy judgment, as seen for example in the Hebraic culture of the Old Testament. I use the term "moral law" loosely. Maximus recognized a *logos* of the law in its written form and in the heart of each person.

I am suggesting at this point that every culture has some seed of the *logoi*, some degree of similarity. Every culture, as an analogue, has a greater measure of dissimilarity and discontinuity with the kingdom of God. Such a notion may be a version of *felix culpa*, an assertion and an argument that needs much more space than what I am permitted in this work. However, I am taking license and making the assertion that the ministry of the Incarnation through to the atonement was didactic, exemplary, curative, and martial (*Christus Victor*) but also prophetic, sacrificial and restorative in regards to the movement of history from creation to lapse to new creation. Within the analogization of creation to the image of Christ, the *logoi* of providence and judgment seeks to lead and shape creation into its eschatological future, judging it in lapse and offering grace and truth in Christ to redeem and to transform. This dynamic of grace within salvation history that I am proposing clearly has strong missional and evangelical tones. I feel these are significant additions to a ontology and theology of participation that so far has looked philosophically and theologically quite cosmic and universal, and may appear to slip into universalist tendencies, as I believe some nuances of Patristic and mystical theology do (i.e. Origen, Gregory of Nyssa, Meister Eckhart etc.). I ultimately owe this missional and evangelical debt to John Wesley who managed to navigate between many of 'rock and a hard place,' including universal atonement and resistible grace and a universal witness and the Great Commission to make disciples of Jesus Christ and prevenient grace and saving grace etc.

An analogical-participation model of Christocentric, critical contextualization would acknowledge a universal witness in every culture of creation, as it reflects Jesus Christ, yet free human response along with God's providence and judgment guiding the Divine-human dialectic. This witness bears some similarity to the *logoi* as revealed in creation (Romans 1:19-20), the "moral law" (Rom 2:14-16 - codified or written on the hearts), and God's providence and judgment in the earth. In light of the last chapter's look at Radical Orthodoxy, I would also like to include within the universal witness of creation, creation or being's necessary predicates, which are analogical to the character and energies of God, the transcendentals of unity, truth, goodness and beauty as cultural touchstones and analogs to God's *logoi*.[15] This addition is not dogmatic but more phenomenological, as it was with Von Balthasar. Of course, the inclusion of the transcendentals may have somewhat of a weak exegetical foundation in the creation accounts of Genesis, though they are present there and throughout Scripture. The transcendentals spring from philosophy and Genesis from theology. However, the transcendentals have strong theological substance and again may be able to serve missionally as a context for theology or at least a context where theology and culture intersect.

Ontological and moral privation require that both similarity and difference are to be assessed. While the similarities offer a contextual point of contact for the gospel, the differences invite the judgment and conviction of the Spirit (the prophetic) and the need to repent and be converted to Christ. In this sense, the *logoi* point to the Logos Christ as he fulfills the will of God within a culture's measure of light and highest moral aspirations and, where it has fallen short. Christ becomes the fulfillment of God's initial grace within all of creation. The similarity and dissimilarity between the beliefs and practices of the culture and the *logoi* need to be examined critically in the full light of the revelation of Jesus Christ, as revealed in Scripture by the Holy Spirit and discerned and interpreted by the ecclesial community both globally and locally, including the church triumphant as a living, holy and canonical tradition. Contextual theology is a work of participation, dialogue, discernment, repentance and construction. I will explore more of this model in Chapter 5.

Next, I will explore John Wesley's theology of universal and prevenient grace as a type of participation and as a further description of Maximus' *metousia Logo*. Wesley's participation in grace will conclude the development of our onto-epistemological model for a theology of mission. Its strong, practical soteriological and missiological concerns bring completion to Maximus' *metousia Logo* and his incarnational theology. By filling in a vision for a theology of mission with Wesley's theology of grace, we will begin to see a more dynamic picture of the cosmo-drama of God's saving work.

Notes

1. The controversy centering around the debate whether Christ had two wills (divine and human) or one will.

2. *Stasis, kinesis,* and *genesis* are Greek words for "steady state," "movement," and "beginning."

3. Greek for "without feeling" and is used in ascetic traditions to refer to denying oneself to the point where one is indifferent to the passions of the flesh.

4. Greek for "ambiguities" or "difficulties" in terms of Maximus' handling of difficult passages from the writings of Gregory of Nazianzus.

5. Maximus believed it was the plan of God through the Incarnation of Jesus Christ to transform the whole cosmic order into the image of Christ.

6. Greek for the "seed of the word," "seed of reason," or "seminal reason" that is shared by everything in the universe.

7. In Eastern Christian theology God's essence is beyond (hyper) or transcends our rational capacity to *fully* understand and remains unknown (apophasis) and is left to our mystical union with God in *theosis*.

8. A ontology directed and informed by theological considerations

9. Latin for the "practical life," the "contemplative life," and the "mystical life."

10. In early Christian sacramental life and still in the Eastern Orthodox Church, the mystagogy involves the catechesis or teaching concerning the sacraments or *mysteria* and the practical life expected to be lived by the initiate into the faith. It also can refer in a broader sense to the teaching concerning the liturgical rites of the church, i.e. the Divine Liturgy.

11. Greek for "the restoration of all things." The version taught by Pseudo-Dionysius and Gregory of Nyssa was condemned by the church for it implied a *necessary* universal redemption. Scholars debate to what extent Maximus taught this doctrine. It is not always clear. It seems that Maximus probably understood the teaching of *apokatastasis* as God's will but not as a necessity, since he clearly taught the freewill of humanity. I make reference in this work to Maximus' belief in hell and God's punishment of the disobedient. The author does not hold to a view of universal salvation but universal atonement.

12. A term coined by Torstein Theodor Tollefsen in *The Christocentric Cosmology of St. Maximus the Confessor* to express Maximus' understanding of God's ultimate purpose in the universe through Jesus Christ.

13. I am following in the spirit and analogical approach of others such as Przywara, Von Balthasar, and David Bentley Hart, among others, and further applying it to contextual mission theology in which analogy becomes a fundamental instrument for critical contextualization, cross-cultural communication, and global theology.

14. There is considerable debate among theologies of religions whether there is salvific knowledge outside of Jesus Christ. I am suggesting that God's universal revelation in creation is real and yet incipient in form to be fulfilled in the Incarnation, Jesus Christ. Other religions, philosophies or belief systems may or may not apprehend and express God's revelation found in creation. This needs to be critically discerned in terms of identifying what God's revelation in creation exactly is according to Scripture and is it revealed in other sources outside of Jesus Christ. Barth says "No!" I agree in part with Barth that religions, even at times certain expressions and practices of the Christian religion, are in opposition to revelation and more of an idol and a condemnation of humanity than a justification. Yet I do not accept this in a wholesale way, as I have claimed a universal witness in creation, and that there may be a case for a universal witness in conscience and culture as well. However, I believe these witnesses, if true, are in an incipient stage, and await that which is perfect. An incipient stage of grace would serve as a point of contact for further revelation. Thus, my position would be of partial or major replacement and fulfillment in Christ, which would include identifying the universal witness, correction of false witnesses, a prophetic judgment against lapse towards the universal witness, and an atonement or fulfillment of that true witness in Jesus Christ.

15. Again this move is nothing original. Von Balthasar's trilogy is in part a phenomenological approach to God through the transcendentals of truth, goodness, and beauty. He grounded this approach in an *analogia entis* theology and metaphysics that did not strictly bifurcate grace and nature but understood nature as a graced nature, and that God's revela-

tion is found in creation and is attested to by Christian witness and reflected in some way by a perennial philosophy of being.

Chapter 5

Participation in Grace (Metousia Chariti)

in John Wesley's Theology

From his fullness we have all received, grace upon grace (John 1:16).

Wesley, Eastern Christianity and Maximus the Confessor

In looking to develop more of the soteriological and missiological details of an onto-epistemology of participation, I turn to John Wesley's theology of grace, specifically its universal and prevenient expressions. A movement from Maximus to John Wesley (1703-1791) is not as far-fetched as it first appears. There are many similarities between the two. Recently, theologians have shown the influences that Eastern Christianity had on Wesley. Albert Outler (1908-1989), an eminent American Methodist theologian, noted that Wesley inherited his vision for the normative pattern for Christian living, perfection, and the divine-human synergism from his patristic studies, specifically from Pseudo-Macarius the Egyptian (Outler believed Gregory of Nyssa was the original source), Clement of Alexandria, and Ephraem Syrus (Outler 1964:9-10,119 and 1991:105). Wesley was a primitivist and in seeking to restore New Testament apostolic Christianity he returned to the early church fathers who were the closest in time to the apostolic church (Outler 1991:103).

Outler argues, convincingly, that one of the most significant features of Eastern Christianity in Wesley is *metousia Theou,* participation in the grace of God, which Outler understands in terms of synergism (Outler 1991:105). There are two energies at work. God takes an active role, and humanity takes a reactive or responsive role (1991:105). Within this dynamic humans have the freedom to resist grace, which is always a constant in Eastern Christian thinking. Outler attributes Wesley's "distinctive pneumatocentric view of grace," that is that God's active grace expressed by his Spirit moves upon the human heart, to the influence of the early church fathers (1991:108). The dynamic of God's grace and human freewill response is foundational to the soteriologies of both Eastern Orthodox and Wesleyan thinking.

United Methodist theologian, Ted Campbell, continues the dialogue between Wesley and the early fathers. Campbell believes that for Wesley, the primitivist, Christian antiquity became a source, among other sources, contributing to a religious vision of the Christian life and how it could be lived in society (Campbell 1991:2). However, the transmission of Christian antiquity to Wesley is held in question by Campbell. He feels it is difficult methodologically to *prove* that those early sources actually shaped Wesley, or if they did, then *how* they shaped various doctrines for Wesley (1991:3). If there is a dependence on these sources, often it is also difficult to demonstrate how they came to Wesley, either direct or mediated, and how Wesley understood them (1991:3). Thus, Campbell examines the way in which Wesley *conceived* of Christian antiquity, and how he used these conceptions to depict and implement a vision for cultural change (1991:4). For Campbell, Wesley's utilization of Christian antiquity becomes *programmatic* for his vision for the Methodist societies (Heitzenrater 2002:29).

Richard Heitzenrater, one of the foremost Wesley scholars, set out to research and confirm Outler's conclusions only to find them wanting. Although Wesley's literary corpus makes numerous references to the early fathers, those references were often general, interpreted in a Western light, and probably not from primary sources (Heitzenrater 2002:30-31). Heitzenrater does not deny the influence that Christian antiquity had on Wesley but questions the transmission and interpretation of the ancient sources and believes that precise nature of that influence has yet to be fully researched (2002:31). On the other hand, United Methodist theologian Randy Maddox sides with the growing number of scholars who find a significant influence, whether direct or indirect, from the early Greek fathers on Wesley (Maddox 1994:23). Maddox sees Wesley as preferring Greek writers over Latin writers and thus tending to favor an Eastern therapeutic soteriology over a Western juridicial one (1994:23). In fact, Maddox traces the Eastern therapeutic and synergistic or co-operant dynamics of salvation throughout his systematic treatment of Wesley's theology in his *Responsible Grace* (1994:92). However, I believe the connection between Wesley and Eastern Christianity is based more on theological analysis and comparison than historiographical analysis.

In this light, this author would tend to agree with Maddox that although Wesley theologically is a *via media* between east and west, he seems to favor more of an Eastern depiction of Christianity rather than a Western one, at least in terms of his view on sanctification. However, the one problem I have in Maddox's work is his reference to Wesley's similarities with Eastern *Orthodoxy*, which is a later development, when it is probably more appropriate to attribute the influences to Eastern *Christianity*. Besides these major scholars, other work has been done in a similar vein to Maddox. Several scholars from the Wesleyan Theological Society have made erudite efforts to draw parallels between the Eastern view of *theosis* and Wesley's view of entire sanctification (Bundy 2004:104-136; Christensen 1996:71-94; King 2003:103-123).

In terms of comparing Wesley to Maximus in particular there has not been as much research. It is doubtful whether Wesley ever read Maximus, but the comparison is worthy. Kenneth Carveley's essay entitled "From Glory to Glory: The Renewal of All Things in Christ: Maximus the Confessor and John Wesley" is one of the few studies available. Carveley notes the typical similarities between Wesley and Eastern Christianity and between Wesley and Maximus as well. Carveley cites numerous passages from both writers to show how they embraced a comparable vision of Christianity in terms of the love and grace of God bringing universal restoration through the Incarnation and sanctification or deification. Carveley's essay picks up on the parallel themes that highlight the overall structure, movement and content of Maximus' and Wesley's theology. Some of those themes include: Incarnation and deification, God's love, *kenosis,*[1] circumcision of the heart, perfect love, and salvation as a universal and cosmic process (Carveley 2002:173-188). He finds that both theologians seek a religion of the heart that recapitulates all things in Christ (2002:173-174).

I tend to agree with Maddox's view that regardless of whether the connection was direct or indirect, Wesley shares a similar theological vision of grace, participation and sanctification with the Eastern fathers, especially Maximus. My own insights are similar to Carveley's. The parallels between Maximus and Wesley are striking. Both were compilers and interpreters of the traditions that they inherited. Maximus compiled, interpreted and edited Origen, Gregory of Nazianzus, Pseudo-Dionysius, and Evagrius, while Wesley did the same with the traditions he inherited, including the early fathers, the Catholic mystics, the Puritans and others in *The Christian Library* as well as other works.

Both served as theological bridges between the Christian East and the Christian West. As was noted above Maximus, an Eastern Christian, aligned himself with the papacy and fought to keep the East from slipping into Monothelitism. Wesley's soteriology draws from an Eastern framework of grace, participation, and sanctification and an Augustinian view of anthropology and sin serves as a *via media* between East and West (Collins 1997:31-38. Collins shows the Augustinian influence).

Both men preached and lived disciplined lives of holiness. Both men were theologians as well as practitioners. Maximus was an ascetic monk and a defender of the faith whose theology was lived out in ascetic practice. Wesley was an itinerant evangelist and apostolic organizer whose "practical divinity" was done "on the way" in the form of journal entries, letters, sermons, essays, and everyday ministry. Both leaders were caught in the middle of theological controversy, especially in terms of debates between monergism and synergism. Maximus challenged the Monothelite view that Christ had one will. He agreed with a Chalcedonian logic that understood that Christ had both a divine will and a human will working together. Wesley's debate with monergism had to do with salvation. The Calvinists of his day held that God's sovereignty was solely at work in salvation, while Wesley recognized that human response was necessary for God's grace to be appropriated (see Coppedge 1987 *John Wesley in Theological Debate).*

The most pronounced theme shared by the two theologians is the vision of recapitulation in the new creation. Maximus' *theosis* can be compared to some degree to Wesley's view of entire sanctification. Both visions are interested in the transformation of humanity into the full image of God. Both visions extend to the entire universe transfiguring it into a cosmic icon of God. The fundamental similarity between the two that I will focus on and develop is the idea of participation as it relates to grace and sanctification or *theosis*. It is important to note early on that Wesley the theologian draws from a diversity of sources and is too complex to reduce to any one or even a few sources or influences. There are as many Wesleys as there are Wesley scholars. George Croft Cell portrays a Calvinist Wesley. Lindstrom portrays a Lutheran Wesley. Cobb depicts a Process Wesley. Coppedge identifies a Holiness Wesley. Maddox highlights an Eastern Orthodox Wesley. Theodore Jennings favors a Liberationist Wesley. Borgen depicts a high church liturgical Wesley. And the list goes on and on. I do not feel this is always the *culpa* or fault of the Wesley scholar. Wesley was a synthesizer and somewhat of an eclectic thinker.

Ken Collins, a historical theologian and Wesley scholar, warns us not to view Wesley through any one stream of tradition (Collins 1997:205-207). Yet, at the same time, we always approach reality with some interpretive framework and theory. Owning my theory-laden views, I recognize that I am looking for parallels between Maximus and Wesley and am assuming that there are, though my assumptions need to be proved. I will factor in Collins' warning and realize the polyvalence of Wesley and will try not to *force* him into an Eastern mold. However, I will commit a *venial* sin and still look at "participation" in Wesley's view of grace. In my efforts, it is not that I seek to make Wesley an Eastern Orthodox Christian, which he is not, but it is a theological effort to examine if Wesley's dynamic of grace can contribute to the discussion of participation.

Wesley and Participation in Grace (*Metousia Chariti*)

In his systematic study of Wesley's theology, Ken Collins understands grace as the "key theme in Wesley's theology" (Collins 1997:19). Collins sees the abundance of this theme from Wesley's treatment of creation to salvation to glorification and structures his study of Wesley around it (1997:19). For Wesley grace is a primary theological category. Wesley, in part, held to the traditional Reformed view of grace as the "undeserved favour" of God (1997:19). Yet he also understood grace in terms of "participation in and empowerment through the life of God" (Collins 1997:20). Wesley is often seen as a *via media*[2] between the Protestant concept of grace and the Catholic understanding of holiness through participation in the life of God (1997:20).

Maddox also recognizes that Wesley's view of grace holds this tension together. For Maddox, Wesley emphasized "the divine initiative expressed in Christ and the divine empowerment available through the Holy Spirit" that enables *"responsible human participation in this gracious work"* (Maddox 1994:141). However Maddox does not see this tension as merely one between Protestant and Catholic view, but he sees the integration of Western juridical concerns with Eastern therapeutic ones (Maddox 1994:142). Salvation is not merely one-sided, that is depicting God's unilateral grace that results in legal righteousness. Salvation is also concerned with imparting grace to a responsive heart that results in transformation and holiness.

Outler's thinking, predating Maddox's, is similar. He identifies the "forensic-pardon" themes stemming from Latin Christianity and also found in classical Protestantism, and these are set apart from the Greek ontological vision of *metousia Theou* (Outler 1991:92-93). According to Outler, Wesley integrated the two themes in a "pardon in *order* to participate" motif or "faith alone, working by love aimed at holy living" (Outler 1991:94). Outler notes that Wesley acquired his participation motif from the mystics like de Renty, as well as Scripture (Outler 1991:93). In fact, Wesley began the day of his Aldersgate experience with 2 Peter 1:4, which speaks of being "*partakers* of the divine nature" (Outler 1991:32,166).

In Wesley, grace requires participation, a response (Maddox 1994:143). Outler calls this response "participation" and also uses the term synergism (Outler 1991:32,105). Maddox calls it co-operant or responsible grace and even participation (Maddox 1994:92, 147-148). At times Collins uses the term participation, claiming that for Wesley all of creation participates in the natural image of God (Collins 1997:22). For Wesley all of creation participates in God's grace. Here *metousia chariti,* participation in God's grace is a theo-ontological category. Grace, often synonymous with the Holy Spirit in Wesley, has a universal ontological function. Wesley's sense of grace is not only theological but metaphysical, since all of nature or creation is an expression of grace. Reality. Similarly, Maximus' understands grace working from the *Logos* through the *logoi* in all of creation. The *telos* of creation is to express the will of God, the *logoi*, the grace of God. Of course, in Wesley, we do not find the strong philosophical orientation that we find in Maximus, but there is philosophical relevance in Wesley that I will briefly explore.

Although Wesley engaged the deism and science of his day, Wesley speaks primarily a Scriptural dialect and not a philosophical one, or a philosophical theological dialect as did many Greek, Christian theologians. Wesley by nature was not speculative but more practical, he did stress the proper and balanced use of reason along with revelation for example in his sermon "The Case of Reason Impartially Considered" (Wesley 1985:2:587). He was well read in philosophy, being trained in Aristotelian logic at Oxford, and he read the philosophy of his day, i.e. John Locke (Wesley 1985:2:589). Thomas Oord claims that some of the philosophers that Wesley read were Aristotle, Augustine, Bacon, Berkeley, Boethius, Robert Boyle, Joseph Butler, Cicero, Samuel Clarke, Descartes, Jonathan Edwards, Erasmus, Hume, Francis Hutcheson, Leibniz, Locke, Malebranche, Cotton Mather, Newton, Pascal, Plato, Thomas Reid, and Voltaire (Oord 2004:155). Thus Wesley had some exposure to philosophy. It is more difficult to tell where he stood in terms of schools of philosophy.

Epistemologically, Maddox sees Wesley as an empiricist in the Lockean tradition yet with a spiritual twist, holding to the idea of spiritual realities being apprehended by spiritual senses (Wesley 1991:154; 1991:339; Maddox 1994:27). Gunter agrees with the assessment of Wesley as an empiricist but with a "Platonic twist" (Gunter 2000:135). Although empirical knowledge of the world is sensed based, knowledge of God is not restricted to the same. Gunter, like Maddox refers to the "spiritual senses" in Wesley (Gunter 2000:137). Through the spiritual senses, we gain experiential knowledge of God. Gunter claims that for Wesley "the spiritual senses are the gracious work of God through the Holy Spirit" (2000:137). The spiritual sight allowed by Wesley is the Platonic twist that expands the senses past the physical realm, enabling experiential knowledge of God (2000:138).

Rebekah Miles would agree. She identifies Wesley's empirical heritage rooted ultimately in Aristotle, but she notes Wesley's understanding of our "spiritual senses" that apprehend the transcendent realm gives him an appearance as a Platonist (Miles 1997:86 and 91). Wesley's "Aristotelian empiricist way leads to a Platonic destination (Miles 1997:93). Wesley is an empiricist because knowledge comes to the mind via the senses. Ideas are not innate. However, Wesley has a Platonic streak in him because the nature of the senses is not only physical but spiritual as well. These senses come in contact with a transcendent realm accessing experiential knowledge of God. I would agree that Wesley seems to have elements of both Aristotelian empiricism and Platonic transcendence.

I would propose *prima facie* that Wesley appears to hold to a position of soteriological epistemology that can best be described as spiritual empiricism. In "An Earnest Appeal to Men of Reason and Religion," Wesley equates the spiritual senses with faith (1872:8:4). He states that faith is:

> "the demonstrative evidence of things unseen," the supernatural evidence of things invisible not perceivable by the eyes of flesh, or by any of our natural senses or faculties. Faith is the divine evidence whereby the spiritual man discerneth God, and the things of God. It is with regard to the spiritual world, what sense is with regard to the natural. It is the spiritual sensation of every soul that is born of God. (1872:8:4)

Thus for Wesley faith is the "eye of the new-born soul," the "ear of the new-born soul, whereby a sinner 'hears the voice of the Son of God and lives'," the "palate of the soul; for hereby a believer 'tastes the good word, and the powers of the word to come'," and "the feeling of the soul..." (1872:8:4). When one is born of God, the ontological shift from *death* to *life* and from *in Adam* to *in Christ* brings about a parallel metaphysical shift from the *visible* world to the *invisible* world and an epistemological shift as well from our *natural senses* to our *spiritual senses*. It is not to say that creation is not of grace and only the new creation is of grace. For Wesley all is of grace, but the natural senses perceive the visible, and the spiritual senses perceive the invisible.

Wesley further explains his spiritual empiricism whereby reason is illuminated by the knowledge of God from the invisible world through the spiritual senses:

So you cannot reason concerning spiritual things, if you have no spiritual sight; because all your ideas received by your outward senses are of a different kind; yea, far more different from those received by faith or internal sensation, than the idea of colour from sound. These are only different species of one genus, namely sensible ideas received by external sensation; whereas the ideas of faith differ *toto genere* from those of external sensation. So that it is not conceivable, that external sensation should supply the want of internal senses; or furnish your reason in this respect with matter to work upon.

What then will your reason do here? How will it pass from things natural to spiritual; from the things that are seen to those that are not seen; from the visible to the invisible world? What gulf is here! By what art will reason get over the immense chasm? This cannot be till the Almighty come in to your succour, and give you that faith you have hitherto despised (1872:8:13-14).

For Wesley, his "spiritual empiricism" is of a totally different order than any natural empiricism that operates in the visible world strictly through the five senses. An ontological change in one's spiritual status initiates one into a new metaphysical reality, an invisible world that can be experienced empirically by faith. Faith becomes the faculty of perception in the new creation. We noted earlier a similar "transcendence," for lack of a better term, in Maximus who through contemplation ascended past the sensible and the intelligible realms. In Wesley, faith seems comparable to Maximus' *theoria* or contemplation. Like Maximus' ontology of participation through the Logos, Wesley's theology of grace contains a similar relational dynamic where creation participates preveniently in God's grace through the unconditional benefits of Christ's atonement. Both reject any natural autonomy of creation but recognize its dependence on God's grace for creation to exist and to fulfill what God intended. God's grace is active in all of creation, whether one is spiritually asleep in the old or awakened in the new.

While many see Wesley in the empirical tradition or even as a spiritual empiricist, Oord recognizes four other traditions with which *Wesleyanism* is often associated; Reid's common sense, pragmatism, Bowne's personalist school, and process philosophy (Oord 2004:158-159). Thus not only was Wesley not strongly philosophically oriented in his writings, which was probably more due to his makeup and context then his ability, it is difficult to locate him philosophically with certainty. Though it seems he favored the empirical approach yet with a spiritual component as referenced prior that allows for transcendent access and experience, a spiritual empiricism out of a theo-ontology of *metousia chariti*.

In some ways, Wesley anticipates the concern of Radical Orthodoxy in terms of reason and revelation in that these categories are not seen as mutually exclusive or separate realms. Wesley's training in Aristotelian logic, his layperson's interest in philosophy and science and his pietistic and experiential spirituality combined for an approach to the faith that integrated revelation and reason with Wesley's empirical approach. Reason was not an autonomous source of knowledge but was a "tool" or a "processor" of knowledge (Miles 1997:78; Maddox 1994:40). Wesley employed reason to organize and draw conclusions from revelation (Maddox

1994:41). Maddox states that for Wesley "When reason is construed in this regulative sense, the polarization between it and revelation breaks down (Maddox 1994:40). There is no inconsistency between reason and faith in Wesley (Miles 1997:79). Wesley recognized the severe limitations of reason even as believers, as exemplified in his sermon "The Imperfection of Human Knowledge," and at the same time he corrected those who undervalued the ability of reason in light of supernatural guidance in his sermon "The Case of Reason Considered" (Wesley 1985:2:590). In the latter sermon, Wesley brings a needed balance to the use of reason and revelation in which there is no inconsistency.

All of that said however, it is difficult to allow Wesley to speak purely in terms of philosophical categories as Maximus often does due to their different contexts. Yet it is the contention of this writer that Wesley speaks of grace in primordial and universal terms, with seemingly 'ontological' implications, that is the Holy Spirit or work of the Spirit as the one who is synonymous with grace. In his sermon "Salvation by Faith," Wesley attributes to God's grace the bestowing of all blessings, forming man from dust of the earth, sustaining all things, working whatever righteousness may be in us, and even giving us salvation through faith (Wesley 1991:40-41). God's grace creates all things, sustains all things, and provides salvation for all things. For Wesley, as with Maximus, nothing exists in a pure state of nature or by its own merit (Lossky 1998:101). Even in our sin, we are not in a "state of mere nature; there is no man, unless he has quenched the Spirit, that is wholly void of the grace of God. No man living is entirely destitute of what is vulgarly called *natural conscience.* But this is not natural: It is more properly termed *preventing grace*" (Wesley 1986:3:207). God's grace has given to all in some measure a universal knowledge of his being and attributes and the knowledge of the "difference between moral good and evil" (1986:3:199). He cites references from John 1:9 and Romans 2:14 to support his claims (1986:3:200). These claims come from his sermon entitled "Working Out Our Own Salvation" using as his primary text Philippians 2:12-13: *"Work out your own salvation with fear and trembling: For it is God that worketh in you both to will and to do his good pleasure."* Wesley's thesis is that the grace of God goes before us and gives us the desire and the power to fulfill his will if we respond to the grace given to us – "God works; therefore you can work" (1986:3:206). This dynamic is often called synergy. I call it participation, participating in God's grace, *metousia chariti.* The term synergy implies that both parties are working and often working equally.

In this sermon, Wesley emphasizes how God's grace initiates salvation in our lives through the universal knowledge of his existence and attributes as well as the discernment between good and evil. Wesley employs the term *preventing* or *prevenient grace* which comes from the Latin *prevenire* which means "to come before." Most likely Wesley was previously exposed to the term through Augustine and Article Five of the thirty-nine Anglican Articles. *Preventing grace* is "the first wish to please God, the first dawn of light concerning his will, and the first slight transient conviction of having sinned against him" (1986:3:203). In his sermon "On Conscience," Wesley also subsumes conscience under prevenient grace, claiming conscience is "not natural, but a supernatural gift of God" or "that supernatural gift of God we usually style preventing grace" (1986:3:482,484).

All of our knowledge of God is a revelation from God's grace, even the initial universal knowledge of God that comes through creation and conscience, claims Wesley in "The Imperfection of Human Knowledge" (Wesley 1985:2:571 and Maddox 1994:28-29). It seems with Wesley that to think of nature as a sphere devoid of grace is non-existent or at best an abstraction. All of creation participates in the universal grace of God. Grace takes on a universal character and function, not in a classic sense of a "universal" or "particular," because God's grace is not created nature. Remember, for Maximus, the *logoi,* though not philosophical universals, were universal in that they transcended and interacted with all of creation. The universal character of God's grace is that it takes on a mediating function so all of creation can participate in God. Outler similarly refers to grace as a universal function in Wesley (Outler 1964:33).

As for Maximus, created being ontologically participates in God through the *logoi,* so for Wesley, creation participates in God through grace. In Maximian terms, Wesley's understanding of grace seems to be comparable to the *logoi,* which are the energies of God working his will in creation. In terms of Maximian *kinesis* and the dynamic initiative of the energies of God in creation, there seems to be a similar function in Wesley's understanding of grace (possibly grace and *wisdom* would equate more formally with the *logoi.* Again, Wesley did not work out of a Patristic Logos grammar). Outler says of Wesley that the Christian life "is empowered by the energy of grace: prevenient, saving, sanctifying, sacramental" (Outler 1964:33). Clearly the terms "grace" and *"logoi"* are not synonymous because Wesley did not think in the same terms as Maximus nor to the philosophical depth as Maximus. Nonetheless, both have identified God's universal movement of love in creation that requires a response, and this universal motion or willing is not of nature but a gift of grace in which creation participates. Grace, like the *logoi,* relates to and expresses the primal will and motion of God in the world. The *logoi,* as the energies of God, express God's will and work in creation.

In many ways, for Wesley, grace is similar. In the Palamite dichotomy, the energies of God are God (his presence) but not his hyper-essence. In Orthodox thinking, God's hyper-essence is to know God's self as God knows God's self. Wesley does not operate out of this dichotomy but often uses grace synonymously with the Holy Spirit, giving grace not merely a universal function but an ontological character or presence in the person of the Spirit. In the sermon "The Witness of Our Own Spirit" grace is God's empowering presence in the Holy Spirit:

> By "the grace of God" is sometimes to be understood that free love, that unmerited mercy, by which I a sinner, through the merits of Christ, am now reconciled to God. But in this place it rather means that power of God the Holy Ghost, which "worketh in us both to will and to do of his good pleasure." As soon as ever the grace of God in the former sense, his pardoning love, is manifested to our souls, the grace of God in the latter sense, the power of his Spirit, takes place therein. And

now we can perform, through God, what to man was impossible. (Wesley 1984:1:309)

If grace is a primary and possibly ontological category for Wesley that has a universal influence on creation, then it may be possible to see Wesley's understanding of grace as a type of participation. Participation is an ontological category and structure for analogous being, which Wesley held to as opposed to a univocity of being (Maddox 1994:49). Since the initial knowledge of God for Wesley did not come from autonomous ratio-empirical inferences drawn from a state of nature but from partaking of prevenient grace, that is shed in the hearts of all persons, then Wesley's religious epistemology is not an empirical, natural theology but an ontologically based epistemology of participation in the grace of God from which all things come – a spiritual empiricism that is rooted in participation in God's grace, a theo-ontology or even a onto-epistemology of *metousia chariti*.

The Radical Orthodox charge of univocal, autonomous reason cannot be brought against Wesley's apparent *de facto* epistemology. Wesley's sensory-based empiricism is rooted in a creation that is an expression of and participates in the grace of God. As humanity responds to God's grace, it is awakened in its spiritual senses to the invisible things of God (Wesley1991:339). The spiritual senses apprehend the one who transcends all, the one who is invisible. Wesley's empiricism is within a larger ontological and analogical relationship between God and creation that is facilitated through grace. As with Maximus, so it is with Wesley that epistemology is ontologically dependent. Maximus' *metousia Logo* and Wesley's *metousia chariti* are examples of onto-epistemologies with their root in God, that is, theologically based onto-epistemologies.

In examining participation in grace, it goes without saying that Wesley did not hold to the Reformed monergistic view of grace or a Pelagian view of natural human freedom. To repeat his statement in "Working out Our Own Salvation," "God worketh in you; therefore you can work" (Wesley1986:3:206). Although synergy is a word that is often avoided for this dynamic because it may imply equal effort from two wills as opposed to primacy given to God's grace, the point is that grace requires a human response, "responsible grace" (Maddox 1994). Human response does not originate from a natural human effort to do good, i.e. the charge of Pelagianism, but Wesley asserts in "Predestination Calmly Considered" that "there is a measure of free-will supernaturally restored to every man, together with that supernatural light which 'enlightens every man that comes into the world'" (1872:10:230). In order for human freedom to respond to God, it is restored in some measure to fallen humanity through prevenient grace through Christ. Hence, participation in grace is not monergistic or of the natural human will which for Wesley was depraved and only evil, but co-operant, a cooperative participation (Wesley1991:329; Outler 1964:33; Maddox 1994:92).

Participation in grace, epistemologically considered, is not merely rational, a matter of ideas or pure reason. Nor is it deontological, as was Kant's means of transcendence. Wesley considered "a religion of opinions; or what is called orthodoxy" and "a religion of works" to be "false religion" (Wesley 1987:4:66-67). In his sermon "The Unity of the Divine Being," Wesley also warned against a "religion of nature," that was gaining ground in his own day, or what we call natural religion, i.e. Hume (Wesley 1987:4:67-69).For Wesley true religion is an *experienced* religion of a circumcised heart with "right tempers towards God and man" (Wesley 1987:4:7:66). Wesley on numerous occasions condemned the reduction of religion to systems of propositions or to outward forms and rituals (see Wesley's *Character of a Methodist* 1872:8:340-341). Wesley's understanding of the knowledge of God cannot be reduced to merely propositional, deontological or external categories. Outler identifies Wesley's "theory of *religious* knowledge" as an awareness or experience of the presence of God's grace (Outler 1964:29). Like Maximus, Wesley understood the knowledge of God as *experiencing* or participating in God's grace. In Charles Wesley's sermon "Awake, Thou That Sleepest," he asks "Dost thou know what religion is? That it is a participation of the divine nature..." (Wesley 1991:90).

Participation as an ontological category carries the understanding that any rational or epistemic structure depends on and is preceded by a transcending ontological relationship. For Maximus it is a *metousia Logo*. For Wesley it is also a participation in God through Christ. As participation relates to the energies of God as in Maximus' doctrine of the *logoi*, it is a participation in grace, a *metousia chariti*. Maximus understood the *telos* of participation to be *theosis*. Wesley also understood the purpose of participation in grace to be holiness or entire sanctification. For both men the ascent to Christ-likeness was a growth in grace.

Human response to grace will bring more grace (Wesley 1986:3:208). In the sermon "Working Out Our Own Salvation," Wesley lays out his *ordo salutis* (Some argue for a *via salutis* or "way of salvation"– Maddox 1994:157-158). Prevenient grace brings one into convincing grace, termed repentance. Following repentance and faith, one is brought into justification, which saves from the guilt of sin and restores the favor of God. Continued growth in grace and repentance of inbeing (inbred) sin brings one into (entire) sanctification which saves from the power and root of sin and restores one to the image of God (1986:3:204).

This growth and transformation in grace of course occurs *in Christ*. Being in Christ marks a new ontological-relational status for the believer and ultimately for the new creation. *In Christ* is the new relational ontological status that realizes the new eschaton of the Kingdom. The believer has a new relative position of righteousness in Christ and is born of the Spirit. In Wesley's sermon "The New Birth" he describes spiritual birth as being born of God (Wesley 1991:339). Just as a newborn child's senses begin to see and to hear, so one newly born of the Spirit has the "eyes of his understanding opened," and their ears are opened to hear the inward voice of God (1991:339). The newborn believer is "sensible of, the graces which the Spirit of God works in his heart" (1991:339). Prior to saving grace, one is blinded by a "thick veil between him and the invisible world," Wesley claims in "On Living Without God" (Wesley 1987:4:171). One "*tastes* nothing of the goodness of God, or the powers of the world to come. He does not *feel* (as our Church speaks) the working of the Holy Spirit in his heart" (1987:4:171).

Wesley uses sensory language to describe the experience or the inexperience of the knowledge of God. This knowledge is not abstract or ideal but spiritually *tangible* or *perceptible* (perceptible inspiration of which Wesley was often accused). Wesley can use sensory and empirical language because he is describing experience in a new spiritual world, the new creation, through a new ontological status in Christ. Since Wesley held to more of an Augustianian and Reformed view of original sin and justification by faith than an Eastern view, he claims imputational righteousness and the *relative change* in status that comes from justification. Of course, Wesley also believed in a *real* change through regeneration and impartational righteousness as well. But in his *ordo salutis,* justification logically preceded such a real change, whereas in Eastern Christian terms justification is rarely discussed.The defining of markers is the primary soteriological difference between Maximus and Wesley. Wesley clearly marked points of process-crisis-process along the *ordo salutis* that integrate both Eastern and Western hamartiological and soteriological concerns. With Wesley's prevenient grace, from the sermon "Justification by Faith," persons participate in initial grace, but they still have not experienced pardon, reconciliation, and a change of status (Wesley 1991:115). Regeneration has yet to occur even in a "rudimentary form" (Collins and Maddox 2000:73). Convincing grace deals with one's transgressions under prevenient grace and points to the need for saving grace in Christ.

Maximus' marked points are more levels of ascension to *theosis; praxis, theoria,* and *theologia.*[3] They are not necessarily crisis points of salvation that deal with different aspects of and responses to sin, i.e. justification from sins committed and sanctification from inbeing sin. The Eastern view looks at the entire journey of salvation as an ascetic and sacramental participation in grace unto *theosis.* Rarely is justification mentioned in an Augustinian-Reformed sense. Nonetheless, for both Wesley and Maximus, the *telos* of the Christian life is holiness. Wesley said in his sermon "On Charity," "that true religion, in the very essence of it, is nothing short of holy tempers," or a holy heart, character and will (Wesley 1986:3:306). "Holiness of heart and life," as the old Wesleyan holiness slogan goes, which is received through *participating* in God's grace is the teleological thrust of Wesley's *ordo salutis.* Maddox stresses the participatory element in that "Wesley's holy tempers would not simply be infused by God's sanctifying grace in instantaneous completeness; they would be developing realities, strengthened and shaped by our *responsible* participation in the empowering *grace* of God" (Maddox 1994:179). Much debate in Wesleyan circles has gone on as to whether Wesley understood entire sanctification to be crisis, process or both, but regardless of where one stands, though I believe it to be both, sanctification is relational and participatory. Entire sanctification is *in Christ.*

Participation and Recapitulation in the New Creation

As holiness is the *telos* of the Christian life for Maximus and Wesley, it is the experience of God's transfiguring presence now and yet to come. Maximus' cosmic liturgy and Wesley's *ordo salutis* are eschatological maps of the coming of the Kingdom into the universe, the participation of the cosmos in the divine. Wesley's vision of holiness not only was intended for the individual but also for the whole of society. He created intense discipleship structures, i.e. societies, classes, bands, select bands etc., for each juncture of the Christian life to nurture growth in holiness, which he ultimately saw as social, that is, loving one's neighbor as one's self. In fact, Wesley saw the Methodist Society as a type of eschatological community, a new creation (Meadows 2004:74). Wesley understood the whole project of holiness as God's design and mission for the people called Methodists. He records in his "Minutes of Several Conversations," that God's design in raising up Methodist workers is "to reform the nation, particularly the Church; and to spread scriptural holiness over the land" (Wesley 1872:8:299). Wesley sought to train and equip believers to live out and promulgate the message of holiness with the expectation that it would bring great transformation.

His vision of holiness was not merely personal but necessarily implicated social holiness, which for Methodists originally meant that the Christian religion was expressed in *koinonia* in discipleship groups and not in isolation. However, Methodist societies also took social action and were responsible for opposing public ills like slavery and alcoholism and supporting prison reform. They also set up credit unions and systems for employment, schools, as well as dispensed medicine, food and clothes among many other services (See Marquardt 1992 and Jennings 1990). Wesley may not have had the sociological insights into systemic sin as we do in our day, but, in his sermon *Divine Providence,* he still was able to identify the "complicated wickedness" that affects humanity beyond the individual will. As a response, he sought to apply the gospel's social ethics in a variety of realms within society (Wesley 1985:2:540). It is true that Wesley's political conservatism often inhibited thinking that would have initiated fully-orbed socio-systemic changes, and that Wesley believed that social transformation began individually; nevertheless his *vision* of holiness entailed an ultimate triumph of grace in cosmic redemption (Marquardt 1992:123-134 and Maddox 1994:253). Like Maximus, Wesley understood that one of the primary purposes of the Incarnation was recapitulation, the gathering together of *all* things in Christ. In his sermon on "The Holy Spirit," Wesley penned that:

> When he was incarnate and became man, he recapitulated in himself all generations of mankind, making himself the centre of our salvation, that we lost in Adam, even the image and likeness of God, we might
> receive in Christ Jesus. (Wesley 1872:7:513)

Participation in Wesleyan grace is an eschatological crisis-process-crisis into the new creation, where all things become new. In this sense, participation conveys the mission of God's grace to bring transformation to the cosmos. Wesley's sermon "The General Deliverance" describes God's plan to redeem the whole of creation. Maximus made the connection between the transformation of humanity and the transformation of the rest of the cosmos. Humanity serves as a microcosm of the universe and in this priestly role would affect the cosmos. Wesley also states that "man was the great channel of communication, between the Creator and the whole brute creation; so when man made himself incapable of transmitting those blessings, that communication was necessarily cut off" (Wesley 1985:2:442). Wesley finds in Romans 8:19-23 a promise of deliverance for the entire created order (Wesley 1985:2:445-447). Wesley enumerates the extent and scope of deliverance in "The New Creation." A new heavens including the stars, the atmosphere, and the climate, the transformation of the waters, a healing of the plant and animal life, and a deliverance of humanity from sin into holiness characterizes this cosmic transfiguration in Wesley (1985:2:502-510).

Wesley does not specifically address millennial positions, but he appears to hold to some version of recapitulation through the universal spread of the Gospel. In his sermon entitled "The General Spread of the Gospel," Wesley envisions the leavening of the "pure and undefiled religion, of the experimental knowledge and love of God, of inward and outward holiness, will afterward spread" to "every nation under heaven," resulting in "the times of universal refreshment from the presence of the Lord" (Wesley 1985:2:493-494). Although Wesley recognizes God's plan for " a universal remedy, for a universal evil," in his sermon "Causes of the Inefficacy of Christianity," he sees "the disease still remains in its full strength; wickedness of every kind; vice, inward and outward, in all its forms, still overspreads the face of the earth" (Wesley1987:4:87). Sin, especially in the church, seeks to impede God's work. This is Wesley's explanation for the "Causes of the Inefficiency of Christianity," the title of this sermon. His homiletical focus here is on the people called Methodists. Their self- indulgence and growth in wealth impeded the spread of scriptural Christianity among themselves and those around them (1987:4:90-95). Hence, Wesley understood this mission primarily as *God's work, missio Dei*. In "Causes of the Inefficiency of Christianity," he stresses God's work in the church, and how the church becomes God's instrument in the world (1987:4:87-90). The church's participation in the Trinity and transformation through the grace of God allows the Lord to work through the church to have an impact on the world.

In the *missio Dei* of both Maximus (cosmic *theosis*) and Wesley (general spread of the gospel), God's grace is actively working in creation and specifically through humanity to bring cosmic transformation. The extent of God's work is not reduced to a "spiritual" salvation sometime in the distant future. Maximus' sacramental worldview prevents bifurcating spirit and matter. Wesley's realized eschatology advances the Kingdom at least in part into this spatio-temporal order as a personal and social reality. Both men hold to a worldview that is holistic, which is programmatic in their doctrines of *theosis* and entire sanctification. Salvation (*soteria*) involves total health in terms of physical, mental, emotional, spiritual, relational, social, and global. As highlighted by Maddox, the nature of transformation for Wesley reflects Eastern themes. Salvation is not understood primarily in juridical, legal or forensic terms but in curative, medicinal, and therapeutic terms. Sin is a sickness or disease that impedes health and vitality. It is an evil that destroys. Christ is then our healer and victor (*Christus Victor*) who cures our sin sickness and destroys the power of the devil and the power of injustice and evil in the world. In this sense evil is seen as the spiritual sickness that opposes health and shalom. Thus healing and warfare motifs can be seen as compatible with such a vision of mission and are themes that need to be researched more by scholars (see Boyd 1997).

The theologies of both men are strongly Christocentric. Maximus' theology of Incarnation drives nearly every category of his thinking, even his epistemology, which is Logos-based. Wesley's epistemology is indirectly tied to his Christology, in that the saving knowledge of God is available *in Christ*. However, Wesley spiritual empiricism is directly tied to the work of the Holy Spirit who regenerates the individual and opens their spiritual senses to the invisible world and the experiential knowledge of God. Together these themes in Maximus and Wesley could serve a Spirit-Word Christology in terms of religious epistemology in a theology of mission. There is ongoing debate as to the extent of the saving work of God in terms of universalist and particularist views (See Okholm and Phillips 1996; see also Knitter 2002). Also, there is debate concerning the work of the Spirit in initiating salvation outside of or not restricted to Christocentric structures (see Karkkainen 2003).

A Spirit-Word Christology identifies Christ in terms of *both* the Logos *and* the Spirit, as opposed to only the Word. A Spirit-Word Christology that combines the epistemic work of the Spirit *and* the Word in creation through prevenient grace can function as a global point of contact for the knowledge of God in mission. God's Spirit is working in creation preveniently to prepare persons for Christ. The consubstantiality of Spirit and Word recognizes the synthesis of the two working together (Zizioulas 1985:126-132). The Spirit gives birth to and fills Christ; Christ sends the Holy Spirit, and the Spirit leads persons to confess Christ, and bears witness to Christ. There is a mutuality of economies. Pinnock states that "Spirit Christology and Logos Christology are complementary, not antithetical" (Pinnock 1996:91).

Such a Christology would recognize God's cross-cultural universal witness in various contexts as points of grace and contact for mission. Cross-cultural forms that would be outside of a Christocentric structure would be examined critically and analogically for their resonance and compatibility with a Spirit-Word Christology. For example, a Spirit-Wisdom Christology would critically examine wisdom traditions for analogies found in a culture's narratives, epics, proverbs, fables, etc. Such analogies can be made based on a few assumptions. Laurie Braaten's essay, "The Voice of Wisdom: A Creation Context for Proto-Trinitarian Thought" (2001) lists several of them. I will list a few in my own order.

First, Christ *is* the Wisdom of God as revealed in Scripture, specifically in the Christological hymns of John and Colossians and in the teachings of Jesus in the Synoptics (Braaten 2001:52). As wisdom, Christ "proclaims and embodies God's work of ordering and sustaining creation, the bringing of order out of the chaos that disrupts and threatens life" (2001:52). Creation represents the beneficent order established by God (2001:53). Second, "if Wisdom is the revelation of God and God's way in creation, then the study of creation in and of itself is a worthy task" (2001:43). In such a study one can find the revelation of God's wisdom and workings, since all truth is God's truth (2001:42 and 44). Third, "Wisdom is a model for us of the freedom to expand our understanding of God by hearing the truth that others have found in God's good creation" (2001:54). Fourth, a critical listening to traditions of wisdom in creation provides a common ground with other cultures for mission (2001:54).

Examining wisdom traditions cross-culturally would be an example of how an onto-epistemology of participation could be used in a theology of mission. In the final chapter, I will look more in depth at the missiological implications of the findings of this research. At this point prior to applying the research, it will be convenient to summarize the development of an onto-epistemology of participation.

Summary

In the Introduction and in Chapter One and Two, I took a cursory look at some of the problems found in modern mission. Split-level Christianity, syncretism, imperialism, colonialism, and other aberrant forms were cited. Among the multiple causes, one was discerned to be an epistemological crisis. Some of the problems in mission are directly connected to the epistemologies and views of reason that theologies of mission have incorporated. Examining the cause further, I felt that the issues in epistemology ultimately had their roots in ontological concerns. Modern and postmodern epistemologies no longer had their mooring in any transcendent ontology, which resulted in autonomous structures that took on the form of hegemonies.

In the Second Chapter, I critiqued modern and postmodern epistemology through the framework of Radical Orthodoxy. Radical Orthodoxy similarly recognized the problem located in a detached ontology, a univocity of being. The genealogy of univocal being gives rise to the increasing focus on epistemology and reason to bear the weight of reality, meaning and certainty. The problem is that a univocity of being detached from God leaves the created order with no transcendent reference. A univocal being in such a state becomes a univocal non-being. This ontological implosion into non-being leaves a wake of nihilism that leaves behind many modern and postmodern epistemological endeavors.

Radical Orthodoxy suggests returning to a classic vision of reality that depicts creation participating analogically in God. Participation puts the created order back in connection with the transcendent through an analogy of being. In this way, creation is not seen as an autonomous realm, a realm that gives birth to the secular. With the construct of participation, epistemology is closely connected with an overall ontological framework in this case the created order participating analogically in God. The *analogia entis* is able to capture both the similarities and difference in predication. Analogy allows for cataphatic and apophatic knowledge. The latter is ballast providing epistemic humility in seeking knowledge, especially the knowledge of God. Reason is forced to take a subordinate role as it participates in a larger transcendent structure that informs and shapes it. It is the corrective of Radical Orthodoxy to bring autonomous realms, especially reason, into participation.

The Radical Orthodox project seeks to realign all truth within the domain of Christian revelation. It has a vision to comprehend all reality in a theological sense as participating in God. I used the Radical Orthodox evaluation as a critical apparatus to analyze modern and postmodern epistemology. I applied its conclusion that there are problems with modern and postmodern ontology (univocity of being and the detachment of ontology from the transcendent) to further critique these movements in terms of closed hermeneutical systems. I adopted the Radical Orthodox solution of *methexis* or participation to construct an ontologically oriented epistemology, which is based on the revelation of creation, in order to serve a theology of mission.

In the Fourth Chapter, I developed the participation model of epistemology further than Radical Orthodox by integrating specific Christian sources, namely Maximus the Confessor and Wesley. In Maximus I found a more "Christian," or incarnational, version of participation that had been purged of its Neoplatonic vestiges. Maximus' understanding of participation is centralized in the incarnate Logos. Through the *logoi* in creation, all things in their order, meaning and purpose find their origin and destiny in the Logos, Jesus Christ. Ultimately, through the Incarnation, God seeks to gather all things unto himself in a cosmic transfiguration.

In the Fifth Chapter, I found similar themes in Wesley as well. Wesley, who did not speak in the same philosophical terms as Maximus, seems in some sense of dynamism to have given a similar function to God's grace that Maximus gives to the *logoi*. Wesley understood grace in a universal sense in that all of creation and all knowledge of God spring forth from grace. Prevenient grace goes ahead of us drawing us into greater grace with its goal entire sanctification. Grace even has ontological characteristics as Wesley often used the term synonymously with the Holy Spirit. Through saving grace, one is born of the Spirit and receives a new ontological and participatory status in Christ. One's spiritual senses are awakened to an invisible world where the believer has access to empirical knowledge of God. Wesley's spiritual empiricism through participation in grace is a type of onto-epistemology, like Maximus' *metousia Logo*, whose function is based on dependent relations with the transcendent. There are no autonomous rational structures.

Through the conjoining of the constructs of participation of both Maximus and Wesley, it is possible to understand the nature and scope of God's cosmic plan of transfiguration, which serves as the basis for a theology of mission. God desires that all of creation experience participation in the transforming grace of God through Jesus Christ in becoming a cosmic icon of God. This is the *missio Trinitatis* and the work of the church. In the next chapter I will be exploring the implications of participation for a theology of mission.

Thus, my original contribution so far to this research is an ontological critique of modernism and postmodernism beginning with Descartes and ending with Baudrillard in terms of deflationary ontologies. I also applied Radical Orthodoxy's ontological conclusions about modernism and postmodernism and used them to critique these systems in more detail, describing what ontological detachment looks like in nominalism, rationalism, empiricism, idealism, existentialism, nihilism, and postmodernism. I also added an insight to the Radical Orthodox critique, and that is that when ontology implodes, epistemology takes a central place, resulting in closed hermeneutical systems that are often found guilty of reductionism.

My further contributions to this research are the integration of Maximus' doctrine of the *logoi* and his cosmic vision to the Radical Orthodox construct of participation. Further I have integrated Wesley's theology of grace into this same model of participation and its cosmic vision. Bringing together the work of Radical Orthodoxy, Maximus and Wesley for a theology of mission is an unprecedented and challenging integration. My final contribution is the application of this onto-epistemology of participation to a theology of mission, which will be in the following chapter.

Notes

1. A Greek reference to Christ's emptying himself of his heavenly glory in order to assume humanity.
2. Latin for "the middle way."
3. Greek for "practice," "contemplation," and "theology"

Chapter Six

Participation and Some Implications for A Theology of Mission

I am the vine, you are the branches. Those who abide in me and I in them bear much fruit, because apart from me you can do nothing (John 15:5).

Characteristics of Participation as an Onto-Epistemological Vision

As I explore the implications of participation for a theology of mission, it is important to identify some of the elements of an analogical or onto-epistemology of participation; the precision of language is really not imperative. In looking at the one term "onto-epistemology" that I have designated to describe the nature and function of participation, I note participation does not serve an autonomous epistemic role. Participation seeks to avoid all modern and postmodern constructs that claim self- reference or autonomy. "To participate" is to recognize that nothing created stands alone. We are a "part" of God's greater picture. We are also "partakers" of God's Divine nature. In line with Radical Orthodox thinking, there are no secular or autonomous realms. As was once said, "All space is God's space." As a divine favor, God is allowing us to share in his creation.

A shared ontology does not permit any epistemological quest to be central and function as a primary interpreter of reality or a first philosophy. Human knowing is a complex activity that takes places within a larger ontological context containing multiple, even innumerable factors that cannot be reduced. Participation puts a primacy on that ontological context which is transcendent in nature and specifically divine, hence participation is qualified as an "onto-epistemology," an epistemology that is ontologically connected, informed and shaped. The claims of participation made in this research are Christian employing Eastern and Western sources, and are specifically Triune – a Trinitarian Ontology.

Even the term "participation" is not primary or primordial but reflects a relationship and a tie to that which is prior and transcendent. God is first, and then we participate in God as creation. Our being is relational and relative. The object of creation, as an epistemological, ontological or even theological category, is not primary or given priority. Creation in its fullness and overflow points upwardly. The semiotic, semantic, analogical and ontic excess and overflow burst doxo-liturgically outward and upward from creation's saturation into *theologia*. The *logoi* acknowledge and recapitulate in the Logos, rapturing the cosmos with them.

What is the nature of our participation? Some participatory frameworks like those influenced by the Palamite distinction of God's apophatic essence and cataphatic energies and activities locate divine ontology in the energies and the ontology is economic (oikonomia), while any purely Trinitarian ontology remains immanent within itself and is unknowable beyond that it is Trinitarian. Participation then is in the being of God's energies and activies and not in the hyperessense of the Trinity. This viewpoint, at least in part, was probably held by early Eastern fathers, such as Gregory of Nyssa, Pseudo-Dionysius and Maximus the Confessor and other Eastern theologians, such as Gregory Palamas and Vladimir Lossky.

Another view of participation would be that the immanent Trinity, at least in part, is understood in the economic Trinity. Hence, we could understand and participate in part, or analogically, in the ontology of the Triune life. This more mildly apophatic view would be held somewhat by Augustine, Aquinas, Von Balthasar, John Zizioulas, and David Bentley Hart among others. I am not pronouncing either dogmatically but would contend for a fair synthesis of the two that would recognize that God apophatically is above and outside being and non-being (*superessence or supernihil*) but can be truly known analogically by revelation as Trinity. Also, God can be known analogically in the *oikonomia* of the persons of the Trinity, specifically in the historical and canonical tradition of Israel and the church, which at least includes Scripture, its symbols of faith, its worship and mission, its Holy Tradition, and its faithful witnesses.

With this introduction, I hope to have established that "participation" is a relative term, and our starting point ontologically, epistemologically, and theologically is with the Triune God, as primarily revealed in the Incarnation of Jesus Christ. With this starting point assumed, we can move on to creation and its participation in God and examine some characteristics of participation. There are at least *eight characteristics* to identify in an onto-epistemology of participation. They are *analogy, epistemic virtue and humility, difference, relationality, experience, faith* or a *fiduciary component to knowledge, privation*, and *incarnation*.

Analogy

Radical Orthodox sources have characterized a *metousia Theou* as being one that speaks of God in terms of the *analogia entis*. Our understanding and speech about God is in terms of analogy, for God as being and the created order as being are expressed merely in *comparable* terms not equal or singular terms or totally unequal terms. Using a Radical Orthodox remix of Aquinas, I extended the analogization process to the created order within itself. Meaning is not so much deferred (Derrida) as it is shared. We understand things within reality as they participate in the divine according to their original purpose in God. I follow Maximus in his analogical understanding of created being according to its *logoi*. The analogous relationship between God and creation found in the *logoi* can be expressed semiologically and textually. The semiotics and text of analogy, metaphor, model, and symbol are used to express our knowledge of created things in a *type* of critical realism, a realism that is analogical rather than univocal. Our knowledge is real but contextual, provisional, partial and expressed in symbols and models.

I will try to avoid the Scholastic taxonomy of types of analogies, including analogy of proportionality, relationality, concept, meaning etc., as I move from an analogy of being between God and creation to also the analogical nature of language and meaning. Modern reason and some forms of univocal logic sought to express meaning in terms of a digital logic or representation, as is expressed mathematically and in computer technology today. However, this sort of black and white representation does not hold beyond realities that are not in complete binary opposition. Even Derrida's deconstruction presupposes a modernist dichotomy of structural, binary opposition and can be limited and reductionistic. Analogical logic and analogical sets are better suited to understand and express realities that are flawed, flexible and fluid in nature, especially in working with language, translation, form and meaning and other cultural categories.

Although we can create a digital representation of images of the world, the world is not digital. Surely, it has a digital component to it in the nature of mathematical expression, but we cannot create the modern fallacy of making a reduction the totality. Such an automated, flat representation is painfully limited in its groping to capture the inherent excess of phenomena that is saturated with the aesthetic, the moral, the unity, and the real, revealing the transcendence of all being. What we grasp is an analogue and is known in part. Digital may prevail over analog for television reception but not so for culture and language.[1]

The mathematics of flesh and blood at best is a fuzzy enterprise. The freedom of the humanities will always be marginalized and alienated in a global takeover by technological totalization. There is a certain fascism and hegemony in the regime of digital, mathematical expression. The system though dissected incessantly refuses to bleed. It fails to capture us and our relationships. Between divine being and created being is the real ontological difference, the *diastema*,[2] the ontological gap of privation, the space between God as he is in himself, and the creation.The flexibility and flux of space-time, energy and form act within the ontological *diastema*, the analogy, the real ontological difference. Analogy marks the forgiveness of the Divine and the error of the human. It is the *diastema* of the Divine and the human from which spawns all creative interaction, choice, meaning and interpretation. It is in the *diastema* of similarity *and* dissimilarity between divine and created being and the differentiation among created being as well where digital logic fails and analogical reasoning communicates the ontological difference. The "either/or" of the digital gives way to the "both/and" on the infinite continuum of meaning and its approximation scale of interpretation.

Analogical expression within the ontological difference allows for a continuing and ongoing descriptive model of truth that approaches the eschatological real and an ongoing living out of that truth. An epistemology of participation through analogization not only seeks to understand and describe the way we think and speak of God and the way we analyze the created order, but also that way in which we participate in God. Humanity is made in the *imago Dei* (image of God). In one sense, the *imago* is an analogue to God. Humanity is *like* God. Our *logoi* or reason for being and purpose is to be completely conformed to God's *likeness*. Eastern theology understands this as *theosis*. Epistemologically and theologically, it is the proper function[3] or "proper participation" of the *imago* to become more like Christ.

The process of *theosis* is an analogization of creation to the image of Christ. We grow in perfection until that day when we see God face to face. Participation recognizes analogy as the fundamental descriptor of predication in our knowing and being. Analogy allows for similarity and dissimilarity, continuity and discontinuity, particularity and unity and other "antinomies" that make it difficult for pantheism, radical monism, pure hegemony and other totalizing structures to survive. Our apprehension of knowledge and truth is real and yet in eschatological process, as we pursue God and his will (*logoi*) as revealed in creation, in scripture, and ultimately in the incarnate Logos, Jesus Christ.

Throughout this discourse, it has been made plain that participation in God functions analogically, and this analogical function plays off the continuity and discontinuity expressed in the divine-human encounter, the experience of the ontological difference, as well as sharing of meaning. Everything sensible and intelligible and visible and invisible in the creative order is a metaphorical affirmation of God and God's work. The continuity of God's reason and purpose is revealed in its nascent form in the created order and realized in history unto its *pleroma*. The *logoi* inspire creation to move forward and upward in history into the fullness of times with the Incarnation. The incarnate Word expresses hypostatically the continuity between God and humanity.

However, the *via negativa* in such analogical discourse reveals the dark, vast, transcendent discontinuity, the *diastema*, between God and creation. The *diastema* is that incalculable and immense analogical interval between the otherness of God's super-essence and created nature *ex nihilo* (see Hart 2003:300-318 for discussion of "analogy"). As an interval it is also space, extension, and distance where motion (*kinesis*) and change (*trope*) take place; from purpose to realization, from privation to *pleroma*, from origin to eschaton under the impetus and drive of love and desire. *Diastema* is that analogical interval of ontological proportion between God and creation. *Diastema* is also creation *itself* as a space-time extension, describing creation's allotted finitiude (Gregorios 1996:83). It is our *diastemic* existence that prevents us from knowing God as God is in God's self, the claim of total knowledge. It is within that interval of analogical discontinuity stemming from our very created nature, which in change and motion starkly contrasts the one who is wholly other, that the silence of apophasis must quiet our minds and senses and lift us up in our unknowing into union with God (*theologia*). Within *diastemic* existence there is an infinite play of continuity (participation) and discontinuity (*diastema*), similarity and dissimilarity, and cataphasis and apophasis expressed in the semiotics of analogy that allows us to struggle, rest, struggle and become in God forever, *epektasis*.[4]

We experience God's immanence in God's descent. God's transcendence is forever attempted in our ascent, while in this *epektasis* we are humbled and emptied (*kenosis*) in our understanding. The play is never exhausted. The desire never consumed, let alone digitized. The signs are always signifying in their fullness and yet ineffably falling short of the one who surpasses totalizing signification. The limits are stretched beyond epistemic horizons in claims of touching infinity only to give praise and glory to the infinite one through its faltering - the *epektasis* of analogy, the space of perfecting perfection, the doxological interval of eternal cascades and crescendos.[5]

For a theology of mission, it signifies our openness to learn and our refusal to totalize. God reveals God's self within different cultural contexts through different worldviews and sign systems. We do not fall into epistemic pride and seek to convert people to our own worldview, culture or forms, but we let God speak analogically through different cultural systems. The challenge in an epistemology of analogy is to identify the timeless theological truths of Christ's supracultural gospel and allow them to be communicated in indigenous semiotic expressions of locality that are analogically faithful to the gospel.[6] Ultimately, Jesus Christ, who is the local, historical, hypostatic concretization of God and also the transcendental signified and signifier, is to be the true mediator of all semiotic expression both globally and locally. A Christocentric critical contextualization employs Christ as the standard of any cultural critique, in terms of its purpose and analogy to Christ.

With Maximus we noted that the *logoi* represent God's universal will as expressed in creation, conscience, culture and ultimately in the Incarnation of Jesus Christ. The revived transcendentals (being, true, good, unity and beauty) of the Ressourcement and Radical Orthodoxy, which are the essentials of the *logoi*, to some degree point to the *telos* of being as critically considered and revealed in cultural attempts at the true, the good, the beautiful and the one. The transcendentals are *a priori* "intentions" of all *gnomic* (post-lapsarian will) will and being but are rarely realized and only fully realized in Christ.They convey our highest ideals in our failed attempts but are fulfilled in God's revealed being, truth, goodness, beauty, and oneness in Jesus Christ. The *logoi* and their transcendental analogues have universal expression and witness and are realized only in Jesus Christ. Christ is the fulfillment and end of the *logoi* for all who believe.

A people and its culture are judged by Christ in terms of its analogical expression of the *logoi* of Christ and his royal attributes of being reflected analogically in the transcendental and other cultural expressions. As cultural expressions are compatible with their *logoi*, its forms can be used to express the truth of the gospel and its requirements, and in a culture's lapsarian differentiation, that differentiation is judged and found in need of God's mercy and redemption, and in its continual transformation its reflection is measured by the nature of Christ himself and the work of the Spirit. Analogization becomes a means of both prophetically engaging a culture and expressing the gospel through Christocentric critical contextualization. Analogy becomes the primary vehicle for communication.

Epistemic Virtue and Humility

Some analytic philosophies speak of the means of the justification or warrant of knowledge in terms of "proper function"[7] and others in terms of "virtue."[8] An onto-epistemology of participation sees the need for both. "Proper" participation understands that the knower (the *imago Dei*) is to function according to the *logoi* (reason and purpose) of the knower that is to be conformed into the image and likeness of Christ (*theosis*). The process of *theosis* is in itself a cultivating and yielding of the fruit and virtue of the Spirit in our lives and in our knowledge. Epistemology as participation involves properly "functioning" in Christ-likeness or holiness according to God's plan. Proper participation and holiness teleologically go together.

This dynamic bears strongly on our understanding of reason itself in terms of an epistemic humility towards the function of reason. Participation contends for a "soft" use of reason rather than a "hard" one. Reason is a function that does not stand alone but works in concert with the human condition within creation as it relates to God. As referenced above, that relationship is analogical. We are *like* God and relate to God through our limited creatureliness. Knowledge is a gift from God, and reason is one of the faculties God has equipped us with to know God. Though we can know God in truth, our knowledge is qualified. Our knowledge is relative to our relation to God. It is limited and finite due to our nature and perspective as humans – *I Corinthians 13:12 For now we see in a mirror, dimly, but then we will see face to face. Now I know only in part; then I will know fully, even as I have been fully known.* Due to the fall, sin often skews knowledge, specifically because we are "curved" onto ourselves or perpetually serving ourselves and cannot see others and God in love as God would have us. Knowledge is also within a temporal perspective and thus provisional and progressive.[9]

I believe that the Eastern dynamic of cataphasis and apophasis is an effective model for expressing the illumination, progression, and limitation of our knowledge, especially towards God. Cataphasis and apophasis characterize our ascent in knowing the knowable unknowable. What is knowable is cataphatic and by revelation and illumination. It is real experiential knowledge of God though revealed contextually. What is unknowable is apophatic, and that is the knowledge of God's hyperessence or to know God's self as God does. However, some knowledge is apophatic not because it is unknowable, but because it has yet to be revealed to us, or we have not come to it yet. It is due to God's will, our limitations or our sinfulness.

Within the metaphorical continuity of our understanding there are unbridgeable gaps of perspectival obscurity merely due to our humanity and location, let alone our depravity. The darkness also looms over our temporality that providentially allows our understanding to serve *provisionally*. The renewing of the mind as a function of the ontological shift in the new creation in Christ is clearly an eschatological function and tension (II Cor. 4:16 – "*the inward person is being renewed daily*"). Thus, in some sense all true knowledge in its analogical ascent and scope is real and yet provisional in its *desideratum* for pleromatic realization at the *parousia* of his glory. We are practicing the symbolic art of knowledge and along the way are often corrected by its apophasis, and yet still inspired by its function and satisfaction to create and further signify in our eschatological quest for fullness.

The New Testament uses the metaphor of disciple, *mathetes,* signifying a "learner" or a "student" of a master. More and more, we are learners of the way of the cross, learning obedience through humility, lack, sacrifice and suffering, so that in participating in Christ's suffering and death, we may attain to the resurrection and the full realization of God's kingdom. Our learning of Christ in the way of the cross becomes an epistemology of the cross, knowing through suffering and dying. Suffering is a universal experience of the human condition that weighs on all of our knowledge. Whether one lives in constant abject poverty, is diagnosed with a fatal disease, lives in mental anguish or depression as a white collar Wall St. criminal, faces the everyday anxiety of facing the future, suffering probably impacts our experience of life more than any other. As Christians, we suffer in the flesh from resisting sin, sacrificing, and stretching towards the goal of our high calling in Christ in our daily life. Our baptismal participation in the death, burial, and Resurrection of Jesus Christ is a command to follow Christ and be a learner of Christ and his way, a *via crucis*.[10] Theology becomes participation, participation in the life of Christ, and not merely an academic exercise or a scholarly game of cat and mouse, chasing the latest ideological or cultural innovations for the sake of relevance alone. Participation is also not a sacramental exercise in *ex opera operato,* or a once for all easy-believism of saying a salvation prayer or responding to an altar call, though I regularly participate by faith in the sacraments and have regularly offered altar calls in my preaching. The Holy Spirit is making disciples of Jesus Christ and nothing less. We are learning to be like Christ. There is a vital connection between participatory knowledge and participatory holiness.

For both Maximus and Wesley, humility and other virtues were an integral part of knowledge. In repentance and ascetic practice, one contemplated the knowledge of God that would ultimately lead to sanctification. Both men realized that knowledge was meant to bring one to holiness. For Maximus and the Eastern Christian monastic tradition, "theology" was *theologia,* a spiritual union with God. It was the highest state of one's journey in *theosis.* The believer begins in *praxis* (ascetic practices and spiritual disciplines of repentance and consecration) and moves to *theoria* (contemplation and meditation upon the truth of God) in order to arrive at *theologia* (spiritual experiential knowledge and union with God). Notice in this process that actions of repentance and humility precede contemplation of truth.

The mind is humbled and purified that it may openly receive with meekness God's word. *Theoria* is not "theory" as we know it, a conceptualization, a principle, a proposition or a formula, but it is the open heart engaging the living truth of Christ through the Spirit.

Also, *theologia* is not "theology" as we often use the term in the West. The Eastern Church has always shunned and condemned what it felt to be dry and reductive scholasticism. It has sought to make room for the work of the Spirit in the human heart. Theology is not reduced to abstractions, but, as *theologia,* it is a holy union with God. Participation embraces an epistemic humility as a spiritual discipline that works through virtue and develops further virtue. In fact, the scriptural tradition reveals a virtue tradition of holy men and woman who have carried out the practices of self-denial, courage, love and sacrificial service on route to and out of a union with God. Virtue tradition may be one of the oldest and longest standing systems or traditions of "warrant" or "verifiability" in the history of humanity, and it may be the most universal today and needs to be further explored in terms of the "ethos" of our message and the messenger.

The goal of knowledge is not knowledge but Christ-likeness and Christopraxis, *theosis,* because our primary conviction about the knowledge of the truth is that Jesus Christ, the God-person, is the truth. The incarnation of truth is not merely reduced to truth as proposition, though it contains it. A mission of theology *is* concerned about propositional truth, scriptural theology, and a congruent biblical witness in many forms like narrative or wisdom. The church's orthodox witness is much broader than conceptualization and comprehension. The witness is the Spirit of God revealing Christ in and through the church in its worship and mission. When the church understands its witness of the truth as the work of the Holy Spirit, then it can bypass constructing purely schemes fashioned for a conversion of mental assent. Instead, we can opt for a community practice of virtue and witness that demonstrates the reality of the Spirit by providing the receptor community with a more tangible and accessible means to discern the truth of the message in the *praxis* of the community of faith.

Difference/Differential Unity

While analogy can allow for human limitations in understanding God, univocity [11] has a tendency in its extreme to totalize into an *ad nauseam* of sameness.[12] With epistemic humility, we not only approach the Divine with unknowing, attentiveness and, at times, kenotic silence but similarly we approach that which is *different.* Analogical participation is compatible with an ontology of peace not differential violence. Difference does not necessarily entail violence within analogy. The structure of analogy is partly based on difference, as opposed to univocity. An example of difference within unity would be within the Triune life of God. There are three *hypostases* or persons in one *ousia*[13]. In an Eastern Christian understanding of person (*hypostasis* and *prosopon*)[14] there is difference. Each person is uniquely different, and yet there is differential unity in the life of the Trinity, beginning with the second person who is God, the Other, and the Spirit who is God, Another, and yet the three are eternally one.

The Christian revelation ontologically understands and lives out of differential unity, an ontology of peace, a unity even in difference. In another example, the Incarnation of Jesus Christ expresses a similar differential unity. Chalcedonian logic conveys that Christ is two natures hypostatically united in one person. One nature is human, and one nature is divine. There two natures are quite different and find unity in one person, differential unity. The church, the body of Christ, and all of creation are called through the Incarnation into a similar union with Christ, *theosis*. In this process, we become like God, holy icons. *Theosis* is analogical, and it unites that which is different, yet not in confusion or absorption but in the uniqueness of identity. An ontology of peace allows us to approach other cultures, forms and meanings with greater respect and discernment. Univocal methods like *tabula rasa* may not be so kind. Translation cross-culturally is not a matter of one to one correspondence. Instead, the Christian faith can be expressed in analogical forms that are critically derived within other contexts. For example, in employing the transcendentals, we note that all being commonly shares in these attributes. Yet being in the classic sense is also differentiated in terms of uncreated and created being, substantial and accidental, universal and particular, genus and species etc., and these can also be seen culturally between West and East, North and South, and local and global and need to be factored into our cross-cultural communication.

The church is one, holy, universal and apostolic, but has many locations and expressions. With Orthodox, Catholic, Lutheran, Presbyterian, Anglican, Baptist, Methodist, Wesleyan, Pentecostal, Charismatic, non-denomination, independent etc., there are many tribes in our one ecclesial nation.[15] Historically, the church is being critically perfected. We have the real flesh and blood church on the earth, not just a spiritual ideal somewhere in the sweet by and by, but that real church is a work in process. The church eschatologically is a critical, real body that is open to process, progress, growth, change and difference. Its difference expressed in its culture and theology actually adds to its greater sense of unity. Difference becomes a positive sign of the church's depth and relevance, whereas the opposite would be indifference.

Relationality

Analogy is also a relational species. Derrida insists on the deferral of meaning in what is called a "metaphysics of absence" (Derrida 1997:22-23,73,152- 157; see also Milbank 1990:307). This is a partial truth. A further description would include deferral to the *other*, "shared meaning" out of a totalizing absence in a creation *ex nihilo;* yet shared in an analogization of transcendent presence signified in incarnational language and embodied *logoi*. Shared meaning sees the "trace" of absence left behind by Derrida's deferral as more of a distribution and participation in meaning. The meaning of the text is deferred because it is shared, as we participate in meaning, in the *logos*. Meaning is not endless references to absence that are generated out of the void but shared signs that participate in the mediation of the *Logos*. Participation, or participatory knowledge, is a relational process that is shared. We know in community, and we know as community. We are not Cartesian cognitive atoms or even Leibnizian monads of windowless independence of self-sufficiency observing the objective universe in our solitary confinement laboratories of personal perception, recording the data and constructing models of our own idiosyncratic universes. We know in community, and are known in community. The very process of creating knowledge is a dependent and relational art and science. Knowledge is acquired in relationship, for we perceive the *imago* in others and ourselves and the *logoi* in all things that God has given meaning, and we are also known in the same way. As *koinonia* is at the core of the Triune God, creation is a dependent complex eco-sphere not only relying on the divine who holds all things together but also relying on its own manifold internal relations.

We are social beings, and we know in relationship, especially ourselves. As I write, I am disturbed by the grammar-check function of my Microsoft Word program that does not permit passive voice, even in this sentence. In this Western, high-tech world, there is only room for an active voice. However, I know that as I am known, I have identity according to 1 Corinthians 13:12 and 1 John 3:1-2. It is when God knows me that I am known and have identity in Christ, and it is when the community knows me that I am known and have identity in the love of another and then know myself.

Participation gives importance to communal structures of understanding and an ear to the totality of voices in a culture, subcultures, traditions (folk, ethnic, academic, research, ecclesial, organizational etc), local epistemologies, and other forms that are the study of cultural anthropology, and the relation between the local and the global (glocalization). Participation in any community-tradition within a culture realizes the epistemic function of relationality. Participation in the church, the body of Christ, and its participation in the *missio Trinitatis* manifest a holy canonical community-tradition that serves as a historical, doxo-liturgical, missional, narrative, hermeneutical, socio-rhetorical, semiotic-textual and testimonial community of knowledge. Such a community establishes and confirms God's revelation of truth through its theological reflection, worship life and mission practice. We know as we participate together. Much of the Western, analytic tradition of philosophy that is caught in the individualistic culture of Cartesian cognition and linguistic reification of reality has basically ignored the communal dimensions of knowledge.

One of the perennial sins and a sin of modernism is excessive individualism. The heart of the fall of humanity in scripture for Orthodox Metropolitan Bishop of Pergamon John Zizioulas (1931 -) is the rupture between being and communion (Zizioulas 1985:102). With the fall, being becomes no longer dependent on communion but is given priority over communion (1985:102). One has to know the being of something *before* a relationship of communion can occur (1985:102). As a result, each individual being is given its own ontological status *in se*[16] to be recognized prior to communion. Epistemic notions of subject and object and the primacy of individuality in ontology are created, whereas, in an ontology of participation, knowledge occurs in relationship, in a relational context (1985:102-103).

For Zizioulas knowledge is not acquired *solo* or in isolation without relationship and influence but in community and in community traditions. In community, we share life and experience, dialogue, challenge, disagree, struggle together, heal, and learn in a process that develops virtue, wisdom[17] and trust among the community as it pursues the knowledge of God and the practice of God's mission in the world. For the believer, that community tradition is the church, though not the only one. It seems that the history of authority for Christianity can be crudely broken into three periods. The first period is the Catholic-Orthodox era or premodern period that looked to the *church* for authority. The second period is the modern period or Protestant Reformation that looked to *Scripture* for authority. The third period is the postmodern period or Pentecostal-Charismatic period that looked to the *Holy Spirit* or experience for authority. These three sources need not be in opposition. The model of participation is one of *participating* in the Life of the Spirit. The Spirit's life extends to the birthing, sanctifying, worshipping and equipping of the church for the glory of God. It is the Spirit who both birthed the church and inspired scripture in and through the apostolic church. It is the work of the Spirit in Scripture and in illumination that is interpreted (a hermeneutical canonical community) and lived out (a *praxis* community) in the worship and mission of the church that is the authority for our faith and practice. Participation realizes the importance of working out our understanding and practicing of God's word within the community-tradition of the church, not in isolation *sola scriptura solo*. This is a radical challenge to the church that claims to participate in the Holy Spirit and in truth, to be a community-tradition that demonstrates a virtue tradition that is reliable, credible and responsible in its testimony of Jesus Christ. Too often, the church has claimed this position propositionally but has failed as a *praxis* community. As a doxastic community, we are accountable to God and the world to live out the mission of God faithfully, if we are to be acknowledged by the world as a community-tradition that embodies the truth and carry any weight as a canonical-tradition.

Experience

Being relational in nature, participation deals with the *experiential* dimension of knowledge. We experience moving and living and having our being in God. Reality as a univocal rational abstraction is not an accurate and full picture of what is before us but is a reduction and a dangerous caricature. Reality is something we know through experience. Often Christian life is reduced to scholastic theology.[18] Jesus is the Word of Life according to 1 John1:1. He is a living Word that gives fullness of life to those who believe. We cannot reduce that promise of life to mere abstractions and propositions. It is a life that we are to experience in the Spirit with all of the fruit of the Spirit. The Holy Spirit is the Spirit of life (Romans 8:2).

Both Wesley and Maximus depict a religious knowledge that is experiential. Participation is ontologically based and so has that dimension of transcendent and immanent interaction of *beings* not just ideas. 'I am; thefore, I think.' Wesley's emphasized the source of knowledge as the grace of God imparted through the Holy Spirit. Wesley recognizes a pneumatic empiricism in which the spiritual senses perceive invisible reality and acquire experiential knowledge of God.

Participation in the *oikonomia*[19] of the Triune God works within the presence of God, the energies of God - the Holy Spirit. Emphasis on the Holy Spirit and the work of the Spirit through grace in the cosmos, preveniently in all persons and fully in the church needs to be part of a theology of mission that incorporates participation. Such a pneumatology works consubstantially with a Christology that is faithful to Scripture, affirms Chalcedonian logic and recognizes the Logos of creation *and* salvation. In this eschaton, the church needs to recognize that in mission it participates in the mission of the Holy Spirit. The Holy Spirit sets the agenda of mission in the earth. We are to follow the lead of the Spirit, as we recognize God's existing witness throughout the world and in the church and as we faithfully proclaim Christ with signs and wonders following.

A Fiduciary Component

In conjunction with Wesley's spiritual empiricism that was elaborated earlier, there is a fiduciary mode of knowledge apprehension in Wesley as well.[20] Wesley seems to work from the Augustinian tradition of *fides quarenes intellectum*.[21] Faith is seen as a spiritual faculty of perception as well as a primary willing and desire of the heart which is the human response to participating in God and in knowledge in general. In some sense all knowledge has faith as its base (Polanyi 1962:266). A fiduciary component of knowledge owns up front our personal commitments in knowing and strips us of pretenses to pure reason or any other appeals to illegitimate authority that we use to control. Faith as trust puts a face on knowledge and a love for neighbor, adding a human dimension to the epistemic task that has often been calculated in cold, de-personalized logic. Not only knowledge but being in life has a fiduciary component, as faith is the intuitive transcendental connection of the heart to being and truth that precedes the motions of knowledge. By faith I am not appealing to a pure *fideism* or subjective belief but a critically tested commitment to revelation that is worked out in the thought and practice of the church and the world.

Often modern theories of epistemology are built from the bottom up and are framed by questions surrounding foundationalism, justification and warrant of belief. I am not against propositional truth and its justification, especially in theology. It has its place in proper perspective and balance. These questions are valid but only address half of the picture. Our picture is larger than a sense-perceived, rationally-constructed world or even a world reduced to logical propositions or language. This sort of foundationalist blueprint for knowledge is a product of modernism and has questions in mind that presuppose reason as having an autonomous or self-sufficient nature. This blueprint also presupposes the ability for one epistemological theory to cover all scenarios and to provide absolute certainty in each case. I do not believe that there is one theory of knowledge that absolutely covers all cases. I am not contending for that kind of knowledge or justification. I leave that to God.

Saying that does not mean we become relativists or skeptics. Some beliefs are basic and can be justified. Some beliefs are not. I believe at the penultimate level, the universe is basically rational, or to a degree comprehensible, to our fallen and limited reason in that we can symbolically describe, interpret and explain it in a limited way if we pursue truth in community and through epistemic virtue.[22] However, reason is a mode of apprehension that works with other modes of apprehension, like faith, that also rests in larger interacting contexts that are situated within creation.[23] Creation operates under the grace and providence of God. Faith and reason work together. What we know, we believe we know. The Triune God is above all and suspends creation according to his will; revelation is the ground of our knowledge, and faith may be the first floor, but our knowledge is also at *some* level and to *some* degree reasonable and reliable in order to function in creation and relate to God.

Thus although we hold to a real external world that is ratio-empirically as well as contextually known in truth and in part, does not mean that that knowledge is built on *purely* rational and self-evident foundations. In an onto-epistemology of participation, the vision of reality is much larger. Whatever penultimate "foundation" we rest on in our basic, reliable and responsible beliefs about the external world is within the context of the created order that is "suspended" from God the Creator. Our picture includes a transcendent dimension in God. "Suspension" rather than "foundation"[24] is the more appropriate metaphor for describing how knowledge is positioned and functions in the larger cosmic vision. Movement within reality is from top to bottom to top again and not from bottom to top, as if the bottom, the Cartesian Archimedean point,[25] is truly immovable and certain. God initiates movement towards creation, and creation responds.

In such an ontologically informed vision of knowledge, divine revelation by grace through faith seeking understanding becomes a primary dynamic. The created order is a grace gift from God that reveals God's love and purpose for creation. We come to understand these things through a faith commitment and through the conviction and evidences of a reliably functioning reason, both working together. Reason cannot work alone or unaided. Ultimately, nothing is autonomous or self-sufficient but God. Left to ourselves, or our own reason, we cannot understand God or God's world as God intends. In I Corinthians 2:14 Paul declares that the "natural man," the one who is not under the influence of God's Spirit, cannot understand the things of the Spirit, because they are revealed by the Spirit and are spiritually comprehended. In God's eyes, we are justified by faith, and not justified by reason.

Privation

Since we participate in God in terms of being and goodness and our participation is never complete, there is an understanding of privation or lack in our being, knowledge and sanctification. Privation can refer to an ontological lack that is not due to lapse. God is forever God, and we are forever not. There will always be a distance in being in this sense. There is also a natural distance in our becoming like God, as we assume one point in space-time and move to another, eschatologically. Pannenberg recognizes our knowledge is provisional. There is also a sense of privation that is due to lapse that impacts not only our participation in knowledge but in holiness, as well. Sin as missing the mark of God's goodness is an absence of the good. There is a privative context to who we are, and what we know.[26] Wesley did not understand prevenient grace as an improvement of our existing nature but as the power to move closer to God through repentance, pardon and regeneration. Both ontologically and in a lapsarian sense, we operate out of a state of privation. The *diastema* between God and humanity exists by our created nature and is exacerbated by our sin. We lack full being like God and are caught in a tension of being and non-being as we choose to become what God intends. The analogical distance between God and creation is the real ontological difference, not Heidegger's being and beings. Morally we have inherited and often choose corruption, misusing our freedom and choosing a self-centered life of idolatry rather than serving God and others. Our natural limitations and our sin affect our noetic structure so that we are impeded, weakened, and bent towards ourselves even in the process of knowing (Plantinga 2000:213-217).

Limitation and lapse greatly hinder our ability to know in the way God would have us to know, and so we stand in need of epistemological redemption. Our intellectual capacities and processes are often infected by unbelief, pride, injustice, selfishness, covetousness, ambition, and hatred, which blind and limit them from their purpose in knowing and loving God and loving others. Hence, any naïve and ideal notion of any evolutionary perfection or deification within the capacity of the human nature itself to respond does not contain a drop of reality. Although as Wesley noted, depravity has not obliterated the image of God in humanity, and God's grace provides us with a universal witness, sin is all too real and often hinders us from realizing God's vision in our own lives and in our world. They say that children and the news are the two most powerful witnesses for inherent sinfulness.

Our sin is also communal and consequential. It is not just personal as in popular Enlightenment based understanding of moral agency and revivalism. Although we participate in God, in some sense, we universally participate in sin (Suchocki 1995:101). Our organic solidarity with the human race enables sin to touch and affect others outside of ourselves (1995:101). In a participatory scheme reality is relational, and Marjorie Suchocki believes "every act of violence reverberates throughout the race" (1995105). By limits of our human nature and our solidarity in fallenness, we stand as *the poor* in need of participation in Christ's righteousness and life that we may move from non-being to being, privation to *pleroma*, and death to life. This is not just a post-colonial revelation, but I think both Paul and Augustine were privy to it as well.

It is important to note that neither the Maximian vision of cosmic *theosis* nor the Wesleyan vision of entire sanctification are a process of 'pure becoming' in either an evolutionary, Hegelian or natural sense or as a necessary universalism. Although for both thinkers all of creation is an expression of grace, there is a sense where the grace in creation is incipient and incomplete. Prevenient grace needs to progress to saving and sanctifying grace for Wesley. Knowledge as an eschatological function goes from the old to the new and thus from creation to new creation. There is an implied *first* order of grace in the creation prior to the fall and a *last* order of grace with Christ, "the old" and "the new" in Pauline terms.

Even though nature is "graced" for Maximus, he realizes a process and crisis in the knowledge of salvation in which the reason moves from "natural reason" under the "law of nature" to "supernatural reason" under the "law of grace," to use Maximus' terms (Maximus 2003:169). This transformation occurs through Christ in the Incarnation. Again the center for Maximus is always the Incarnation. We are not talking about an undifferentiated participation that has no center, *contra* Reno's charge against Radical Orthodoxy (Reno 2002:72). Christ, the incarnate Logos, *is* the participatory center.

Wesley and Maximus also realized the presence and activity of evil and sin in the world and in the human heart and the need for grace and a response from the human will. Wesley frequently and undisputedly preached on sin, evil, and eternal punishment.. Maximus along with his doctrine of the *logos* of providence recognized the collateral working of God's judgment that "punishes by word and deed those who deserve it..." (Maximus 1996:133). He seems to reject the 'Origenist version' of the *apokatastasis* (unconditional universal restoration). In his *Ascetic Life*, Maximus quotes from Scripture concerning eternal punishment (Maximus 1955:118-119). The economy of salvation works *with* the human will and not around it. Evil, though non-being, is not a gloss but a choice against God's will that results in corruption and destruction but is overcome in Christ's death and Resurrection. Maximus' *ontology* of differential unity is part of the created order of the *logoi* in the *Logos* and is good. However, a *morality* of difference comes under the *logoi* of providence and judgment, and human choices for evil are punished and corrected for converting purposes (Thunberg 1995:69-70). Neither Maximus nor Wesley's vision of salvation is in any sense a natural process of pure becoming or a necessary universalism determined by the will of God. Yet, both recognize our common human location in relative privation as a starting point in this world.

Incarnation

Finally, participation is inherently incarnational. Our participation is not initiated by an ascent and reaching up to God, as much as it is the grace of God through creation reaching down to us in redemption and fellowship. Incarnation is God's initial move in descent. Participation is our response in ascent. We only participate in the creation because *God* has created us. Similarly, it was Christ who became flesh and had fellowship with our humanity so that we may be like him in his divinity. Participation is initiated by the grace of God as he invites us into communion with him. Maximus believed that Jesus "incarnated," in some sense, in creation, Scripture and in the flesh. For us, participation is fulfilled in Incarnation. God became man so we can partake of the divine, paraphrasing Athanasius. For us, for the church, for mission, participation means to "be there." It means to be concretely present, spirit, soul, and body with God and others, participating in his grace and love. It means to be contextual without confusing, changing, combining or mixing the Logos with what is enfleshed.[27] The Incarnation informs the church that it does not cling to a theology of glory but finds its mission in a theology of the cross. The mission is to be sent out from glory into the world to seek and find the lost. Following the Resurrection and the witness of the glorified Christ, the disciples were empowered to witness of the exalted Christ by the power of the Spirit.

Differential unity describes the Chalcedonian logic that allows for Christ to be one person and have two natures without confusion. Although we can never be incarnations of God the way Christ is the Incarnation, we are called to be Christlike, *theosis*. For Maximus, this occurs because of the Incarnation. Because Jesus, who is divine, became human, so we who are human can become like the divine. *Theosis* occurs through the Incarnation, because we are joined with Christ, and are deified through him. However although we are united to Christ and are one with God through the Incarnation, we are distinct from God in our humanity, a differential unity.

As we communicate the gospel in mission with Christ, we are called to reflect and manifest the Kingdom as a "theophany,"[28] as well as to communicate it. We become living epistles read by all. Yet, our unity in Christ and our witness is contextual and thus differentiated. Its differentiation occurs in the expression of our own cultural context and when the message is contextualized in the culture of others. Difference is not *necessarily* violence, in the Nietzschean and Focauldian sense. The message of Christ and our unity in Christ is a constant, though its expression is differentiated across cultural lines, less it be an indifferent gospel. Participation is the call and the freedom to be in Christ in any context as we are in mission with the Triune God. Critical contextualization of the mission has always been God's work in history. As we participate in this effort, we are invited to explore what the Word becoming flesh looks like cross-culturally.

An onto-epistemology of participation is characterized by these features and others, as it attempts to portray in human language the cosmic drama of God's grace. What is offered is not so much a philosophical system as it is a philosophical and theological *vision*. I believe the term *vision* more accurately depicts the work of both Maximus and Wesley. I will look at the implications of such a vision within a theology of mission. As all mission begins with God, I will begin with the Trinity and how its *oikonomia*[29] gives shape to the mission of the church. Following, I will examine participation as it bears on three key elements in a theology of mission, creation, Incarnation, and new creation.

Participation and *Missio Trinitatis*

This research unintentionally took on somewhat of a Trinitarian form. My work with Radical Orthodoxy focused on reconnecting the cosmos back to God its creator. I then sought to develop that nascent form of participation through Maximus' theology of Jesus Christ the Logos, and finally follow through with the soteriological consequences of participation by examining Wesley's *ordo* of grace and the work of the Spirit in the knowledge of God. My trinitarian scheme was at first laid out unwittingly, but there has been an intentional return to the Trinity and Trinitarian structures in recent theological endeavors[30], especially in missiology. In accordance with Christian revelation, the Trinity is beginning to take a primary and formative role in how we do theology and mission.

In this past century, the notion of beginning theology with God, theology proper, may be best represented by the Swiss theologian Karl Barth (1886-1968). In the second chapter of this work, I explained the Radical Orthodox understanding of correlation. Part of this movement's purpose is to return theology to the roots of revelation and remove the hybrid influence of "secular" thinking. I propose to call this process "de-correlation." Barth may have been "de-correlating" before any of us, as he sought to return purely to the revelation of the Word of God. Barth's concern was to let God speak and act for God, and God does this through his Word. Karl Barth read a significant paper in 1932 at the Brandenburg Missionary Conference in which he repudiated the notion that mission or its conception was a human activity or a work of the church. Barth affirmed that mission was the activity of God who sends God's self in mission through the *oikonomia* of the Son and the Spirit (Bevans and Schroeder 2004:290). Mission became an enterprise authored by God and not the church. Barth, the neo-Reformer, brought a critical insight into the church's understanding of the nature of mission, similar to other theocentric and Christocentric insights that Barth was accustomed to bringing.

Earlier I had alluded to the Radical Orthodox critique of the secular as a product of the univocity of being. The Enlightenment idea of the nation-state, and the notion of national and even autonomous churches echo a univocal expression of being, as the church is able to declare itself in national terms and speak for God on its own terms. The autonomy of the national church and the subsequent splintering into a plethora of denominations may be one of the most poignant religious expressions of a univocity of being – the autonomy and space to speak independently for God. Thus, in these Enlightenment terms the church *owns* the mission.

The mission becomes the mission *of* the church. It took a "de-correlationist" like Barth to relocate salvation and mission back in God by removing the exaggerated anthropomorphic moves and errors in liberal and evangelical theology. Later in 1934, Karl Hartenstein would take Barth's idea and attach the term *missio Dei* (mission of God) to it, as opposed to *missio ecclesiae* (mission of the church) (Bevans and Schroeder 2004:290). The *missio Dei* conveys the idea that not only the mission is of God, but also that mission comes from the very nature of God. God is a missionary God (Bosch 1991:390).

In 1952 at the Willingen Conference of the IMC, the notion of the *missio Dei* was put clearly in the context of the Trinity. Bosch states:

> The classical doctrine on the *missio Dei* as God the Father sending the Son, and God the Father and the Son sending the Spirit was expanded to include another "movement: Father, Son, and Holy Spirit sending the church into the world...Willingen's image of mission was mission as participating in the sending of God. (Bosch 1991:390)

The *missio Dei* is a paradigm shift in mission from being church or human centered to being God centered. God is already in mission to the world through the *oikonomia* of the Trinity. The church is called to *participate* in this mission. If God is truly the one in mission, and we merely are called to participate, the mission is a part of the *oikonomia* of the Trinity expressed through the Incarnation and the sending of the Holy Spirit and the Spirit's work with and through the incarnated and ascended Word. There is a parallel between the *processio* and the *missio* of the Trinity, the eternal procession and the temporal mission. The Son is eternally begotten in love from the origin the Father, as the Word of God and also the Other(ness) of God expressed. The Spirit eternally proceeds from the Father through the Son reflecting back on that same Word and proceeding through Him in love and back to the Father. There is an eternal perechoretic dance of mutuality and communicating of persons and sending and receiving of God's love and glory. These eternal movements of begetting and proceeding, and revealing and reflecting among the Trinity suggest God as a social or communal being of perfect wisdom and holy love, as well as God with a purpose and mission to communicate and share God's self.

The economic Trinity reveals and defines these eternal intimations through the history of salvation. The Triune God is a mission God in the communication and mediation of the person of Jesus Christ. As the Word proceeds in eternity, he is sent and is incarnated in humanity in time for our salvation, and as the Spirit proceeds from the Father through the Son, the Spirit is sent into the world by the Father to bear witness to the incarnate Word in the world. There the church, the Spirit-filled body of Christ, born according to the will of the Father from the womb of the Son, through the dynamic power of the Spirit, is in union with Christ and is led by his Spirit and participates in his mission. The mission of Christ is simply to do the will of the Father. We appropriate what Von Balthasar instructs us about

Christology and its missiological identity. Jesus was sent to fulfill the mission of the Father that was to not only do his will but to reveal his person. The identity of Christ is summed up in his missional realization personifying the Father specifically by doing his will. Jesus as the exegesis (John 1:18) or revealer and interpreter of the Father concretely carries out both his person and his mission. They are inseparable (Von Balthasar 1978:149 IIB). The mission of God is revealed through the economic working of the Divine persons in the world. Christ demonstrates through his own person and work that the mission is participation in the Triune life of God. This is the sending and the receiving of the mission. Jesus Christ functionally participated in an earthly manner in the will and person of the Father, so that we may be united to Christ and his fellowship with the Father. We see this expressed in Jesus' sacerdotal prayer in John 17. Here, the Triune God, mission, Christology. atonement, covenant, union, pneumatology, sanctification, and ecclesiology intersect.

All of our understanding, theology and work come out of our participation in God's mission in us and in others. Bosch puts it this way: "The *missio Dei* is God's activity, which embraces both the church and the world, and in which the church may be privileged to participate" (Bosch 1991:391). "Mission as participation in the mission of the Triune God," to use the phrase of Bevans and Schroeder, is also thematic to the *Ad Gentes* mission document of the Second Vatican Council:

> The church was now understood as a people, a communion, and mission   w a s conceived as the participation in the dynamic communion of God's triune life, that is, the church was a sacrament of salvation, a sign and instrument of God's saving presence toward and within all of creation. (Bevins and Schroeder 2004:286)

Mission was understood, in *Ad Gentes,* as God's self revelation through the Son and the Spirit manifested in the history of creation to humanity who is formed by the Spirit into a community as an icon of the Trinity and is equipped by the Spirit with gifts to participate in God's mission (Bevans and Schroeder 2004:287).

The Orthodox Churches in 1986 put together a mission document entitled "Go Forth in Peace: Orthodox Perspectives in Mission" which similarly reflects the theme of participation in the *missio Dei* (Bevans and Schroeder 2004:289). The Orthodox statement explores the "radical communal nature of God" as the wellspring for mission. The life of the Trinitarian community is the revelation of God through Christ and the Holy Spirit to the world (Bevans and Schroeder 2004:288-289). The mission of God is the sharing of God's abundant life of communion with creation (2004:288). The church participates in this overflow of life, and from this participation comes its missionary nature (2004:289).

More recently, there have been emphases placed on a Trinitarian approach to the *missio Dei* with Catholic missiologists like Robert Schreiter. Schreiter "has indicated that the Trinitarian understanding of the *missio Dei* might hold out a new direction for mission theology" (2004:292). Schreiter echoes some of the insights that I have made from Radical Orthodoxy in terms of an ontology of difference and peace and the differential unity of the Trinity. Schreiter believes that the unity in diversity expressed in the Trinity will be central to a theology of religious and cultural pluralism in response to postmodernism (2004:293). Bevans and Schroeder claim that "much of the renewal in Trinitarian theology in the West owes its inspiration to Orthodox theology" (2004:294). This author would at least agree to its influence in his own theology. The Trinity, as communal being in Zizioulas, provides a theological model for *koinonia*, relationships, freedom and difference in personhood, diversity in community, and participation, in which the world is invited to share (Zizioulas 1985). This model is at the core of an Orthodox theology of Trinity and mission and is best expressed through the church in the Liturgy and the Eucharist, for the church participates in the Triune God when it participates in the Eucharist (see Stamoolis for elaboration -1986:94-95). The limited scope of this research prevents further development, but an ecclesiology of Eucharistic participation is foundational to the church's identity as a doxo-liturgical being and to mission.

Eastern Orthodox contributions to Trinitarian theology also involve tying together the economies of the Son and the Spirit. Often the Western church tends to be Christologically dominated over against pneumatology (Zizioulas 1985:129). As referenced above in a Spirit-Word Christology the two being consubstantial work together in God's overall economy. Luke-Acts reveals a Spirit-Christology in which Christ is born of and empowered by the Spirit to do the work of the Father (Yong 2005:86-87). A Spirit-soteriology and ecclesiology understand that the Spirit births and empowers the church as a corporate personality of Christ (Zizioulas 1985:130-131; Yong 2005:88-91). Papanikolaou paraphrases Zizioulas on the Holy Spirit that "the Holy Spirit accomplishes the identification of Eucharist, church and the eschatological Body of Christ. It is by the power of the Holy Spirit that the Eucharistic community becomes conscious of their unity in Christ and of their participation in the triune life of God" (Papanikolaou 2006:33). For Zizioulas and Eastern Orthodoxy it is important that there is a synthesis between Christology and pneumatology. Wesley also connected the two with his theology of grace. The Spirit begins to work early on in prevenient grace with the purpose of ultimately bringing one to Christ and continuing in grace to transform one into Christ's image. Participation in the *missio Trinitatis* needs to recognize the *oikonomia* of God in the work of the Son and the Spirit not in exclusion of each other but in conjunction. Trinity then becomes our root metaphor for all of our theology and mission.

God the Father: Creation and Participation

A theology of mission from the *Missio Dei* begins with the Trinity. The Son is eternally begotten from the Father of origin, and the Spirit eternally proceeds from the Father through the Son in a perechoretic community of holy love. God's motion and mission of love is from eternity and is self-sufficient and in need of nothing. It is not for lack, need or privation or necessity that God creates or moves outside of God's self. The Triune community freely expresses its love, grace, and wisdom through a desire to extend *koinonia* to another, the cosmos *ex nihilo*. In fact, the cosmos itself is a free gift of God's grace and divine speech of love and purpose. It is also an icon of the communion and participation in the Triune life of God. The eternal communication of the person in the processions and reflections express the mission through its own doxological attraction of beauty. The creational Word first utters this sound of eternity economically. In the beginning, an invitation and gift are spoken. The invitation, from the beginning to the end, is to participate in the Divine life. The gift is the invitation and manifestation of the Divine life in creation, a seed that will grow in creation's womb until the fullness of time. The origin of the mission is in the Father who communicates to the Son and the Spirit eternal love that freely chooses to give of that gift that is the act of creation and its participatory nature in the Divine life. Creation is a grace-gift, as is its participatory nature to experience the Triune life, all of which is mediated by the Word, the mediator of all textual reality as its transcendental signifier. Outside of the Word there is nothing made that has been made (John 1:3).

Creation in its existence, expression, and purpose participates in the life of God. God's economy begins in history through the *logos* of creation as an extension of the divine abundant life. Creation is therefore sacramental and the beginning of a sacramental theology that achieves its purpose and reaches its height in the Incarnation and is expressed globally in the Eucharistic theology, witness, and community of the church.

Both Maximus and Wesley recognized that creation houses the universal witness of God and all things harmoniously join in on the Triune chorus of redeeming love. Maximus saw that the contemplation of created things could lead to the understanding that their reason and purpose (*logoi*) could all be traced to one God, the Logos, because God created all things by his Word (*creatio per verbum*). For Wesley, creation and conscience were both expressions and instruments of God's prevenient grace that identified his existence, attributes, and a fundamental discernment of good and evil. Neither man thought of this knowledge in terms of "natural theology." Creation was a work of the grace of God, and humanity was never truly in a state of pure nature. All nature is graced in some sense. The theological then holds primacy not only in heavenly but also in earthly matters.

I again echo Von Balthasar's and Radical Orthodoxy's call for the theological *a priori*, a theological sensibility in all knowledge. The notion of a universal witness to the knowledge of God and a capacity to receive it is compatible with an onto-epistemology of participation. It is in creaturely dependence and by God's grace that the universe participates in God. The imprint of the Divine is on all of creation and thus theology shapes all that we are. Radical Orthodox "decorrelation"[31] made it a point to demonstrate the nihilistic fate of giving creation the ground of its own being. There is no space in the cosmos for autonomy except in the realm of deception. The Christological hymn of Colossians reminds us that "everything was created through him and for him" and "he holds all things together." Creation does not have its own ground but participates in God.

A theology of mission needs to develop a high theology of creation; not one that diminishes the uniqueness and exclusivity of Christ, but one that is compatible with it, bringing the God of creation and salvation together as Maximus did in his theology of the Logos. Catholicism and especially Liberal Protestantism may have a tendency to disconnect creational grace with the fall and the Incarnation, while Evangelicalism may have a tendency to disconnect the God of Incarnation and redemption from the God of creation. Both creation and redemption reveal the Word, and the Word is God. The revelations may differ in content but are similar in origin and nature and unified in purpose.

Due to the grace manifested in both creation and the Incarnation, there is a special blessedness about the cosmos, in that it participates in the holy grandeur of God and is the object of his plan of restoration. Manichean, Docetic, and Gnostic dualisms do not cloud the vision of a sacramental universe whose very spatio-temporal grounds were fashioned for doxo-liturgical celebration. The incipience of the grace and glory of God is manifested in the first day of creation and is restored in the new creation, a glory whose beauty elicits from our hearts a liturgical response of obedient praise. God sets the tone on that first day for our doxo-liturgical purpose and its fulfillment in Christ.

Along with other scholars, Bruggemann notes that the creation narrative in Genesis chapter one was formed in the Priestly tradition for *liturgical* usage (Brueggemann 1982:22). God as designer and artificer built creation as a cosmic temple, metaphorical of his Kingdom, in which all the inhabitants of the universe are to praise and worship according to the liturgy of his word revealed in creation (Middleton 2005:81-88). Middleton also suggests that humanity, representing by analogy God as King in the *imago Dei,* imitates and carries out God's rule of justice and order through a royal and priestly function in which humanity impacts and blesses the entire created order, as organizers and "culture shapers" (2005:88-90). This view of humanity is similar to Maximus' view of humanity as microcosm and mediator of the cosmos. The implication is that God seeks to accomplish his purposes or mediate them through culture, and humanity is called to represent the will of God as a "culture shaper" by manifesting his Kingdom.

A high view of creation bears witness in an ontology of participation and in the Scripture record of creation. Creation begins the mission of God revealing the grace, love and wisdom of God in all things. In its beauty, creation reflects the sublime majesty of God and commands that its inhabitants glorify the one who has made all things. Creation provides the sacramental context for the work and acts of God in history, specifically culminating in the Incarnation. The revelation of that work is written in the *logoi* of creation's order, and creation becomes an icon of its maker. Applied to a theology of mission, a high view of creation acknowledges that through creation, although hindered by sin, there is a universal witness of God and a theological *a priori* and capacity in humanity that has gone ahead of the church in every land among every people. This witness needs to be discerned, interpreted, and evaluated in every culture. As Middleton indicated, humanity as part of the created order is given the divine task of "culture shaping" according to God's purposes. Culture shaping is God's will and purpose in making humanity in the *imago Dei*, and it is his command in ordering humanity to extend God's shalom to the earth. I believe there are many starting-points in communicating the Gospel cross-culturally, but one starting point is the witness of God in creation and through culture that is received as a theological *a priori* and is to be discerned critically.

The doctrine of *tabula rasa*, which is based on a preferential option of Western culture due to its assumed superiority, comes from a low view of creation and a high view of reason. The sacramental nature of creation makes for a level ground for all cultures. Each culture can be a vehicle through which God speaks and reveals God's self. Stephan Bevans refers to these respectively as the "transcendental model" and the "anthropological model" (Bevans 2002:55). Their focus in contextualizing theology is on culture and its transcendental experience of the divine. The anthropological model in particular is creation-centered, as it looks to human experience in culture as the starting point (2002:57). For example, theologian James Cone (1938 -) has modeled this approach. His theology of liberation *begins* with blackness and the experience of blackness and its connection with the heart of God (Cone1986:23-24). There he touches on the heartbeat of an oppressed and suffering community. Participation in our theology of mission looks for places where God's grace is operating preveniently in the midst of our culture and experience. Cone finds it in a Jesus whose "righteousness is inseparable from the weak and helpless in human society" (Cone 1986:5). He finds it in the 'blackness of God," who identifies "with the oppressed to the point that their experience becomes God's experience" (1986:63).

Cone continues that "the blackness of God means that God has made the oppressed condition God's own condition" (1986:63). He sees this echoed in the Exodus and Gospel traditions where "by electing Israelite slaves as the people of God and by becoming the Oppressed One in Jesus Christ, the human race is made to understand that God is known where human beings experience humiliation and suffering" (1986:64). Kelly Brown Douglas picks up on this same type of identification found in the grace of God through her depiction of the "Black Christ," who found solidarity with the slaves and in the black experience of oppression and struggle (1994:20-21,54-55).

In the case of the Black Christ and Black theology, the point of grace was found in the cultural experience of the people. Within the narratives of privation and suffering, the voices crying injustice were heard. It was in the midst of those cries that Blacks, themselves, heard the voice of grace and God's identification with their suffering. God had already gone ahead and not only was touching the culture where it was hurting but was preparing a way of liberation and a place of peace. Black theology found participation in God's blackness and in God's empathy for the suffering and the oppressed. It is at that point that *critical* contextualization is necessary to begin to employ the meaning and truth of the Gospel in indigenous and culturally relevant forms (see Hiebert on Critical Contextualization 1985:171-192). I will look more in depth at contextualization in the next section. However,

Cone used the cultural experience of "blackness" as a point of contact and even the core for his theology of mission. There are multiple models and points of entry that can be used, but in a theology of mission with a high theology of creation, the anthropological model is effective at finding God's universal witness in the very experience of the people.

One of the primary benefits of a high theology of creation, its theological *a priori,* and an anthropological model of mission is that it works from an ontology of analogical participation. The context of creation and the universal theological *a priori* are a basis for revelation, though only a starting point, as well as a basis for human value, freedom and equality before God There is a vital connection between God and creation and between the God of creation and the God of salvation. Although the revelation of creation and salvation may differ in time, purpose, and content, both share a common nature in grace. As I have noted, an ontology of analogical participation does not see the differences in creation as *inherently* oppositional, as is the case in a univocity of being. Analogy comprises differential unity and expresses an ontology of peace. Creation expresses a differentiated unity of peace, cosmic shalom. Difference is honored and respected though not diluted or blindly accepted in terms of cultural relativism. In a participatory scheme, creation is sacramental and has been fashioned for God's use and glory. It is doxo-liturgical and sacred. Of course, in creation I am including culture critically considered.

With creation as a basis and starting point for communication mission, many models and opportunities arise (See Bevans 1992). For example, analogical models found in creation can be effective starting points in contextualizing and communicating the Gospel. Don Richardson's *Peace Child* has popularized the potential of "redemptive analogies" and "functional equivalences" to reach a people group (Richardson 2005). While often, we seek a literal or formal equivalence, which ultimately stems from a univocity of being, when communicating texts, form, meaning and messages it is an unrealistic expectation in a created world of analogical expression. Further research needs to be done exploring analogy as a primary method of cross-cultural communication. Analogical communication and evaluation becomes a more tedious and critical task than univocal cross-cultural expression. Analogization is an *epektasis* towards perfection, a straining towards more accurate expression and meaning, a tightening of the diastemic gap of dissimilarity and similarity.

One example of analogical expression and the theological *a priori* is wisdom. Out of a virtue construal of reality, we are summoned to pursue and incarnate virtue that will transform our character and our practice, until in practicing wisdom, we embody and reflect wisdom. Wisdom, as a category, is an active expression and manifestation of *Logos, Logos* as *Hokmah-Sophia*[32] . It can be argued that Jesus Christ came primarily as the fulfillment of the wisdom tradition. Christ personified, revealed, and interpreted Wisdom. [33] Thus, a primary contact point and analogy for the gospel can be the critical use of wisdom, especially local wisdom.

Robert Schreiter in his *Constructing Local Theologies* comments that sapiential knowledge functions analogically (Schreiter 1985:86). Sapiential knowledge is creation-based. God leaves vestiges of himself (*vestigia Dei*), specifically his creativity and order, in type and antitype configurations, patterns in the world, hierarchical orders, controlled allegory, and the hidden in the visible in creation (1985:85-86). These are all analogical forms that function to lead us upward towards God through the things we know in creation. Schreiter observes the cultural conditions where sapiential theology is receptive. First, wisdom predominates "in those places where human life is seen as a unified cycle, marked by progressive development" (1985:86). Second, it occurs in cultures where both the visible and the invisible are seen as a unified whole (1985:86). Third, cultures that appreciate the underlying structures and patterns in the universe that serve as a pathway to human growth are open to sapiential theology (1985:86). Fourth, wisdom theology prevails in cultures that tend to focus on the inner way which leads to the outer reality (1985:87). Fifth, "cultures that adopt a two-level approach to ultimate reality, an exoteric and an esoteric one, are likely to follow the patterns of a wisdom theology (1985:97).

Sapiential traditions become a way to approach certain cultures analogically. For example, much work has been done to approach Asian cultures that have a strong orientation towards Taoism, which is a wisdom tradition. *The Tao of Jesus* and *The Tao Te Ching* are examples of inter-traditional attempts to communicate within wisdom traditions. Both texts use the *Tao Te Ching* by *Lao Tzu* and dialogue with the sayings of Jesus. Since the study is analogical, both similarities and differences are brought forward in an attempt to find mutual understanding through the common medium of wisdom. Through the reading of the text, points of grace in the Taoist tradition become clearer and clearer, providing a lens to see and interpret the culture as well a starting point for communication and contextualization. The emphasis in this section of participation in the Father is that creation, specifically culture, needs to be explored as a starting point for dialogue and contextualization in a theology of mission.

Mission Implications:
1. There is a universal witness of God across cultures in creation because of God's grace.
2. The universal witness opens the door to an anthropological model of communication and mission in other cultures. Cultural anthropology and its participant-observation are effective in discovering that witness.
3. One can employ a culture's wisdom tradition as a means of mutual understanding and communication in a culture.

God the Son: Incarnation and Participation

As the Son is eternally begotten of the Father, so the mission of the Father is generated in the Son by the Spirit. Eternal generation is expressed economically in the generation of the created world and the Incarnation. Another key element in a participatory theology of mission along with the Trinity and creation is the Incarnation. I hold to the Incarnation in its scriptural form as symbolized in the Chalcedonian formula. As a note of conviction, I do not hold this form to be aberrant or syncretistic in any way. I do not hold this form to be merely a cultural expression or a purely absolute form without cultural expression. I hold it to be both the tradition's faithful interpretation and expression of faith concerning Scripture's witness of Jesus Christ in the language of that day and is part of the tradition's canon of interpretation for all time.

Recalling what was said by Von Balthasar in alluding to John chapter one, he indicated that the person and work of Jesus Christ *is* the mission of the Father revealed economically. Von Balthasar's thesis is that the mission, person and identity of Jesus Christ are all interrelated and defining Jesus Christ as person and mission. The person and mission of the Father are communicated through the person and mission of Jesus Christ. The Father generates the eternal person of the Word who reveals the Father. The Father sends the Son, the Incarnate Word to exegete the Father by missionally embodying his will. The Son of Man came to do the will of the one who sent him. The eternal generation of the Word gives economic expression to the Incarnate Word whose Word is Life, the life of the Triune God. The Triune life of God is the communication of love in Divine persons. Through the mission of the person of Jesus Christ, humanity is invited into the life of the Triune God by uniting with the person of Jesus Christ. We participate in Jesus Christ, and Christ dwells in us by the indwelling Holy Spirit who communicates the sanctifying presence of Jesus Christ to our own personhood, and we become more like Jesus and a more authentic and perfect expression of personhood through his person.

Von Balthasar comprehends the mission of God economically as cosmic *drama* (Theo-Drama) and *dramatis personae* (Jesus Christ). *Processio* and *missio* are interrelated and inseparable (Von Balthasar 1983:63,80 & 81). Ultimately, in terms of the Word, *processio* directs *creatio,* and *missio.*The eternal generation of the Son corresponds to the Word of creation and the Word being the firstborn of all creation and the first born from the dead, and thus the generation of the new creation (Von Balthasar 1983:61-62). Mission, personhood and identity are interdependent, and the mission of the Triune God defines who Jesus Christ is. Even Jesus' economic sense of "who he is" is defined by his self-understanding of "being sent". This sense of mission alone explains his "coming," and why the Son of man came into the world. The gospels are full of "coming" language in reference to the Son of man, including the Johannine "sending" formulas (Von Balthasar 1978:152-153). There are defining consequences that need to be explored at some point by the church as it compares the ontological and functional dimensions of Christology with its parallel ontological and functional dimensions of its own ecclesiology in terms of person and mission. [34]

Returning to the mission of the Son, the Logos is the exegesis of the Father, and the incarnated Word reveals and interprets the person and mission f the Father economically. *Processio* defines and inspires *missio* (Von Balthasar 1978:427). This is the exegesis of Jesus Christ communicated in the person and mission of the "Son of God," Sonship, and thus the contiguous call to be born of the Spirit (John 3) and to be called the sons of God (John 1:12). The sending and the invitation are embodied in Christ. The gift is appropriated in our covenantal union with Christ and in his fellowship with the Father through the Spirit. Participation and union in the Triune life through Jesus Christ by the indwelling and sanctifying Spirit is the mission. Thus, our new life and offspring mission stem from our new ontological status *en Christo* ("in Christ" – 2 Cor 5:17 *So if anyone is in Christ, there is a new creation: everything old has passed away; see, everything has become new.* NRSV).

Revisiting Maximus and Wesley, their theologies are characteristically missional. Salvation history takes on the form of transformational grace from incipient to deifying. Maximus and Wesley are missional theologians in plotting out the course of grace from creation to new creation with Christ as the soteriological *locus*. Both missional theologians rightfully connect the work of the God of creation with the work of the God of salvation For Maximus, the Logos of creation is the Logos of Incarnation. For Wesley, prevenient grace purposes to move persons to saving grace. The Incarnation of Jesus Christ, which for Eastern Christianity includes Christ's life, death, and Resurrection, is central to Maximus' theology and should be to any Christian theology. The Gospel is Jesus Christ. He is the Word of God. Velli–Matti Karkkainen in his *Christology: A Global Introduction; An Ecumenical, International, and Contextual Perspective* states that "Jesus Christ stands at the center of Christian faith and theology" (Karkkainen 2003:9). Although this study is claiming a central position for Christ in a theology of mission, this study is not intending to explore the range of intercultural, contextual Christologies. It is my intent to work within the simple framework of participation and its interaction with a classic Christian formula, the Incarnation, to uncover its implications for a theology of mission. I will briefly review Maximus' and Wesley's Christologies for this purpose.

Von Balthasar comments that "Maximus builds his whole doctrine of salvation, with great consistency, on the basis of his formal Christology" (Von Balthasar 2003:256). Thunberg states that, for Maximus, "the doctrinal basis of man's deification is clearly to be found in the hypostatic union between the divine and human nature in Christ" (Thunberg 1995:430).For Maximus, the Incarnation is tied directly to the fulfillment of God's purpose in the cosmos, that is, deification. The Incarnation and its trajectory of *theosis* is the mission of God and characterize the sweep of Maximus' theology, which is clearly missional and eschatological. God is joined with humanity and thus to the world through the microcosm of the person Jesus Christ. Through his identification with and defeat of sin and death, Christ has offered deliverance to the cosmos from non-being and chaos and restoration to life, according to God's original intentions. Christ's redemptive work is healing and restorative for creation, as creation is renewed to its natural capacity and original purpose. (see Maximus *Ad Thalassium 21* for his understanding of *Christus Victor* and restoration).

Although Maximus addresses the issue of redemption from sin and its nexus with the Incarnation, he more so stresses the connection of the Incarnation to the overcoming and healing of the divisions of being that prevent cosmic unity (Von Balthasar 2003:272-273). There is a therapeutic strategy of reconciliation within the healing work salvation. Divisions are united as God and humanity are united in Christ. Those divisions are male and female, earth and the *oikoumene,* heaven and earth, the sensible and intelligible realms, and finally uncreated and created being (God and creation) (Louth 1996:72-74). One can see Maximus wrestling with the inherited philosophical problem of the one and the many in his theology. The purpose of the Incarnation and the restoration of humanity in *theosis* to its original microcosmic position are to heal, mediate and synthesize these fundamental divisions. The one and many were purposed in Adam the microcosm and are restored in their unity in Christ. Differential unity is perfected in *theosis* (Thunberg 1995:427). Meyendorff sums up Maximus' Christology and its relationship with salvation or *theosis:*

> This essentially dynamic doctrine of salvation supposes a double movement: a divine movement toward man consisting of making God partakable of by creation, and a human movement toward God, willed from the beginning by the Creator and restored in Christ. The hypostatic union of these two movements in the incarnate Word constitutes the essence of Maximus' Christology: two natures imply two energies or will meeting one another. (Meyendorff 1987:143-144)

In *kenosis,* God descended into the human condition of suffering and death to make himself "partakable" through the Incarnation. Creation's participation in God as an ontological order cannot change, but its participation in God's *telos,* life and community was sabotaged by the fall. God's grace and love in Christ calls creation back to reunite with him..The mission of God is to bring restoration and reconciliation within the created order and also to perfect or complete what began with creation. Of course, the Eastern view of creation would not comprehend creation as a finished perfection without the capability of growth, as expressed in a more Western view. The Eastern view understood creation as perfect and finished in a limited sense, because it saw creation in its incipience with the full potential to grow in grace in the image of God.

This double movement of healing within the dynamic of salvation is similar to Maddox's depiction of grace and salvation in Wesley, as we explored in chapter five. Both Maximus and Wesley held to the orthodox Chalcedonian formulation of the Incarnation. In Wesley, there is an integration of Eastern and Western themes in his soteriology and thus one would expect those same themes to correlate to his Christology. In terms of Western themes, Wesley's view of the Incarnation strongly relates to the purpose of the atonement and its juridical orientation (Maddox 1994:96-97). Atonement brought pardon from sin, removal of guilt, imputation of Christ's righteousness and adoption as children of God to corresponding to justification in Wesley's *ordo*, which was basically a Western and Reformed construal, except for his understanding of universal atonement in which the benefits of the atonement were appropriated in particular by faith. In terms of Eastern themes, Wesley's understanding of salvation as primarily holiness, that is deliverance from the power of sin, healing and wholeness, is more of a Catholic and Eastern Christian focus. For Wesley, sanctification like justification finds its basis in the atonement. However, except for his emphasis on holiness and his basic adherence to Chalcedon, Wesley's Christology is primarily Western. He does not correlate many of his Eastern soteriological convictions to his Christology, which in terms of atonement is juridical (Maddox 1994:96).

Of course, both of these analyses of Maximus' and Wesley's Christologies are at best cursory. However, I summarize that the purpose of the Incarnation is directed toward salvation, which is holiness, although Wesley did not develop the relationship between Incarnation and salvation as extensively as Maximus. The Incarnation calls us to partake or participate in the divine nature and call others as well to participate in the divine nature. Incarnation shapes our theology of mission. God has come to us on our own terms in our own condition to reconcile the world unto God's self. God calls us to participate and be joined together with Christ that we may be transfigured and be God's agent to transfigure the world. Incarnation, *theosis,* and mission are teleologically connected in the mind of God. Our baptism is a baptism in Christ in union with his person and in union with the Triune God, in both the life and mission of the Triune God. [35]

The church is called in its baptismal participation in Christ to call others to participate in Christ and be transformed into his likeness. This functional understanding of the church does not take away from its everlasting ontological identity as the body of Christ in which the Triune community is in hypostatic *koinonia* with his people through the Incarnation and is celebrated in the Eucharist. The limitation of this study prevents clarifying the link between the Incarnation and ecclesiology, but the relationship is fundamental and paradigmatic. For this research, it is enough to link, yet not equate, the mission of Christ to the mission of the church in terms of participation. That the kenotic Christ has immersed himself in the human condition of privation, depravity, oppression and suffering to bring liberation and restoration is an indication to the church of the nature and thrust of mission. The Spirit of the Lord anoints and empowers the church for this mission of liberation, healing and restoration, for this is the ministry of Christ as depicted in Luke 4:18. The church is in mission *with* Christ when it takes up the mission *of* Christ. Maximus in his "The Church's Mystagogy," makes this startling statement concerning *theosis* and participation in the mission of Christ:

> For if the Word has shown that the one who is in need of having good done to him is God – for as long, he tells us, as you did it for one of these least ones, you did it for me – on God's very word, then, he will much more show that the one who can do good and who does it is truly God by grace and participation because he has taken on in happy imitation the energy and characteristic of his own doing good. And if the poor man is God, it is because of God's condescension in becoming poor

for us and in taking upon himself by his own suffering the sufferings of each one and "until the end of time," always suffering mystically out of goodness in proportion to each one's suffering. (Maximus 1985:212)

Following the doctrine of the *missio Trinitatis*, a theology of mission is grounded in our participation in mission *with* the Trinity out of our experience in the life of the Trinity through the person of Jesus Christ as revealed by the Holy Spirit. Participation begins with baptism, as we participate in the death, burial, and Resurrection with Christ and are gifted with the sacrament of the Holy Spirit who anoints us for holy living and service. Our participation in baptism and the chrismation of the Spirit[36] mark us and call us into mission with Christ, just as Jesus began his ministry at his baptism in which the Spirit descended upon him. We join Christ in proclaiming the fullness of his Kingdom to the world. Christ allows us to participate in his eschatological Kingdom through baptism and the gift of the Spirit. We witness to Christ and the fullness of his coming when we remember and fellowship with his body and blood and celebrate his Resurrection and his Kingdom through the Eucharist. The Eucharist brings us into unity with the Triune God and each other, a participatory ontology in Christ, in his divine life, in his body and in his mission. We partake of new eschatological being *en Christo* that is the new creation. We participate in the death, burial, and Resurrection with Christ and are filled with the Spirit of Christ for our transformation and for service with Christ.

Christ calls the world to come unto him, learn of him, and be healed by him that it may be like him and reflect the light of his person into the world, doing what he did, even greater works. When we partake of Christ, we partake of his person and his work through the indwelling Holy Spirit. Identity and mission are interrelated. Christ calls us to participate in his sufferings by participating empathically in the suffering of those around us. The prevenient grace of God in Christ is upon the poor with Good News as it was when he was on the earth. Luke-Acts scholar Joel Green indicates that Jesus' ministry was a Jubilee of release, reversal and comprehensive restoration for the poor, involving forgiveness, healing (physical and social), deliverance from the demonic, and total wholeness (Green 1995:78-79). Green understands Lukan soteriology as preeminently status reversal (1995:94). A kenotic church also empties itself of sin, corruption, privilege, inward focus, parochialism, and ethnocentrism through Christ and is filled with the Spirit to be transfigured in his image and be sent into in his mission. The church is then prepared to be enfleshed in the world for a ministry of liberation, healing and restoration. The participation of the church in Christ for the purpose of Christ revealing himself through the church to the world conveys the nexus between Incarnation, *theosis* and mission. The incarnate Logos fulfills the *logoi* (a *preparatio evangelica)* for a particular people.

Participating in Christ's comprehensive mission of liberation involves the implications of the event of the Incarnation. Christ by the Spirit incarnates within the context of a people. In missiology, the terms indigenization, acculturation and contextualization have been used to describe the church's participation in Christ's Incarnational mission. Christocentric critical contextualization is that process that analyzes and evaluates a given culture in terms of its forms, meanings, and practices in light of phenomenology, Jesus Christ, Scripture, and reality. It seeks to employ forms, meanings and practices that are indigenous and rooted in the local context and owned by local leadership – self governed, self propagating, self supporting, and self-theologizing (Hiebert, Shaw and Tienou 1999:21-29). David Hesselgrave defines critical contextualization as the "properly applied means to discover the *legitimate* implications of the Gospel in a given situation" (Hesselgrave 1991:136). Critical contextualization is the balance of communicating and living the truth through culture-specific forms that do not change the meaning of the truth.

At times, there is a debate as to whether mission should contextualize or not. The problem is that there is no debate in Scripture. God has already contextualized when he decided to work through a *specific* nation, Israel and through a *specific* language Hebrew. In the New Testament, God specifically contextualized his eternal message through Judeo-Hellenistic forms and the Greek language. In fact, the Incarnation is an extreme form of contextualization. When God becomes human, he becomes a *specific* human within a *specific* culture and genealogy. The Incarnation of Jesus Christ is the canonization of contextualization and localization in mission. The particularity of Christ and the particularity of the gospel narratives are all indications of contextualization. Study the global mission document entitled the Acts of the Apostles and its mission theology to continue the discussion. The point is we always experience God's self-revelation in a context. The question is whose culture will we communicate the gospel in theirs or ours?

The missional fact that the Word became flesh indicates not only the locality of God in space, time, history, culture, and physical hypostasis, but also the locality of mission as a conjunction of both the target and starting point of mission. God targeted humanity and began with humanity in his Incarnational mission. The transglobal became local, so the local can move to the global and beyond. The locality of culture, form, narrative, wisdom, sign and symbol must become the seedbed for the mustard seed of the kingdom of God, and we must become its cultural agronomists. The "smallest" seed must take the smallest ground. We need to go local and as local as we can get. We need to go local enough to touch the root metaphor and core grammar of the culture's unique sound and allow it to syncopate with the primary colors and invisible waves of the gospel message.

Participation as a theology of mission must involve local contextualization. Christocentric, critical contextualization allows for an authentic, powerful, and liberating witness of Christ in the smallest segments of society for the purpose of transforming the world. Localization in mission is for local and global transformation. Note that today our penetration of the local will inevitably touch the global as the two meet in the glocal, the spatial hybridity of culture in this age. The global dimension makes translation and communication easier on one level and more difficult on another when we deal with cultural identity and worldview conversion.

In his book *The Celtic Way of Evangelism,* George Hunter III recaptures how contextual and local strategies were employed in, a somewhat, Roman global world in the conversion of the Celtic people to Christianity (Hunter 2000). Hunter contrasts the Celtic way of evangelization with the Roman way. The Roman way was to "civilize," a people by forcing the adoption of Roman customs, then they would "Christianize" them by forcing them to adopt Roman Christian customs (Hunter 2000:17). The Roman model of Christianizing was basically present the Christian message; invite the people to a faith decision; and welcome them into the fellowship of the church – basically believe first and then belong (2000:53). The Celtic model stressed belonging first *before* believing. Persons are brought into the fellowship and accepted; there they interact and engage in conversation and the life of the church; and as their faith develops they are invited to commit (2000:53). Patrick, Columba, Aiden and other Celtic leaders were effective because of their strategy to incarnate and be with the people, creating community, and in that process the people were convinced by the influence of the Christian life, the "ethos" that they lived out (2000:63-64).

Community living was vital for Celtic Christianity, as it is today for postmodern Christianity. Hunter offers five lessons concerning community or missionary ecclesiology to be learned from the Celtic movement. First, evangelization was done in teams not solo, and it involved identifying with the people through shared living (2000:47). Second, the Celts formed monastic communities for discipleship and leadership development that involved shared living with a "soul friend," a spiritual mentor, small groups, and the entire community. Training in these communities not only prepared persons in Scripture and ministry, but it also prepared people to live and serve others in mission (2000:47-48).

Third, the Celts practiced spiritual disciplines, specifically "imaginative prayer," which was a creative experience of the contemplative life whether in solitude or with others. This indigenous form of prayer released the poetic creativity of the Celtic soul to strengthen their fellowship with God. Out of these experiences, Celtic Christians wrote new prayers and psalms, again illuminating a natural cultural inclination in the Celtic people. Thus they employed spiritual disciplines in indigenous forms (200:48-39). Fourth, the monastic community practiced radical hospitality to seekers, visitors, refugees and other guests (2000:52). They would be welcomed with a foot-washing from the journey, food, sleep, and Christian community. The final theme is the "belonging" before "believing" principle mentioned above.

Within the community life of the Celtic movement contextualized forms and practices were employed. Patrick and other apostolic leaders incorporated Celtic cultural forms into the life of the church. Hunter elaborates:

> Philosophically, the Irish were accustomed to paradox, which prepared them to appreciate some of Christianity's central truth claims. Their belief in Ultimate Reality is complex, and their fascination with rhetorical triads and the number three open them to Christianity's Triune God. Christianity's contrasting features idealism and

practicality engaged identical traits in the Irish character. No other religion could have engaged the Irish people's love for heroism, stories, and legends like Christianity. Some of Christianity's values and virtues essentially matched, or fulfilled, ideals in Irish piety and folklore. (Hunter 2000:20)

As a result, the Celtic movement intentionally adopted Celtic rather than Roman forms. Leaders would explain God in terms of Trinity because of the Celtic predilection to the number three and paradoxes. The clover was used as a natural analogy (2000:72). The creation-based Celts often drew natural analogies. This tendency may have stemmed from their roots in Druid natural mysticism (2000:87). Hunter claims "the doctrine of the Trinity became the foundational paradigm for Celtic Christianity (2000:82).

The Celts seemed to be a more of an expressive people than their colder British counterparts. Hunter remarks that they were more of a "right-brained" people, that is intuitive, emotional, imaginative, artistic, and experiential (2000:72). As a result, contextualized approaches that appealed more to the right-brained Celts than the left-brained logical and abstract Romans were used. Among the forms employed were analogies, poetry, storytelling, music, nature, visual arts, symbols (2000:72-74). Truth was communicated in Celtic poetic verse and rhythms as well as through the storytelling of bards. Even the death of Christ was communicated through Celtic sacrificial traditions (2000:83). Celtic evangelization engaged all of the senses and thoroughly used the forms of the culture.

Hunter explains that such contextualizations are not just lessons from the past but need to be applications for today. The once Christianized West has become the "New Barbarians" of postmodernity. Like the barbarians that were converted through the Celtic Christian movement, Westerners with "no Christian memory" need to be reached once again (2000:96).

As the Christian movement is becoming more centralized globally in the South and the East, the West has opened up once again as a mission field. Christianity as a global movement is living in strategic times, as the West needs to be reached in its post-Enlightenment, post-critical context. Attempts are being made by "younger evangelicals" to rethink their theology in light of its encounter with postmodernism through the lenses of classic and patristic Christianity (Webber 2002*)*. However, in the South and East, although the Christian movement is advancing, there is still a greater need for Christianity to express itself in non-Western forms. The global South and East are faced more with post-colonialism than postmodernism (Jenkins 2006:5). Their concerns are not how to respond to nihilistic rationalism and its accompanied forms: global market capitalism, the bureaucratic nation-state, and the secular university and media, all of which produce unbelief and skepticism. Issues involving poverty, injustice, sickness, famine, racial and gender oppression, political violence, corruption, and chaos need to be addressed by faith (2006:5). It is no surprise that Pentecostal and charismatic type churches that address needs through the teaching of a comprehensive salvation that includes signs, wonders, healing, and transformation are flourishing.

As the gospel continues to spread in post-colonial settings, contextualization becomes more and more significant, especially in Christology. How is Christ incarnated among the people? Since Christ is the center of the gospel and the means of salvation, contextualized Christology is a major challenge for a theology of mission. Karkkainen affirms that "Incarnation is God's highest self-expression; it is a real meeting place between the divine and the human. Jesus of Nazareth is not only the total and final revelation of God but also of humankind" (Karkkainen 2003:260). Karkkainen lists four basic Christologies in currency:

1. The Incarnational Christology of the early church and Catholicism
2. The theology of the cross of Protestantism, especially of the Lutheran tradition
3. The Resurrection and ascension Christology of Eastern Orthodoxy
4. The empowerment Christology of Pentecostalism and the Charismatic movements (Karkkainen 2003:15).

The fourth Christology listed has been adopted in the two-thirds world by many theologies. In contexts where people have been oppressed and powerless, Christ has revealed himself as a deliverer and a healer (2003:246). In many of these cultures a spiritual worldview is embraced. The spirit world regularly interacts with the affairs of everyday life. The causes of everyday occurrences and problems are seen as spiritual in origin. The Western Jesus of propositional truth will not suffice (2003:248). In Africa, Christ needs to be a wielder of power and a healer. African cultures are searching for both. Healing, as a holistic term covering physical, mental and spiritual, is often sought by the religious specialist (2003:253). The message of Jesus Christ as healer and protector often proclaimed by Pentecostal type churches has been received greatly by indigenous people and has been paramount to the rapid growth of Pentecostal and Independent churches in Africa (2003:253). Another example in Africa is Christ the Proto-Ancestor. The African Christ is the Proto-Ancestor who is "the unique ancestor, the source of life and highest model of ancestorship" (2003:256). He is the essence of all of the "good and positive elements of the African cult of ancestors and serves as the critic of its less honorable features" (2003:257). Christ the Proto-Ancestor becomes the model for living, which is one of the chief functions of ancestry. As the ancestors are invoked for direction and help, so Christ is invoked as the fulfillment of the ancestor cult in all its functions.

Contextualization of key doctrines like Christology and soteriology and contextualization of various liturgical forms are the beginning of a participation theology of mission. Participation and localization is an effective model because it preserves the integrity of the gospel and culture. In Chalcedonian logic the two natures are not changed, mixed, confused nor divided but joined in a perfect union. Incarnation, participation, and contextualization preserve the nature of the gospel and the fundamental nature of the culture. The Spirit and the local and global church prophetically critique all cultural practices since no culture is without sin.

However, the integrity of the culture is preserved in the communication of the gospel and the formation of local churches and theologies.

Participation in the *missio Dei* means that the church seeks to empty itself of its own agendas, participates in the leading of the Holy Spirit, and begins participant-observation within a culture along side the people of that culture in order to find where God is working, and how the Jesus of Matthew, Mark, Luke and John is revealing himself today in that context. We are called to participate with God in this process of contextualization, which for us missionally is Christocentric critical contextualization, transformation and ultimately *theosis,* to be an icon of God. The Incarnation needs to be the key in communicating the gospel. For Maximus it was the key to understanding the reconciling of the world of its divisions. The Incarnation crosses the *diastema* or distance between God and humanity. Mediation in Maximian thought also echoes of a Platonic as well as scriptural solution. Mediation to the One was always the conundrum to solve, especially in Middle Platonism. Yet even today mediation is at the center of our *diastema.* Consider interpretation. Hermeneutics has virtually swallowed up epistemology, thus creating an ontological semiosis. In popular culture, the digital sign is one of our primary mediators, especially via the internet and satellite. The old dictum is true that "the medium is the message." The postmodern world is in search of mediation for its salvation - linguistic mediation, digital mediation, semiotic mediation, mediation to the real. Contextual mission strategy is the cultural mediation of the gospel of Jesus Christ, who is the transcendent signifier and textual mediator of all things. There is nothing outside of the textual mediation of the Logos.

Mission Implications:
1. Through the Incarnation, Christ came into the human context, so that humanity can be transformed in Christ's image (*theosis).*
2. We participate in ministry *with* Christ in a particular context. Critical contextualization of the forms of a culture in order to communicate and live the gospel in a meaningful way to the receptor enables us to better minister with Christ to a people.
3. Learn from the culture and the Spirit find a contextualization for the person of Jesus Christ that is relevant to the culture.

God the Holy Spirit:
The New Creation and Participation

The *missio Trinitatis* is descriptive of the eternal perechoretic movement of love among the three persons of the Trinity. The origin of the Father eternally begets the Son in love, and the Holy Spirit eternally proceeds from the Father through the Son in love. Trinitarian love is sacrificial and self-emptying into the glorifying of the Other, from first to second to third to first persons. There is a dual, reciprocating movement of expression and reception of divine love between the persons. Love freely flows to the "otherness" of person, never closed within itself, but always in motion, the extending and receiving of gift.[37] With creation, God extends God's love to the "otherness" of the cosmos and ultimately in the Incarnation who is offered for the restoration of all things. Participation in a theology of mission begins with the mission of the Trinity in the context of creation in which the whole cosmos is called by its *logos* to participate in God. The Logos of the Trinity is the Logos of creation and is the same Logos of Incarnation, and the Spirit-Logos within the church and released in the world. God's plan in creation is to join creation together with himself. The third person of the Trinity is the same Spirit that descends upon Christ. The consubstantiality of the Son and the Spirit is evident economically and missionally in the virgin conception of Jesus; the descent of the Spirit upon Christ at his baptism for his anointed ministry to the poor and the broken; his resurrection and justification in the Spirit; his breathing of the Spirit upon the disciples; the sending of the Spirit by the Father through the Son; the indwelling presence of the *Parakletos* as another Comforter in the church; and in the endowment of the church with power to witness to the resurrected and exalted Christ. The Spirit is the Spirit of Truth who witnesses to the truth of Jesus Christ and his person and mission that originates in the Father. The Spirit and the Word are one in Jesus Christ in manifesting the will of the Father, and are one in the church is manifesting the will of the Father. The procession of the third person from the Father through the Son is one of person and mission. The sending of the Spirit by the Father through the Son is one of person and mission. The Spirit indwells and reveals the Son who embodies the person and mission of the Father in the church and to the world.

The Triune God accomplishes his purpose in creation through Christ, the incarnate Logos, by becoming human. By the divine becoming human, we are enabled by the Holy Spirit to become like God through union with Jesus Christ. Deification is God's *missio* for creation through the Incarnation. From creation to Incarnation to new creation, the *missio Dei* has worked in history through the economy of the Trinity, bringing in the new eschaton of the Kingdom. All of this is gift, the gift of the Trinity to his gift of creation through the gift of Jesus Christ by the gift of the Holy Spirit as recorded in Acts 2:38. It is the gift of participation in the Triune life of God. I have examined creation and Incarnation, and how they are connected to the mission of sanctification or *theosis*. *Theosis*, in turn, is the penultimate *telos* of God's mission, thus it is the *telos* of the participating church. The glory of God that elicits the transformation into *theosis* is the ultimate *telos*. Yet in some way the two are inseparable, for the participation of the church is the Triune God is a part of his glory. God's primary mission is his glory, followed by the transformation and glorification of all creation, which is also to his glory.

The church participates in the death, burial, Resurrection of Christ (Romans 6:1-6) and in the Spirit of Christ (Rom 8:9), who is the third person of the Trinity, and the Spirit who conceived Jesus in Mary and who descended upon Christ at his baptism. Out of the church's experience of union and transformation in Christ through the Spirit, the church serves as a liturgical and witnessing community of the transforming power of the Resurrection in Christ Jesus. The witness of the church is in fellowship with the witness of the Spirit, as the Spirit goes ahead and orchestrates the agenda of God in the earth to dethrone the powers of evil, heal the sickness of sin, and sanctify the cosmos. The presence of the Spirit of Pentecost himself is the sign of the eschaton. He is the living sign of the resurrected Christ walking among us in this fallen world. He testifies of and manifests the risen and exalted Christ in the church and in the world. The Holy Spirit is *sent* in mission for this purpose. He is the primary missioner in this eschaton, and his mission is to reveal the person and work of Jesus Christ in the world. The Holy Spirit is the master evangelist sent into the world to convict it of sin, righteousness, and judgment and to call all to Christ. Christ then calls his body to be filled with the Spirit of Pentecost and to participate in his work. Thus, the acts of the Holy Spirit become the acts of the church. It is not to say that the Spirit cannot and does not work apart from the church, but that he has elected the church as he elected Israel to embody his person and work, not in a totalizing way but in an exemplary and emblematic way.[38]

The presence of the Spirit in the believer, the church, and in the world is radical. When one *experiences* the resurrected Christ, one experiences an ontological and participatory shift from "the old" to "the new," from death to life, from "in Adam" to "in Christ," *en Christo*. One is a new creation in Christ by the Spirit and abides in the now and not yet of the Kingdom. The new creation is the Pentecostal work of the Spirit, the Spirit who brings the eschatological reign of Christ into the earth. Our participation, as far as the influx of the Kingdom in this world is concerned, is in the economy of the Holy Spirit, who eschatologically carries out the economy of the Son into its *pleroma* or fullness (John 1:14-16). The Holy Spirit is the primary agent and executor of the practice of God's mission in the earth following the ascension of Jesus Christ. Christology and pneumatology work symbiotically as the Spirit is the presence of Christ in the earth to save and the presence of Christ in the church to perfect and to serve. Charismatic theologies of Luke-Acts make no distinction between the work of the Charismatic Christ in the Gospels and the Charismatic church in the book of Acts (Stronstad1984; Lord 2006:68). The Christ who saved the lost, healed the sick, fed the hungry, cast out demons, clothed the naked, and preached the Kingdom is the same Christ living in and working through the church in the book of Acts. Luke 4:18-19 are not only programmatic for the ministry of the Servant Messiah but also his church in Acts 1:8, whose mission program is to do what Christ did to the ends of the earth.

We cannot separate the economy of the Son from the economy of the Spirit. Too long the Western church has operated out of an Enlightenment worldview that has embraced a rationalist's gospel of propositional truth within a closed naturalistic universe governed by the laws of scientism. Kraft calls Western Christians "practicing deists" (Kraft 1989:39). As a pastor, I see "practical atheism" as one of the chief sin among us, living as if the existence of God did not make a difference in our everyday lives. We live as if God does not exist. As in the example that I gave from Charles Kraft in the first chapter, the church is often ineffective in cultures that operate out of a spiritual or supernatural worldview. The mission of the church is reduced to the cognitive transference of information about Jesus Christ. The mission of the church is not an exercise in propositional, syllogistic logic. It is nothing less than a participation in the life and work of the Holy Spirit. Today the two-thirds world, or majority world, Christians understand the everyday working of the Spirit and call the West to return to such a pneumatic faith. The global church needs to allow its eyes to be open to the work of the revitalizing Holy Spirit that goes before her. The work of the Spirit is the fullness of salvation in every aspect of life - conviction, repentance, repentance, conversion, deliverance, healing, and transformation in souls, families, communities, schools, hospitals, clinics, prisons, orphanages, shelters, nursing homes, agencies, and even governments. When the work of the Spirit is minimized or squeezed out of our theologies and lives, we then turn to the idols of our culture to meet our needs and do what only God can do, split-level Christianity. A good portion of what we call Christianity in the West is split-level with cultural evangelicalism on the top and various forms of pop American pragmatism, psychology, and politics on the bottom.

As Paul Hiebert has emphasized, salvation (*soteria*) needs to penetrate to the level of worldview conversion, and ultimately involve every dimension of life, including the physical, spiritual, mental, emotional, familial, relational, social, existential, ecological, global and cosmic dimensions of life. The eschatological reality of the new creation involves every aspect of life in a now and not yet tension of the realized and the hopefully awaiting (See Snyder 1991:16-17). The Jesus who performed miracles and forgave sins also fed the multitudes and honored the status of women and ethnic minorities. Scripture does not operate out of a bifurcated worldview, splitting material from spiritual or personal from social. Both Maximus and Wesley's versions of participation accommodate for a total picture of reality that values physicality and discerns the invisible. Participation in a theology of mission brings an integrated worldview and is open to a complex topography of the cosmos. It recognizes that there are multiple layers to any site of reality. There are an infinite number of epistemic locations within any site. We also operate on many levels as beings that are spiritual, physical and social, and so the grace of God works on some many different levels through a wide variety of standpoints and positions. The church needs to expect the work of the Spirit to touch us at multiple levels and in multiple points beyond what we have calculated in the past.

Participating in Christ through the Holy Spirit, the church and its lens for mission need to be as wide and clear as God's mission. This includes the awareness and cognition of the neglected world of the invisible. One paradigm for approaching spirit-incorporating worldviews is M. Kraft's worldview of "spiritual-power" oriented societies. She lists the basic assumptions that these societies characteristically hold:

1. Spiritual power, both good and evil, exists apart from human power.
2. Spiritual powers are active and involved in human daily experiences.

3. Human beings have limited power and hence have need for spiritual power in many areas of life.
4. Humans need good spiritual power to counteract the evil spiritual power affecting them in life.
5. There are ways for humans to access spiritual power.
6. Evil spiritual power may be used by humans to harm other humans.
7. Some spiritual powers are stronger than others.
8. The strongest spiritual power wins in the encounters involving more than one spiritual power.
9. Good spiritual power is to be drawn in, and evil spiritual power must be dispersed or driven away.
10. The struggle with spiritual powers continues throughout life. (M. Kraft 1995:28-29)

M. Kraft's work along with her husband Charles Kraft's work is part of a growing movement that seeks to work out of a worldview that extends to spiritual powers and spiritual phenomena, as many two-thirds world cultures do.

Another comprehensive work on the subject comes from the Lausanne Committee for World Evangelization, *Deliver Us from Evil: An Uneasy Frontier in Christian Mission*. The work of the writers and practitioners draws primarily from Scripture and secondarily from experience to demonstrate the reality of such encounters and the need to understand the authority we have in Christ to pray for healing, deliverance and other needs in a balanced and scriptural way. The exploration of spiritual power has not just been the focus of Pentecostal-charismatic types but scholars like Walter Wink and Robert Linthicum who come out of more a socially liberal camp have written profoundly and practically on this subject as well. Of course, the whole area of the spirit realm, the demonic and spiritual warfare often stirs controversy, but the church needs to come to a biblical understanding of such phenomena and the power of God if it is to be effective. Too many of our critiques of these movements come from a Western Enlightenment worldview that does not detect the invisible. An ontology of participation in God recognizes both a created world that is *visible* and *invisible*. Enlightenment thinking would tend to demythologize the ontic status of invisible being and an invisible world. Some of this thinking needs to be de-correlated and allow the revelation of God to stands in the power of its own canonical rhetoric and tradition without explaining such phenomena away. We often find this type of thinking in a radical fundamentalism that holds to an Enlightenment worldview that does not allow for the "supernatural," and seeks a more rational explanation for such phenomena.[39] The canons of rational fundamentalism have no need for any expression beyond a literal faith.

Yet ironically, we also can find similar thinking in more "liberal" theologies. One example of a mission theology that in word claims a salvation that extends to the realm of the spiritual, but in practice it often reduces salvation to the socio-political, are various forms of liberation theology. I strongly agree with the liberation impetus to touch and empower the poor. I confirm that there is a gospel-based preferential option for the poor. I also prophetically stand in solidarity with liberation theologies in their indictment of the church (often its conservative expressions) that it not only neglects the poor and the outcast, but also greatly contributes to this marginalization. The Western church has mingled too much and has inbred with the powers of socio-economic and racial oppression. The church itself needs liberation.

On the other hand, if the church proclaims a message of holistic liberation, it needs to deliver on it. Of course, much of liberation theology has its roots in different nuances of Marxist, critical, and social theory. Although it is theistic, unlike Marxism, in practice it operates out of an ontological vision that is more immanent than transcendent. I believe this is due to its genetic makeup that, in part, bears the DNA of dialectical materialism, which is a product of modernism. Understandably then, the *historical* and *socio-political* condition of the poor is the focal point of the theory not the manifestation of the absolute idea, as in Marxism's step-father Hegel's dialectical idealism. Liberation becomes more material driven and moves from the bottom up. Liberation theology's ontological orientation is flipped over from the one proposed in this work on participation. While participation moves from the spiritual to the material, it may be said that in liberation the movement is from the material to the spiritual.

Ultimately, liberation theologians do oppose theologies that bifurcate their metaphysics into spiritual and natural, and define salvation as a spiritual glorification in a transcendent afterlife and neglect the historical, the here and now, and the condition of the poor (see Gonzalez 1988:41-46,83-85 and Boff 1987:91-100). Gustavo Gonzalez expresses some of the twentieth century reaction among Catholic theologians to the neo-Thomist nature-grace dualism by concluding that, "The natural and supernatural orders are therefore intimately unified" (Gonzalez 1988:44). In word, liberation does acknowledge the spiritual, though it seems to be penultimate and at times even absent. Yet in spite of these assertions that allow for the penetration of the "supernatural" into the natural order, liberation theology often expresses a gospel that is merely socio-politically oriented to the exclusion of issues that are usually categorized as "spiritual" or "supernatural" for lack of better terms, such as spiritual warfare, conversion or physical healing to name a few. I am talking about invisible realities even beyond abstraction or even universals, spirit beings and spirit realities. It is not to disregard the socio-political, but to include it, and yet not to reduce the mission to it. Gonzalez, like many liberation theologians, understood liberation primarily in these terms. He states that:

> Everything has a political color. It is always in the political fabric – and never outside of it- that a person emerges as a free and responsible being, as a person in relationship with other persons, as someone who takes on a historical task. (Gonzalez 1988:30-31; see also Chapter Eleven for Gonzalez on the political)

Understanding the intent of Gonzalez in this passage, I realize that he envisions a liberation that is historically conscious and concrete concerning the human condition in its socio-existential context. For salvation to be "real," it must touch us as socio-political beings, where we live. Yet, nowhere in his *magnum opus, A Theology of Liberation,* does he address issues that touch on a holistic gospel, such as forgiveness of sins, spiritual warfare and deliverance, conversion, or physical healing. Even though he condemns the dilemma, "either a spiritual redemption or temporal redemption," it is often the spiritual redemption that suffers loss (1988:96). Gonzalez warns against "excessive spiritualization" and a "disincarnate" spirituality, but we do not find him addressing these issues and needs as they relate to even the temporal realm (1988:96). I do not want to make a blanket statement concerning liberation theologians that they neglect "the spiritual," for there are some in praxis and theory who demonstrate a comprehensive salvation (Costas 1989).Yet, in the major works by other liberation theologians, such as Segundo and Boff, I did not find that to be the case (Boff 1987; Segundo 1976).

A theology of mission that is shaped by the person and work of the Holy Spirit is called to address a broader worldview that includes spiritual powers and demonstrates the full power of God's salvation. The church's witness is vitally connected to the power *(dunamis)* of the Pentecostal Spirit that equips the church with gifts for ministry, a ministry that extends into the heavenly realms. Scripture claims that *God's purpose in all this was to use the church to display his wisdom in its rich variety to all the unseen rulers and authorities in the heavenly places. Eph. 3:10 (NLT).* Cosmic transformation, the new creation, entails a comprehensive work of God, and the church needs to modify its worldview, its theology, and its structures to accommodate for the daily interaction of the spiritual and the invisible in the empirical world.

Andrew Lord outlines a "holistic vision for mission that encompasses: evangelistic mission, healing mission, social mission, reconciling mission, ecological mission, Christian spirituality, and Christian character and relationships" (Lord 2005:63). A holistic work of God requires a holistic worldview and holistic ministry. It may not comprise the entire content of a theology of mission, but a model of *theosis* needs to have warfare *(Christus Victor)* and healing components that are worked out practically in everyday life, not only among those whose worldview operates within those categories but specifically in the West where such categories are ignored.

I have been discussing holistic ministry that has revolved around addressing a variety of needs at multiple levels of life. Much of this discussion ties in with evangelization, seeking to reach people with the gospel, which is followed by the discipleship process. I will examine discipleship later, but it is significant to note that movements, like the "Missional Church" and the "Emerging Church," have come to realize that categories like evangelization, outreach, membership/baptism, discipleship and worship and their order of progression are both somewhat fuzzy. Both of these movements are identifying mission as the DNA of the church. It is who we are as the church. Mission then can include all of these at some level. It is not to say everything is mission, because then mission often becomes nothing. Yet the mission of the church is expressed somewhat in all of these practices. An emphasis of the Missional Church is to begin in service where the community is in need outside of the four walls. It may be then that those who attend church may be in mission practice before they are converted, and then officially discipled. Their discipleship may reside in the prevenient grace that they experience through the call to mission and their experience in serving. Persons then belong before they believe. Others may believe while they belong, while others may believe after they serve.

In all cases, structures within the church, as an ecclesial family, are needed for the development and nurturing of souls within an intentional, participatory community of caring, accountability, instruction, fellowship, and service. We know in participatory community, and we grow in participation. We participate in ecclesial being that is in Christ as the body of Christ that participates in the Triune life of God. Our participatory sanctification is worked out through many practical forms and functions of the church in both its charismatic as well as institutional modes. Wesley called these the "means of grace," those normative practices that the Spirit uses to convey grace. All of these forms and functions that the Spirit uses are essential to the overall spiritual formation and health of the believer and the church. It is when the church has isolated these categories and functions or singled one out to the exclusion of the others that the health of the church has suffered and the mission impaired. Participatory epistemology recognizes that we come "to know," "to experience" and "to grow" in relationship, and we need vital, spiritual, ecospheres or communities of participation in which to grow. Jesus grew his followers within a discipleship context. The discipleship process is a didactic, learning (*mathetes*)and spiritually developmental process that offers context, form, and structure for stability in the Christian life of growing in grace. Jesus as sage called disciples unto himself. Disciple or learner is our primary designation. We are called to learn from Jesus Christ, his person and mission (Matthew 11:29). Discipleship relationships are didactic communities of participation that offer a psycho-social environment for spiritual development in the new life in Christ, and they also can provide unbelievers with both a context for the call to Christ as well as mission opportunities that may bring them to Christ. If both existing and new churches are to be healthy and self- theologizing, self supporting, self propagating, and self governing, then intentional discipleship and leadership development needs to become a vital function in the church.

Both Maximus, who was a monk, and Wesley knew the value of small group structures and community life for spiritual formation and discipleship. Wesley had a small group for every mode of spiritual formation. According to D. Michael Henderson, the Society dealt with the cognitive mode of discipleship (Henderson 1997:83) The Class Meeting was behavioral formation (1997:93). The Band Meeting touched the affective domain of discipleship (1997:112). The Select Society was the training mode for leadership development (1997:121). And the Penitent Bands were the rehabilitative mode of discipleship, for those struggling with social dysfunctions (1997:125). Renewal specialist and Free Methodist theologian, Howard Snyder (1940-) acknowledges the impact that discipleship structures can have on the life of the church. He refers to these *ecclesiola* structures as "new wineskins" (Snyder 1980:53). Snyder, as well as the author, holds a renewal theory of the church. It is evident in the interpretation of the history of the church that the Spirit of God periodically renews the church to vitality for the purpose of mission. Renewal movements often birth new structures or wineskins to hold the new wine. In the case of the Methodist movement, its discipleship structure "constitutes the genius of the whole movement" (1980:53). In studying renewal movements, Snyder identified the *collegia pietatis*[40] of German Pietism, the bands of Moravianism and the small group structures of Methodism as key to the revivals in those movements (Snyder 1989 *Signs of the Spirit)*. These small groups and little churches within the larger church were catalytic to igniting the entire church with the revitalizing flames of the Holy Spirit, inspiring and equipping the church for further mission.

There is a need to create contextualized structures cross-culturally for discipleship. The Chinese house church movement is a good example of contextualizing a central institution for the Chinese, the extended family, into a small group of believers gathered for worship, prayer, and teaching. In the West, there is a movement called "New Monasticism" which is calling persons out of the Empire and into the urban deserts to live together, to serve the urban poor, work for justice, and grow in grace in disciplined communities (Rutba House 2005). This movement is a reflection of the postmodern quest for identity, especially in community. The biblical language and imagery of *oikoniomia* (the household of God) can serve the church well in the process of contextualization and identity development. Metaphors of God as Father, Jesus as Son, the church as the family of God, members as brothers and sisters, and leaders as spiritual fathers and mothers are rich wells to draw from when contextualizing the message in cultures that are centered around the family and community.

Finally, one of the most important implications of participation for a theology of mission is its universal appeal and facile theological contextualization cross-culturally. An onto-epistemology of participation in creation, Incarnation, and new creation has *theosis* as its theological goal. Since many religious systems have 'union with God' at the center of their belief systems, they are inclined to relate to a participatory worldview and theology. Clark Pinnock selects *theosis* as the essence or core of salvation rather than justification in his theology of the Holy Spirit. He views the broad reach of *theosis* as an asset to cross-denominational, and cross-faith communication (Pinnock 1996:149-150).

Echoing Maximus, I am specifically referring to a *cosmic theosis*. This cosmic goal is high but it is broad as well. It is inclusive and comprehensive and touches on the ultimate desire of humanity, union with God. Pinnock claims that "the purpose of life is a transforming friendship and union with God" (Pinnock 1996:152). Karkkainen quoting M.C. McDaniel writes, "All major religions agree on one thing, the deepest desire of the human person is to get in contact and to live in union with his or her God" (Karkkainen 2004:1). Karkkainen continues in his own words:

> Different religions offer distinctive understandings about the nature of that union, and the way to the attainment of salvation. These differences, notwithstanding, it seems reasonable to argue that salvation involves some form of union with God. Thus, the desire for union is the theme of religions and consequently theologies...This search for union with God is undoubtedly the leading motif in religions. (Karkkainen2004:1-2)

Karkkainen's work *One with God: Salvation as Deification and Justification* is an in-depth, ecumenical attempt at uniting Christian soteriologies and Christian theologies of religions under the over-arching theme of *theosis* to construct a global theology. He states, "The idea of union with God has profound implications not only with respect to Christian ecumenism but also for a Christian theology of religions (the relationship of Christianity to other world religions)" (Karkkainen 2004:4).

Another attractive dimension of participation and *theosis* to other cultures is that often other world religions and folk religions share the common theme of some version of apophaticism concerning the ultimate nature of God or what Eastern Orthodoxy calls the hyperessence of God. Hinduism, Buddhism, and other Eastern religions share a similar apophatic sensibility, the unknowing, when it comes to fully knowing God. There is epistemic humility often accompanying a negative theology that reverberates throughout nirvanic (full absence) and even brahmic (full presence) thinking. Transcendence brings one past and out of the illusory realm of senses and thought. Christian apophasis, of course, does not hold to such a low view of the material and sensory world, but it does acknowledge its limitations and temporality. Apophasis characterizes Eastern Orthodox mystical theology as humanity ascends by the Holy Spirit through ascetic practices into union with God, it becomes a process of unknowing. God is not reduced to the sensible or the intelligible realms in any notion of pure immanence. There is always a remainder. In his utter transcendence, God is beyond categories of being and non-being and any other antinomy offered by human reason. Like in other Eastern religions, silence is the only response to having touched the divine. Apophaticism would surely be a surprising expression of epistemic humility for the Asian hearer of Christianity. Often Western Christian knowledge and communication of God is so systematic, scholastic, reduced and even commercialized that it causes people from Eastern cultures to turn to skepticism concerning the overall Christian witness due to any Western form. The idea of knowing God enough to transform one's life but knowingly not being able to know the unknowable is an attractive notion for one who is looking to know but not own God.

I believe that cosmic *theosis* defined by a pneumatologically informed Christology, expressed in Eucharistic ecclesiology and holistic missiology, and developed in communities of disciplined spiritual formation could function as a central theme in a global Christian theology of mission.

Mission Implications:
1. The church is to understand its dependent role in mission as it participates in the mission *of* the Holy Spirit.
2. Let cosmic *theosis* be the measure and scope of our holistic mission to a people.
3. We are called to develop contextual structures of community that foster discipleship, nurture and transformation for mission.

Notes

1. See Paul Hiebert's *Transforming Worldviews*, as it does a much better job at explaining worldview, culture, contextualization, and translation in terms of digital and analogue.

2. Greek – meaning "gap" or "distance."Much of my inspiration concerning the *diastema* comes from listening to Gregory of Nyssa and from listening to David Bentley Hart listening to Gregory.

3. An attempt at a more organic play off Plantinga's more mechanical concept "proper function."

4. A Greek word used by Gregory of Nyssa and other Eastern Christian theologians to describe the ever forward-moving struggle towards union with God in *theosis*.

5. This is my attempt at playing David Bentley Hart on my theological guitar.

6. Critical contextualization is one current practice that allows for this type of faithful witness. I will discuss critical contextualization later in this chapter.

7. Alvin Plantinga has formulated a theory of epistemology known as "proper function," that involves the proper function of the cognitive faculties in the production of belief within an environment designed for truth as a goal in order to establish warrant for a belief. Plantinga's theory is a type of naturalized epistemology that works compatibly within a larger framework of supernatural theism. Plantinga's epistemological theory like this theory of participation is ontologically based, since it is connected with design (*telos*) and reason of being (*logos*) within God's creation. Though there are similarities between Plantinga's "proper function" and my rough sketch of a "proper" participation, the difference is that Plantinga's theory, as well as many analytic theories, reduces epistemology and the knower to individual cognition. It is still locked into the Cartesian model of epistemology as individuated reason or cognition. Plantinga's theory like most naturalized epistemology comes off somewhat mechanical or robotic, though Plantinga at least includes the human factor of the noetic effects of sin on the knowledge process. Proper participation acknowledges the whole *imago Dei*, not just the cognitive-mechanical dimension or faculty, and it recognizes the community-tradition, narrative or social dimension of knowledge and virtue apprehension and production as well.

8. Virtue epistemology is based on the model of virtue theory in ethics. It seeks to resolve the foundationalist and coherentist dilemma and debate concerning justification of true belief by proposing that the nurturing of epistemic virtues within the knower, such as honesty, truthfulness, conviction, diligence, and openness, is integral to developing a reliable process that produces justified belief. Some virtue epistemologists are Ernest Sosa, John Greco, and Linda Zagzebski. The writer does not hold that any one current theory of epistemology provides absolute knowledge, certainty, justification or warrant for every situation

or case. Warrant is in degrees and at times comes in different ways. Participation offers more of an onto-epistemological vision that incorporates and develops different theories as they find compatibility within a larger theological setting. A scriptural, theological vision of reality does not have to hold *necessarily* to one type of theory or model of epistemology, philosophy or science in order to be true.

9. Wolfhart Pannenberg notes the provisional nature of knowledge that unfolds eschatologically until we know in full at the coming of Christ.

10. Latin for "the way of the cross."

11. Univocal being when pushed to its extremes results in either nihilism or pantheism.

12. We had noted earlier how nihilism does not discern difference in its assessment of the history of philosophy. All is a ruse of violence and power.

13. Greek for "substance" or "essence"

14. *Prosopon* is a Greek word that refers to the mask used in Greek theater that represented human freedom and the ability to attempt to escape fate.

15. Many parochial voices within Eastern Orthodoxy and Roman Catholicism would see these denominations as "parachurch," while others would consider them, at best, branches to their one trunk.

16. Latin for "in itself"

17. *Phronesis* is the practice or habits of virtue and wisdom.

18. Throughout history, Christian theology has turned to scholasticism in many forms; Catholic (Scotism), Lutheran (Abraham Calovius), Reformed (Beza), and others. In many cases, it becomes a tedious reduction of the living faith to pure orthodox conceptualization.

19. A Greek word from the New Testament for the "economy," "household management" or "plan" of God.

20. In Chapter Four, I examined Wesley's epistemology which incorporates faith as a mode of apprehension of knowledge.

21. Latin for "faith seeking understanding."

22. Examples of epistemic virtue are humility, honesty, wisdom, and openness. Virtue epistemology finds justification of belief in the reliability and responsibility of the agent.

23. One interacting context is the socio-cultural context, and more specifically, a community tradition like the church.

24. Foundationalism builds its system of truth from the ground up through reason and/or empirical data. Suspension "hangs" creation from a transcendent God. Of course, the dimensional language is analogical.

25. Archimedes was rumored to have said that if he could find a fixed point and a proper lever, he could move the world. Descartes sought such a fixed point in his "I think; therefore, I am" foundation of modern knowledge.

26. "Privation" or "privative" comes from the Latin *privatio* or "private." My context is from the philosophical and Eastern Christian tradition that uses the term to mean "lack" or "without" (especially being – ontological lack), and in other cases, "moral evil due to an absence of good." In embracing evil as privative, I am not denying the existence of "radical evil." Evil originates without cause and is dysteleological. It is also without being, privation. Evil is also not true in nature, but its existence is a fact. Without being, evil is not absolute but relative to what it negates or lacks. As a response to God, it is a misuse of freedom, and a causeless *ex nihilo* anti-creation out of the possibility that freedom provides of not choosing God. Yet after the choice and lapse, remains a created being that still participates existentially in God. A created being made in the image of God then is under the foreign influence of evil, living and making decisions within God's created world. There is sort of an anti-"hypostatic union" between privation (evil) and the *imago* that allows for privation

to become radical, intentional, and seemingly ontic, though it is not. As anti-matter attached to the *imago* it masks itself as having real, ontic status, but though it does exists as the consequence of freedom's misuse within a moral agent, it has no real being that is participating in God. The only participation is in the form of judgment that the agent receives from God.

27. I am suggesting the Chalcedonian logic for Christology as a model of contextualization that protects against syncretism. Incarnation proper, however, is a term and event that identifies only Jesus Christ. We participate in God through the Incarnation, but we never become Incarnation in the Chalcedonian sense.

28. Here, meaning God *appearing* or manifesting through the church.

29. Greek for "economy." In theology it refers to both the total plan and management of God's will in history, and also its implementation through the revelation and ministry of the three persons of the Trinity in history.

30. Stanley Grenz among others has done some quality work in this area.

31. "Decorrelation" is a term I am coining to denote the process of removing a "secular" correlation from theology. See "Correlation" in chapter 2.

32. *Hokmah* – Hebrew for wisdom. *Sophia* - Gteek for wisdom

33. This is the thesis of Ben Witherington's book *Jesus the Sage* published by Fortress Press 1994.

34. See Hans Urs Von Balthasar's chapter called "Christ's Person and Mission found in *Theo-Drama: Theological Dramatic Theory, volume three: Dramatis Persona e: Persons in Christ.* The chapter is a theological analysis of how the identity and person of Jesus Christ is defined in mission. Jesus' self-understanding was as the Son of man sent into the world to save the lost. Jesus' consciousness of his Divine mission defined how he saw himself and the Father and the nature of his purpose.

35. It is possible that we have a connection to both the immanent and economic Trinity, the former is mystical and purely apophatic and the latter is cataphatic One's understanding of the Trinity as ontological, hyperessence, or identical in terms of immanent and economic will define the nature of such an experience. As mentioned prior, we experience the energies of God through the persons economically, yet there is something transcendent to the Trinity that is unknowable and proper only to God's self.

36. Chrismation or the baptism with the Spirit is interpreted differently in many Christian traditions. Lutheran, Reformed, and Baptistic traditions understand the baptism with the Spirit as synonymous with regeneration and the reception of the Spirit, thus tying it to baptism. The Roman Catholic tradition views it as a post-baptismal and post-catechetical sacrament called confirmation, imparted by the laying on of hands of a bishop. Wesleyan and Pentecostal-Charismatic view it as a post-conversional experience for sanctification and/or power for service. Pentecostals include speaking in other tongues as evidence of the experience, while Charismatics expect the gifts of the Spirit, which may include tongues, as one sign of the experience. Eastern Orthodoxy, and recently United Methodism, understands chrismation as the gift of the Spirit received immediately following baptism through the laying on of hands as part of the baptismal liturgy.

37. There has been an ongoing dialogue and debate in phenomenology over the possibility of the "gift". See *The Gift* by Marcel Mauss, *Rethinking God as Gift: Marion, Derrida, and the Limits of Phenomenology* by Robyn Horner, and *God, the Gift and Postmodernism* edited by John Caputo and Michael Scanlon.

38. Following the promulgation of the *missio Dei* revelation, the church was often relegated to the sidelines. Since God was in mission, the church was considered insignificant, irrelevant and even a hindrance to God's work. God was working everywhere else but in and through the church. This extreme position was taken due to prior emphasis placed on

the church as the sole agent for salvation. Outside of the church, there could be no salvation. I contend for somewhat of a *via media* with a tendency to veer more towards the church as God's primary vessel for the work of the Holy Spirit. However, the church needs to be on guard as to how it handles its own power, especially as it addresses the socio-political realm. The whole Constantinian project in which church and state are intermarried and Christendom becomes its offspring has historically proven to be devastating for both church and state. The Constantinian project was probably the most costly error in syncretism that the church has made. The modern empire in the West has had a similar impact on the church throughout the age of exploration, evangelization and exploitation. Today, especially in America, the church needs to guard itself against the excesses of a culture of market-driven capitalism, popular and philosophical pragmatism and Christian America patriotism that have promoted a syncretism of American evangelical Christendom that cannot differentiate between Christianity and American culture.

39. I had made reference to Charles Kraft's experience in Chapter One.

40. Snyder recognized that Pietism's *collegia pietatis* (colleges of piety) or small groups, Moravian *chore* (choirs) or bands, and Methodists (societies, classes, and bands) often functioned as a "church within the larger church," or *ecclesiolae in ecclesia* in order to bring renewal to the church as a whole.

Chapter Seven

Conclusions, Contributions and Questions

What happens when ontology is detached from God and collapses under its own weight of nothingness? The last seven hundred years of philosophy may call it an *epistemological crisis*. I call it an ontological crisis with an epistemological impact on truth, meaning and certainty. One solution offered to this problem has been an *ontological* critique of the epistemological issues within modernism and postmodernism. I have concluded that from modernism to postmodernism ontology has been deflated of significance, while epistemology has inflated and taken on the central role of first philosophy. Even more so, epistemology has morphed into a hermeneutical closed-system that does not allow for the transcendent.

Christian theology of mission has been guilty of co-mingling with such epistemologies in crisis. The Enlightenment up until the end of the modern period of mission best expresses the nature of the problem. Colonialism and Christianity, exploration, exploitation, and evangelism, and hegemony and holiness often went hand in hand, as the Western missiological enterprise collaborated with Western national interests in geo-politics, scientism, technological advancement, and cultural imperialism.

Today in an era of postmodernism, the foundations of modernism have been thoroughly critiqued. Autonomous reason and all of her manifestations have been stripped of her illusions of omnipotence and underneath a will to power dynamic has been discovered by her critics. Postmodernism has taught us to be suspicious of all knowledge claims, doing a clever job of reducing them to various semiotic derivatives. However, in the process, knowledge is not only not what it used to be, it has become nothing. Radical Orthodoxy has hammered out a theo-ontological critique of the stubborn claims of Derrida, Lyotard and Foucault, the postmodern trinity, as well as others in the postmodern camp. Radical Orthodoxy theory has unearthed a nihilistic genealogy of modern and postmodern thinking that goes all the way back to Duns Scotus and his univocity of being. The univocity of being has been the primary gene of nihilism that has allowed its philosophical ancestors to assume ontological autonomy apart from God on the grounds that being is a common predicate shared by God *and* the created order. Thus, the created order has its own being to ground itself. This claim is an illusion, and in fact, the ancestry of a univocity of being actually rests on a univocity of non-being, hence the fruit of nihilism. The theological antidote administered is participation. An ontology of participation brings the created order back into connection with the transcendent God. Within this scheme of ontology, there can be no secular or autonomous domains. Everything is defined theologically.

In response to a critique within their own Radical Orthodox circle by James K.A. Smith, the writer sought to ground the doctrine of participation in a more "Christian" source rather than in Plato and picked that great defender of orthodoxy Maximus the Confessor from out of the patristic closet. Maximus proposed a *metousia Logo,* a participation in the Logos. I attempted to modify Radical Orthodoxy's version of participation by remixing Maximus' theology of the *logoi* and the Incarnation. His incarnationally centered theology provided an alternative for the ontology of participation in a purely Platonic sense. Maximus' construct is rooted and grounded in the Christian revelation of the incarnate Logos. In the process of developing Maximus' ontology of participation in the Logos, the writer drew upon John Wesley to add soteriological and missiological detail to the vision of participation. The writer has attempted to synthesize the work of Maximus and Wesley to put theological muscle on an onto-epistemological frame of participation that would have missional implications. Like Maximus, Wesley focused on participating in the divine nature. His primary theological concept that drove his doctrine of sanctification was grace. Wesley's theology of grace takes on a similar function as Maximus' *logoi.* Wesley's theology of grace is an entire soteriological *ordo* that defines and directs the Christian experience into entire sanctification or *theosis.* Wesley's theology of grace, beginning with prevenient grace and extending to sanctifying and glorifying grace describes the Triune work of God in the world. Along with Wesley's theology and practice of personal and social holiness, Maximus' cosmic liturgy advancing toward cosmic transfiguration depicts a comprehensive vision of recapitulation that provides the scope and trust of a robust theology of mission.

A unique contribution to mission theology is the development and application of an onto-epistemology of participation to a theology of mission. Radical Orthodoxy has talked much about participation but has yet to apply it to mission. Much has been written by Maximus and Maximian scholars on participation, but the author is not aware of any material that applies participation to mission. The author has developed eight characteristics that highlight an onto-epistemology of participation and has then sought to apply it to a theology of mission, using three basic categories that can serve as a global theology: creation, Incarnation, and new creation. With participation beginning in creation and moving to Incarnation and then to the new creation/*theosis,* it is a framework where many past problems and future challenges can be worked out. An onto-epistemology of participation understands mission as God's, a *missio Dei* and not the church's mission. The eternal *processio* informs the economic *missio.* God is a missionary God, and his movement in eternity is extended to creation, as all creation is invited to participate in the Triune life of God. The church is called to participate in God's work of cosmic transfiguration. Creation provides the universal context from which God begins. Incarnation is the climactic cause that makes possible deification, and the new creation is the eschatological reign of Christ through the Spirit in the universe. The new creation is new in every aspect. Only a holistic worldview can comprehend the scope of the nature of the work that God desires to do in the earth, and only a holistic mission that touches every area of life is sufficiently compatible with the *missio Dei*. The Holy Spirit is the primary agent and missionary of this global witness. The Holy Spirit goes ahead of the church working within cultural contexts and empowers the church to participate in the work that will restore people's lives to God's original design. The church is called in this process to discern critically how to communicate the truth in culture-specific, local forms without changing the meaning of the everlasting gospel of Jesus Christ. It is called to find faithful forms of community to serve in nurturing the spiritual growth of others, forms that will further God's mission in the church and in the world. The result is that the cosmos become a living icon of the glorious Triune God. Through and for God's glory, *theosis* is the *telos* of God's mission. God desires to transform us through his glory into his image that we may be one in loving fellowship with God and give God glory throughout eternity.

What are some of the questions that can come out of this research and could further research in the direction of an actual theology of mission? Some questions may be concerned with defining more specifically and exploring the practical consequences of contextualization within an analogical model of participation as applied to local theology. How does one identify a universal witness in a culture? Are the transcendentals reliable phenomenological reflections of a universal witness? How well preserved is such a witness? How does one exegete a culture and discern the Spirit's prophetic work within society using a participatory framework? How does participation relate to God's judgment? How similar or dissimilar (analogical) is a culture's witness to the witnesses in the Hebrew Bible? What is Jesus' relationship to the Hebrew Bible and its salvation history? What continuity and discontinuity does Christ bring to a culture's witness? How is Christ the end and fulfillment of the law or a culture's witness?

The second set of questions would relate to how participation relates to the traditional categories of theology and mission. Further, how does participation interrelate with non-Western categories, specifically local forms, like narrative, proverbial wisdom, filial piety, or ancestral worship? Does participation suggest or even require Western theological specifics, i.e. a certain doctrine of election and condemnation, a particular theory of atonement, a certain soteriology, ecclesiology or eschatology? If it does, then how does it affects the practice of mission cross-culturally?

For example, the view of participation that I have offered is informed primarily by Maximus and Wesley. Sanctification is central to a soteriology of participation. How does this affect justification and regeneration? Maximus and Eastern Orthodoxy do not stress a Protestant-Reformed form of justification by faith. Wesley's *via media* synthesized it with his therapeutic notion of salvation. Its inclusion or exclusion will have an impact on how we understand conversion, and our doctrine and ecclesial forms of post-conversion. Are these views biblical or cultural? An exclusion of a strong justification by faith would be replaced by a gradualism towards *theosis*. Conversion may be understood in a sacramental sense via baptism. Strong catechetical structures would be necessary to promote growth and maturity in the faith. If there is a strong justification by faith teaching and practice, then conversion may be preached and experienced in a more evangelical sense rather than a sacramental one. Yet, strong catechetical structures would still be necessary, as evangelicals have found out through the insufficiency of crusades and revivals. The last thirty years of evangelical discipleship has put a premium on small group structures. Indigenous forms need to be considered as such theology is contextualized.

How can participation be contextualized, especially within religions that already hold to some form of participation or union in the divine, i.e. Hinduism? Would participation become more of a hindrance or a more accessible stepping-stone towards contextualization, localization, and glocalization than other forms would? What distinctions would have to be made between "Christian" participation and other religious notions of participation in God? Are they the same? Why or why not? In our example of sanctification, would indigenous notions of participation and *theosis* have to be distinguished from other religious forms of divinization? What are those distinctions? In Western worldview what is the difference between participation , sanctification and the American Dream, or self-help, self-realization, self-actualization, self-potential and a host of other therapeutic remedies for the self? What are the distinctions between various religious methodologies of sanctification? Would certain indigenous, sociological understandings of communal participation have an impact on the communal nature of salvation and discipleship? These and other questions begin to arise as the notion of theological participation is brought to bear on a theology of mission.

References Cited

Abraham, William, J. 2006. *Crossing the threshold of divine revelation.* Grand Rapids, MI: Eerdmans Publishing Company.
Ahlstrom, Sydney E. 1972. *A religious history of the American people.* New Haven, CT: Yale University Press.
Anderson, Douglas. 2004. Common sense marriage of religion and science. In Cheryl Misak (Ed.), *The Cambridge companion to Peirce.* Cambridge University Press.
Anderson, Walter Truett (Ed.). 1995. *The truth about the truth.* New York: Penguin Books.
Appignanesi, Richard and Chris Garratt. 2003. *Introducing postmodernism.* Cambridge, UK: Icon Books.
Aquinas, Thomas. 1960. *The pocket Aquinas* (Vernon Bourke, Ed.). New York: Washington Square Press.
Aquinas, Thomas. 2003. *On evil* (Brian Davies, Ed.). Oxford University Press.
Augustine. 1958. *City of God* (Vernon Bourke. Ed.). New York: Doubleday.
Balthasar, Hans Urs Von. 1978. *Theo-Drama, theological dramatic theory: III: dramatis personae: persons in Christ.* San Francisco, Ignatius Press.
Balthasar, Hans Urs Von. 1983. *Theo-Drama, theological dramatic theory: V:The Last act.* San Francisco, Ignatius Press.
Balthasar, Hans Urs Von. 1993. *Presence and thought: An essay on the religious philosophy of Gregory of Nyssa.* San Francisco, Ignatius Press.
Balthasar, Hans Urs Von. 2003. *Cosmic liturgy: The universe according to Maximus the Confessor.* San Francisco: Ignatius Press.
Barbour, Ian G. 1997. *Religion and science.* San Francisco: HarperCollins.
Baudrillard, Jean. 1983. *Simulations.* New York: Semiotext[e].
Baudrillard, Jean. 1999. *Revenge of the crystal.* London: Pluto Press.
Berger, Peter, and Thomas Luckmann. 1968. *Social construction of reality.* San Francisco: Harper and Row.
Berkeley, George. 1929. *Berkeley selections* (Mary Calkins, Ed.). New York: Charles Scribner's Sons.
Best, Steven, and Douglas Kellner. 1991. *Postmodern theory.* New York: The Guilford Press.
Bevans, Stephan B. 2002. *Models of contextual theology* (Revised and expanded edition). Maryknoll, NY: Orbis Books.
Bevans, Stephan, B. and Roger P. Schroeder. 2004. *Constants in context: A theology of mission for today.* Maryknoll, NY: Orbis Books.

Bibb, Henry. 1999. Narrative of the Life and Adventures of Henry Bibb, An American Slave. In Yuval Taylor (Ed.), *I Was Born A Slave: An Anthology of Classic Slave Narratives* (Vol. 2, *1849-1866*.. Chicago, Ill: Lawrence Hill Books.
Biddle, Mark E. 2004. *Missing the mark*. Nashville, TN: Abingdon Press.
Blowers, Paul M., and Robert Louis Wilken (Trans.). 2003. Introduction to *On the cosmic mystery of Jesus Christ: Selected writings from St. Maximus the Confessor*. Crestwood, NY: St. Vladimir's Seminary Press.
Boff, Clodovis. 1987. *Theology and praxis: epistemological foundations*. Maryknoll, NY: Orbis Books.
Boler, John. 2004. Peirce and Medieval thought. In Cheryl Misak (Ed.), *The Cambridge companion to Peirce*. Cambridge University Press.
Bosch, David, J. 1991. *Transforming mission*. Maryknoll, NY: Orbis Books.
Boyd, Gregory A. *God at War*. 1997. Downers Grove, IL: IVP.
Braaten, Laurie J. 2001. The voice of wisdom: a creation context for proto-trinitarian thought. *Wesleyan Theological Journal*, 36 (1).
Brueggemann, Walter.1982. *Interpretation: Genesis*. Atlanta: John Knox Press.
Bundy, David. 2004. Vision of sanctification: themes of orthodoxy in the Methodist, Holiness, and Pentecostal traditions. *Wesleyan Theological Journal*, 39(1), 104-136.
Campbell, Ted A. 1991. *John Wesley and Christian antiquity: religious vision and cultural change*. Nashville, TN: Abingdon Press.
Carr, David. 1991. *Time, narrative, and history*. Bloomington, IN: Indiana University Press.
Carveley, Kenneth. 2002. From glory to glory: the renewal of all things in Christ: Maximus the Confessor and John Wesley. In St. Kimbrough (Ed.), *Orthodox and Wesleyan spirituality*, (pp. 173-188). Crestwood, NY: St. Vladimir's Seminary Press.
Cavanaugh, William T. 1999. The city: beyond secular parodies. In John Milbank, Catherine Pickstock, and Graham Ward (Eds.), *Radical orthodoxy: a new theology* (pp. 182-200).
Christensen, Michael J. 1996. Theosis and sanctification: John Wesley's reformulation of a Patristic doctrine. *The Wesleyan Theological Journal*, 21(2), 71-94.
Coady, C.A.J. 1992. *Testimony: a philosophical investigation*. Oxford University Press.
Collins, Kenneth J. 1997. *The Scripture way of salvation*. Nashville, TN: Abingdon Press.
Collins, Kenneth J., and Randy L. Maddox. 2000. Recent trends in Wesleyan Holiness scholarship. *Wesleyan Theological Journal*, 35(1), 67-98.
Comaroff, Jean L., and John L. Comaroff. 1991. *Of revelation and revolution: Christianity, colonialism, consciousness in South Africa*. (Vol. 1). University of Chicago Press.
Comstock, Gary L. 1987. Two types of narrative theology. *Journal of the American Academy of Religion* 55(4), 687-703.
Cone, James H. 1991. *A black theology of liberation*. Maryknoll, NY: Orbis Books.
Copleston, Fredrick. 1962. *History of philosophy* (Vol. 1). New York: Bantam Doubleday Dell.
Copleston, Fredrick. 1963. *History of philosophy* (Vol. 2). New York: Bantam Doubleday Dell Pub. Group.
Copleston, Fredrick. 1965. *History of philosophy* (Vo. 3). New York: Bantam Doubleday Dell.
Coppedge, Allan. 1987. *John Wesley in theological debate*. Wilmore, KY: Wesley Heritage Press.
Costas, Orlando E. 1989. *Liberating news: a theology of contextual evangelization*. Grand Rapids, MI: Eerdmans.
Cunningham, Conor. 2002. *Genealogy of nihilism*. New York: Routledge.

Damasio, Antonio. 1994. *Descartes' error: emotion, reason, and the human brain*. NY: Putnam Berkley.
Damasio, Antonio. 1999. *The feeling of what happens: body, emotion in the making of consciousness*. New York: Harcourt.
Descartes, Rene. 1951. *Meditations on first philosophy*. Laurence Lafleur (Trans.). New York: Bobbs-Merrill.
Descartes, Rene. 1998. *Descartes: selected philosophical writings*. John Cottingham, Dugald Murdoch, and Robert Stoothoff (Trans.). Cambridge University Press.
Derrida, Jacques. 1992. *Derrida: a critical reader*. David Wood (Ed.). Oxford, UK: Blackwell Pub. L.T.D.
Derrida, Jacques. 1995. The play of substitution. In Walter Truett Anderson (Ed.). *The Truth about the truth*.
Derrida, Jacques. 1997. *Of grammatology*. Baltimore, MD: The Johns Hopkins Press. NY.
De Wulf, Maurice. 1959. *The system of Thomas Aquinas*. NY: Dover.
Douglas, Kelly Brown. 1995. *Black Christ*. Maryknoll, New York: Orbis Books.
Flemming, Dean. 2005. *Contextualization in the New Testament*. Downers Grove, Ill: IVP.
Fletcher, Richard. 1997. *The barbarian conversion*. Berkeley: University of California Press.
Foucault, Michel. 1980. *Power/knowledge* (Colin Gordon, Ed.). New York: Pantheon Books.
Foucault, Michel. 1984. *Foucault Reader* (Paul Rabinow, Ed.). New York: Pantheon Books.
Freedman, Jill, and Gene Combs. 1994. *Narrative therapy*. New York: W.W. Norton
Gilles, Anthony E. 1991. *The evolution of philosophy*. Staten Is, NY: Society of St. Paul.
Gilson, Etienne. 1991. *The spirit of Medieval philosophy*. Notre Dame: Uni versity of Notre Dame Press.
Glaude, Eddie Jr. 2000. *Exodus! religion, race, and nation in early nineteenth century Black America*. University of Chicago Press.
Gonzalez, Gustavo. 1988. *A Theology of Liberation*. Maryknoll, NY: Orbis Books.
Green, Joel B. 1995. *The theology of the Gospel of Luke*. Cambridge University Press.
Gregorios, Paulos Mar. 1996. *Cosmic man: the divine presence*. New York: Paragon.
Grenz, Stanley J., and John R. Franke. 2001. *Beyond foundationalism: shaping theology in a postmodern context*. Louisville, KY: John Knox Press.
Gunter, W. Stephen. 1997. *Wesley and the quadrilateral: renewing the conversation*. Nashville, TN: Abingdon Press.
Gunter, W. Stephen. 2000. Personal and spiritual knowledge: kindred spirits in Polanyian and Wesleyan epistemology. *Wesleyan Theological Journal*, 35(1).
Gutierrez, Gustavo. 1988. *A theology of liberation*. Mary Knoll, NY: Orbis Books.
Hallward, Peter. 2003. *Badiou a Subject to Truth*. Minneapolis, MN: University of Minnesota Press.
Harris, H.S. 1995. *Hegel: phenomenology and system*. Indianapolis, IN: Hackett.
Harrison, Alferdteen (Ed.). 1991. *Black exodus. The great migration from the American South*. Jackson, MS: University Press of Mississippi.
Hart, David Bentley. 2002. *The Beauty of the infinite*. Grand Rapids, MI: Eerdmans.
Hart, Kevin. 1989. *The trespass of the sign*. Cambridge University Press.
Hauerwas, Stanley, and David Burrell. 1995. From system to story. In Stanley Hauerwas and Gregory Jones, Ed.), W*hy narrative?*. Grand Rapids, MI: Eerdmans.
Hegel, Georg W.F. 1991. *The philosophy of history* (J. Sibree, Trans.). Buffalo, New York: Prometheus Books.

Heidegger, Martin. 1960. *An introduction to metaphysics*. Garden City, New York: Doubleday.
Heitzenrater, Richard P. 2002. John Wesley's reading of and references to Early Church Fathers. In S.T. Kimbrough (Ed.), *Orthodox and Western spirituality* (pp. 25-32). Crestwood, NY: St. Vladimir's Seminary Press.
Hesselgrave, David J. 1991. *Communicating Christ cross-culturally* (2nd edition). Grand Rapids, MI. Zondervan.
Hiebert, Paul G. 1985. *Anthropological insights for missionaries*. Grand Rapids, MI: Baker Book House.
Hiebert, Paul G. 1999. Missiological implications of epistemological shifts. Harrisburg, PA: Trinity Press International.
Hiebert, Paul G., Daniel R. Shaw, and Tite Tienou. 1999. *Understanding folk religion*. Grand Rapids, MI: Baker Book House.
Holcomb, Justin S. 2005. Being Bound to God, Participation and Covenant Revisited. In James K.A. Smith and James H. Olthuis (Eds.) in *Radical Orthodoxy and the Reformed Tradition*. Grand Rapids, MI: Baker.
Holstein, James A., and Jaber F. Gubrium. 2000. *The self we live by*. Oxford University Press.
Horrocks, Christopher. 1999. *Baudrillard and the millennium*. New York: Totem Books.
Hunter, George, III. 2000. *The Celtic way of evangelism: How Christianity can reach the West again*. Nashville, TN: Abingdon Press.
Husserl, Edmund. 1999. *The essential Husserl* (Donn Welton, Ed.). Bloomington: Indiana University Press.
Jenkins, Philip. 2006. *The new faces of Christianity: Believing the Bible in the global South*. New York, NY: Oxford University Press.
Jennings, Theodore W., Jr. 1990. *Good news to the poor*. Nashville, TN: Abingdon Press.
Jorgensen, Knud. 2001. Spiritual conflict in socio-political context. In A.S. Moreau et al (Eds.), *Deliver us from evil*. Monrovia, CA: World Vision International.
Kant, Immanuel. 1990. *Critique of pure reason* (J.M.D. Meiklejohn, Trans.). Buffalo, NY: Prometheus Books.
Karkkainen, Veli-Matti. 2003. *Christology: A global introduction*. Grand Rapids, MI: Baker Book House.
Karkkainen, Veli-Matti. 2004. *One with God: Salvation as deification and justification*. Collegeville, MN: Liturgical Press.
Kaufmann, Walter. 1975. *Existentialism from Dostoevsky to Sartre*. New York: New American Library Inc.
Kierkegaard, Søren. 1936. *Philosophical fragments*. (David Swenson, Trans.). Princeton University Press.
Kierkegaard, Søren. 1941. *Concluding unscientific postscript* (David Swenson, Trans.). Princeton University Press.
Kierkegaard, Søren. 1980. *The concept of anxiety* (Reidar Thomte Ed. and Trans.). Princeton University Press.
Kimbrough, S.T. 2001. *Orthodox and Wesleyan spirituality*. Crestwood, NY: St. Vladimir's Seminary Press.
King, Rob. 2003. Eastern Patristic Spirit-Christology for contemporary Wesleyan faith practice. *Wesleyan Theological Journal*, *38*(2), 103-123.

Kirk, Andrew J., and Kevin J. Vanhoozer. 1999. Christian mission and the epistemological crisis of the West. In Andrew J. Kirk and Kevin J. Vanhoozer (Eds.). *To stake a claim*. Maryknoll, NY: Orbis Books.
Knitter, Paul F. 2002. Theologies of religions. Maryknoll, NY: Orbis Books.
Kraft, Charles H. 1989. *Christianity with power: Your worldview and your experience of the supernatural*. Ann Arbor, MI: Vine Books.
Kraft, Charles H. 2002. *Confronting powerless Christianity: Evangelicals and the mission dimension*. Grand Rapids, MI: Baker.
Kraft, Marguerite. 1995. *Confronting spiritual powers*. Eugene, OR: Wipf and Stock.
Kuhn, Thomas S. 1962. *Structure of scientific revolutions*. Chicago: University of Chicago Press.
Kung, Hans. 1981. *Does God exist?* New York: Random House Books.
Lane, Richard J. 2000. *Jean Baudrillard*. London: Routledge.
Lifton, Robert Jay. 1999. *The Protean self: Human resilience in an age of fragmentation*. Chicago, Ill: University of Chicago Press.
Linthicum, Robert C. 1991. *City of God, City of Satan*. Grand Rapids, MI: Zondervan.
Locke, John. 1962. Essay concerning human understanding (A.D. Woozley, Ed.). NY: The New American Library Inc.
Lord, Andrew. 2005. *Spirit-Shaped mission: A holistic charismatic missiology*. Waynesboro, GA: Authentic Media.
Lossky, Vladimir. 1998. The mystical theology of the Eastern Church. Crestwood, NY: St. Vladimir's Seminary Press.
Louth, Andrew. 1996. Maximus the Confessor. *The Early Church Fathers*. London: Routledge.
Luibheid, Colm (Trans.). 1987. *The classics of Western spirituality: Pseudo-Dionysius, the complete works*. New York: Paulist Press.
Maddox, Randy L. 1994. *Responsible Grace*. Nashville, TN: Abingdon Press.
Marion, Jean-Luc. 1991. *God without being*. Chicago: University of Chicago Press.
Maritain, Jacques. 1995. *The degrees of knowledge*. University of Notre Dame Press.
Marquardt, Manfred. 1992. *John Wesley's social ethics*. Nashville, TN: Abingdon Press.
Maximus the Confessor, 1955. The Ascetic Life, The Four Centuries on Charity. In Polycarp Sherwood (Ed. and Trans.), *Ancient Christian Writers: The Works of the Fathers in translation*. New York: Newman Press.
Maximus the Confessor. 1981. *Four hundred texts on love, two hundred texts on theology, various texts on theology, and on the Lord's Prayer from the Philokalia: the complete text* (Vol. 1, St. Nikodimos of the Holy Mountain and St. Makarios of Corinth, Compilers, and G.E.H. Palmer, Philip Sherrard, and Kallistos Ware (Eds.). London, U.K.: Faber and Faber Limited.
Maximus the Confessor. 1985. *Selected writings*. George C. Berthold (Ed. and Trans.). New York: Paulist Press.
Maximus the Confessor. 1996. *The Early Church Fathers*. Andrew Louth (Trans. and Ed.). London: Routledge.
Maximus the Confessor. 2003. *On the cosmic mystery of Jesus Christ*. Paul M. Blowers and Robert Louis Wilken. (Ed. and Trans.). Crestwood, NY: St. Vladimir's Seminary Press.
McGill, Arthur C. 1982. Suffering: A test of theological method. Philadelphia, Westminister Press.
McInerny, Ralph. 1956. *Aquinas and analogy*. Washington, D.C: Catholic University of America Press.

Meadows, Phillip R. 2004. Methodist society as the new creation. *Wesleyan Theological Journal*, 39(2).
Metz, Johann Baptist. 1996. A short apology of narrative. In Stanley Hauerwas and L. Gregory Jones (Eds.), *Why narrative?* Grand Rapids, MI: Eerdmans.
Meyendorff, John. 1987. *Christ in eastern thought.* Crestwood, New York: St. Vladimir's Seminary.
Middleton, J. Richard. 2005. *The liberating image: The Imago Dei in Genesis 1.* Grand Rapids, MI: Baker.
Milbank, John. 1993. *Theology and social theory: Beyond secular reason.* Oxford, UK: Blackwell.
Milbank, John. 2000. The programme of radical orthodoxy. In Laurence Paul Hemming (Ed.), *Radical orthodoxy? A catholic enquiry*. Burlington, VT: Ashgate.
Milbank, John, and Catherine Pickstock. 2001. *Truth in Aquinas*. London: Routledge.
Milbank, John, Catherine Pickstock, and Graham Ward (Eds.). 1999. *Radical orthodoxy: A new theology*. London: Routledge.
Miles, Rebekah, L. 1997. The Instrumental Role of Reason. In *Wesley and the Quadrilateral: Renewing the Conversation*. Nashville, TN: Abingdon Press.
Misak, Cheryl. (Ed.). 2004. *The Cambridge Companion to Peirce*. Cambridge University Press.
Montagnes, Bernard. 2003. *The doctrine of the analogy of being according to Thomas Aquinas*. Milwaukee: Marquette University Press.
Moreau, A., Scott., Tokunboh Adeyemo, David G. Burnett, Bryant L. Myers, and Hwa Yung. (Eds.). 2002. *Deliver us from evil: An uneasy frontier in Christian mission*. Monrovia, CA: World Vision International.
Murphy, Nancey. 1990. *Theology in the age of scientific reasoning*. Ithaca: Cornell University Press.
Nietzsche, Friedrich. 1939. *The philosophy of Nietzsche*. New York: Random.
Nesteruk, Alexei V. 2003. *Light from the east: Theology, science, and the eastern orthodox tradition*. Minneapolis: Fortress Press.
Ngugi, Wa Thiong'o. 1986. Decolonising the mind. Oxford: James Currey.
Ockham, William. 1990. *Ockham: philosophical writings*. Philotheus Boehner (Ed. and Trans.). Indianapolis, IN: Hackett Publishing Company.
Okholm, Dennis, L. and Timothy R. Phillips. (Eds.). 1996. *Four views on salvation in a pluralistic world*. Grand Rapids, MI: Zondervan Publishing House.
Oord, Thomas J. 2004. Types of Wesleyan philosophy: The general landscape and my own research agenda. *Wesleyan Theological Journal*, 39(1).
Osa Loya, Joseph A. 1998. *The Tao of Jesus: An experiment in inter-traditional understanding*. New York, NY: Paulist Press.
Outler, Albert C. (Ed.). 1964. *John Wesley. A library of Protestant thought*. New York: Oxford University Press.
Outler, Albert C. 1991. John Wesley's interests in the Early Fathers of the Church. In Thomas C. Oden and Leicester R. Longden (Eds.), *The Wesleyan theological heritage*. Grand Rapids, MI: Zondervan.
Palmer, G. E. H., Philip Sherrard, Kallistos Ware. (Eds. and Trans.). 1981. Maximus, centuries on theology. In *The Philokalia* (Vol. 2). London: Faber and Faber.
Pannenberg, Wolfhart. 1990. *Metaphysics and the idea of God*. Grand Rapids, MI: Eerdmans.
Pannenberg, Wolfhart. 1991. *An Introduction to systematic theology*. Grand Rapids, MI: Eerdmans Publishing Company.

Papanikolaou, Aristotle. 2006. *Being with God: Trinity, apophaticism, and divine-human communion*. University of Notre Dame Press.
Park, Andrew Sung. 1992. *The wounded heart of God*. Nashville, TN: Abingdon Press.
Peacocke, Arthur. 1984. *Intimations of reality*. Notre Dame, IN: Notre Dame Press.
Peters-Golden, Holly. 2004. *Culture sketches: Case studies in anthropology* (3rd edition). New York: McGraw Hill.
Petulla, Joseph. 1998. *The Tao Te Ching and the Christian way*. Maryknoll, NY: Orbis Books.
Pickstock, Catherine. 1998. *After writing: On the liturgical consummation of philosophy*. Oxford: Blackwell Publishers.
Pinnock, Clark H. 1996. *Flame of Love: A Theology of the Holy Spirit*. Downers Grove, Ill: Inter Varsity Press.
Plantinga, Alvin. 2000. *Warranted Christian belief*. Oxford: Oxford University Press.
Polanyi, Michael. 1962. *Personal knowledge: Towards a post-critical philosophy*. Chicago: University of Chicago.
Polkinghorne, John. 1998. *Belief in God in an Age of Science*. Yale University Press.
Pope, Alexander. 1951. *Alexander Pope: selected poetry and prose* (2nd ed.). William Wimssatt. NY: Holt, Rinehart and Winston.
Reno, R.R. 2002. *In the ruins of the church*. Grand Rapids, MI: Baker.
Richardson, Don. 2005. *Peace child*. Ventura, CA: Gospel Light.
Rutba House. (Ed.). 2005. *School(s) for conversion: 12 marks of a new monasticism*. Eugene, OR: Wipf and Stock Publishers.
Sartre, Jean-Paul. 1966. *Being and nothingness*. New York: Washington Square Press.
Schreieter, Robert J. 1985. *Constructing local theologies*. Maryknoll, NY: Orbis Books.
Scotus, Duns. 1987. *Duns Scotus: Philosophical writings* (Trans. Allan Wolter). Indianapolis, IN: Hackett Publishing Company.
Segundo, Juan Luis. 1976. *The Liberation of theology*. Mary Knoll, NY: Orbis Books.
Sherwood, Polycarp. (Trans.). 1955. *St. Maximus the Confessor from Ancient Christian Writers* (Vol. 21). NY: The Newman Press.
Sider, Ronald J. (Ed.). 1980 *Cry justice: The Bible on hunger and poverty*. Downers Grove, Ill: IVP.
Smith, James K.A. 2003. *Introducing radical orthodoxy*. Grand Rapids, MI: Baker.
Smith, James K.A. 2005. Will the real Plato please stand up? Participation versus incarnation. In James K.A. Smith and James H. Olthuis (Eds.), Radical orthodoxy and the reformed tradition. Grand Rapids, MI: Baker.
Smith, James K.A., and James H. Olthuis (Eds.). 2002. Radical orthodoxy and the reformed tradition. Grand Rapids, MI: Baker.
Snyder, Howard A. 1980. *The radical Wesley and patterns for church renewal*. Downers Grove, Ill: Inter Varsity Press.
Snyder, Howard A. 1989. *Signs of the Spirit: How God reshapes the church*. Grand Rapids, MI: Zondervan.
Snyder, Howard A. 1992. *Models of the kingdom*. Nashville, TN: Abingdon Press.
Stackhouse, John G. (Ed.). 2000. *Evangelical futures: A conversation on theological method*. Grand Rapids, MI: Baker.
Stamoolis, James J. 1986. *Eastern orthodox mission theology Today*. Maryknoll, NY: Orbis Books.
Stanley, Brian (Ed.). 2001. *Christian missions and the enlightenment*. Grand Rapids, MI: Eerdmans

Stephanson, Anders. 1995. *Manifest destiny: American expansion and the empire of right.* New York, NY: Farrar, Straus, and Giroux.
Stronstad, Roger. 1984. *The charismatic theology of Luke.* Peabody, MA: Hendrickson Publishers.
Stroup, George W. 1981. The promise of narrative theology. Eugene, OR: Wipf and Stock.
Suchocki, Marjorie Hewitt. 1994. *The Fall to Violence.* NY: Continuum.
Sugirtharajah, R.S. 1998. *Asian biblical hermeneutics and postcolonialism.* Maryknoll, NY: Orbis Books.
Thorsen, Donald. 2003. Sola Scriptura and the Wesleyan Quadrilateral. *The Wesleyan Theological Journal,* 41(2).
Thunberg, Lars. 1995. *Microcosm and mediator* (2nd edition). Chicago, Ill: Open Court Publishing Company.
Tollefsen, Torstein Theodor. 2008. *The christocentric cosmology of St. Maximus the Confessor.* Oxford University Press.
Tsing, Anna Lwenhaupt. 2003. *Friction: An ethnography of global connection.* Princeton University Press.
Van Huyssteen, Wentzel J. 1997. *Essays in postfoundational theology.* Grand Rapids,MI: Eerdmans.
Vanhoozer, Kevin J. 1999. *To stake a claim.* Mary Knoll, NY: Orbis Books.
Von Rad, Gerhard. 1961. *Genesis.* Philadelphia: Westminister Press.
Wagner, C. Peter. 1993. *Confronting the Powers.* Ventura, CA: Gospel Light.
Wallace, Anthony F.C. 2003. *Revitalizations and mazeways: Essays on cultural change* (Vol.1). Lincoln, NE: University of Nebraska Press.
Webber, Robert E. 2002. *The younger evangelicals: Facing the challenges of the new world.* Grand Rapids, MI: Baker.
Wesley, John. 1872. *The works of John Wesley* (Vol. 1-14) (Thomas Jackson, Ed). London: Wesleyan Conference Office; reprinted Kansas City, MO: Beacon Hill Press of Kansas City, 1986.
Wesley, John. 1984-87. *The works of John Wesley* (Albert Outler, Ed.) (Vols. 1-4). Nashville, TN: Abingdon Press.
Wesley, John. 1991. *John Wesley's sermons, An Anthology* (Albert C. Outler and Richard P. Heitzenrater. Nashville, Eds.). Nashville, TN: Abingdon Press.
West, Cornel. 1982. *Prophesy deliverance: An Afro-American revolutionary Christianity.* Philadelphia, PA: Westminister Press.
Willey, Basil. 1952. *The Seventeenth century background.* NewYork: Doubleday.
Wiley, Tatha. 2001. *Original sin: Origins, developments, contemporary meanings.* NY: Paulist Press.
Wimber John and Kevin Springer. 1986. *Power evangelism.* San Francisco: Harper and Row.
Wink, Walter. 1984. *Naming the powers.* Philadelphia, PA: Fortress Press.
Yong, Amos. 2005. *The Spirit poured out on all flesh: Pentecostalism and the possibility of global theology.* Grand Rapids, MI: Baker Publishing Group.
Zizioulas, John, D. 1985. *Being as communion.* Crestwood, NY: St. Vladimir's Seminary Press.
Zohar, Danah and Ian Marshall. 2000. *Spiritual intelligence the ultimate intelligence.* New York: Bloomsbury.

Index

African Independent Churches, 53
After Writing, (Pickstock), 84
Ahlstrom, Sydney, 54
analogia entis, 19, 24, 34, 76, 82-84, 86, 89, 93-94, 110, 127, 130
analogy, 82, 86, 107, 130-133
   analogical apperception, 24
   analogical language, 24, 131
   analogical participation, 74, 83, 85, 101, 107
   analogization, 107, 131, 134, 152
   analogy of being, 71, 89, 93-94
Anselm, 64
apophatic theology, 86-87, 93, 101, 134-135, 172
Aquinas, Thomas, 7, 72, 76-77, 87-89, 93, 130
Aristotle, 62, 115–16
atheism, 17-18
Augustine, 38, 64, 72-73, 83, 93, 113, 115, 122, 130, 143

B
Bacon, Francis, 64,115
Badiou, Alain, 66
Balthasar, Han Urs von, 11, 70, 72, 88, 91–94,103, 108–110,130, 149, 154, 175
Barbour, Ian, 58, 61, 90
Barth, Karl, 51, 94, 109, 145-146
Baudrillard, Jean, 26, 48, 50-51, 63, 92
Beckett, Samuel, 36-37
Berger, Peter, 51
Bergson, Henri, 36, 37, 41
Berkeley, George, 78, 115
Bhaskar, Roy, 61, 90
Bob Jones University, 90
Boethius, 115,
Bohler, John, 62
Bosch, David, 12,20, 28, 53
Boxer Movement, 53
Boyd, Richard, 90
Boyle, Robert, 115

Bultmann, Rudolf, 34, 65, 90
Butler, Joseph, 115

C
Campbell, Ted, 112
Camus, Albert, 36-38, 46
Canonical Theism, 8
Carson, D.A., 90
Carveley, Kenneth, 113,
Catholic Ressourcement, 7, 88, 94, 133
Celtic Christianity, 159-161
China Inland Mission, 53
Cicero, 115
Clarke, Samuel, 115
closed-systems, 32, 57-58, 67, 78, 80-81
Collins, Ken, 113-114
colonization, 32, 53-55
Concept of Anxiety, The (Kierkegaard), 38
Concluding Unscientific Postscript (Kierkegaard), 38, 45
Cone, James, 151,
contextualization, 23, 71, 74, 107, 158-159, 162-163, 171
continental philosophy, 22, 25, 44,
Copleston, Frederick, 62, 78-79,
correlation (Radical Orthodoxy theory of), 71-73
Critical Realism, 41, 58, 60-63, 87, 131
Croft, George Cell, 114
Cunningham, Conor,18, 49, 72, 75, 76, 81

D
Davidson, Donald, 91
deconstruction, 47, 49, 79, 131
deferral of meaning, 49, 65, 137
deism, 32,
Deleuze, Gilles, 75, 79, 92
Derrida, Jacques, 18, 48-50, 65, 75, 79, 92
Descartes, Rene, 16, 28-33, 40-43, 64,77, 115
Dewey, John, 78, 91
diastema, 131-132, 142, 163, 173
discipleship, 170
discourse theory, 47-48,
Donovan, Vincent, 53,
Dostoevsky, Fyodor, 36,
Douglas, Kelly Brown, 16, 151

E
Eastern Orthodoxy, 80, 83, 100, 109, 112, 114, 137, 147-148, 172
Edwards, Jonathon, 115
empiricism, 9, 32-33, 78, 116-117, 120 (spiritual)
Enlightenment, 8-9 , 20, 28, 37, 47, 77

entire sanctification, 112, 114, 121, 127
epistemology
   analogical, 87
      crisis, 9, 17, 26, 36
   positivism, 58
   idealism, 58-61
   instrumentalism, 58-61
   onto-epistemology of participation, 87, 120, 126–27, 129, 131, 144, 149, 171
Erasmus, 115
Erickson, Millard, 90
Evagrius, 97-98, 113
Existentialism, 9, 35-46

F
Fichte, 36, 79
fideism, 44-45, 140
Ford, David, 91
Fosdick, Harry Emerson, 90
Foucault, Michel, 17, 48, 79, 82, 92
foundationalism, 23, 47, 51, 64, 81, 174
Frei, Hans, 91
Fuller Theological Seminary, 90

G
Gadamer, Hans-Georg, 23, 65,
Gasper, Philip, 90
Gonzalez, Gustavo, 168-169
Graham, Billy, 90
Gregory of Nazianzus, 98, 109, 113,
Gregory of Nyssa, 72, 86, 93, 98, 100, 107, 109, 111, 130, 173
Grenz, Stanley, 12, 28, 92, 175

H
Haack, Susan, 91
Habermas, Jürgen, 91
hacceity, 62
Hart, David Bentley, 12, 80, 85-87, 91, 109, 130
Hauerwas, Stanley, 91
Hegel, Georg, 31, 38-39, 51, 75, 78-79
Heidegger, Martin, 18, 31, 36, 39-42, 50, 75, 79, 85, 142
Heitzenreiter, Richard, 112,
Hemming, Laurence Paul, 69
Henry, Carl F.H., 90
Henry of Ghent, 75
Hiebert, Paul, 12, 57-62, 87
Hobbes, Thomas, 9, 51, 73
Hume, David, 64, 78, 115
Hunter, George, 159
Husserl, Edmund, 31, 40-44

Hutcheson, Francis, 115
hyperrealism, 26, 50, 63

I
Iamblichus, 84, 96, 98
instrumentalism, 39, 58-61

J
James, William, 78,91
Jaspers, Karl, 36
Jennings, Theodore, 114
Jesus Seminar, The, 65, 90

K
Karkkainen, Veli-Matti, 171-172
Kaufmann, Walter, 36, 39
Kant, Immanuel, 18, 33-36, 41-43, 64-65, 67, 75, 79
Kierkegaard, Soren, 35-40, 44-46, 51
Kimball, Dan, 92
Kraft, Charles, 57, 165
Kuhn, Thomas, 51

L
Las Casas, Bartolome de, 53, 83
Leibniz, Gottfried, 33, 38, 51, 115
Leplin, Jarrett, 90
Lessing, Gotthold, 45
Lessing's "Ditch," 45
Liberation Theology, 8, 151, 167-169
Lindbeck, George, 91
Linthicum, Robert, 167
Locke, John, 51, 64, 78, 115
logocentricism, 47, 49
logoi, 10-11, 13, 99-111, 115, 119, 121, 127
Lonergan, Bernard, 91
Lord, Andrew, 169
Lossky, Vladimir, 100, 130
Louth, Andrew, 97,100
Lubac, Henri de, 72
Luther, Martin, 39, 51,
Lyotard, Jean, 48, 65, 79, 92

M
Machen, J. Gresham, 90
Macintyre, Alasdair, 91
Maddox, Randy, 112-116
Malebranche, 115
Manifest Destiny, 54,
Marion, Jean-Luc, 23, 50-51

Marx, Karl, 35, 50, 73, 168
Mather, Cotton, 115
Maximus the Confessor, 10-11, 22, 75, 93, 95-110, 113, 117, 119, 121, 125, 127, 143, 155
McArthur, John, 90
McClaren, Brian, 92
McClendon, James William Jr., 92
McGrath, Alistair, 90
Meister Eckhart, 107,
Merleau, Ponty, Maurice,36
metanarrative, 47, 73,79
Milbank, John, 19-20, 24, 42, 65, 72-74, 79, 81, 83, 87-88, 92
Miles, Rebekah, 116
missio Dei, 124, 146-148, 164, 175
missio Trinitatis, 11,22-23, 128, 138, 145, 148, 158, 163
Missional Implications of Epistemological Shifts (Hiebert), 58,
Modernism, 7
    defining, 9

N
neo-Orthodoxy, 91
neo-Platonism, 84, 95, 97-99, 104
Newton, Isaac, 30, 32, 73, 115
Ngugi, wa Thiong'o, 56
Nietzsche, Friedrich, 17, 18, 36, 40, 47, 71, 75, 79-82
nihilism, 19, 52, 75, 79-81, 85
nominalism, 18, 24, 77-78
nouvelle theologie, 72

O
Ockham, William of, 7, 18, 31, 75-78
Oden, Thomas, 91
Olson, Roger, 90, 92
ontology
    analogical model of, 71, 74, 83-85
        creational ontology, 51, 66, 102
        delation(ary) ontology, 8-10, 17, 26, 41, 48-49, 51, 77, 83
    of participation, 11, 22, 48, 58, 66, 69, 74, 76, 81-87, 101–103, 117, 131, 150, 167
        of peace, 19, 79-83, 85, 136-137
        of violence, 19-20, 24, 56, 67, 76, 79-81
        onto-epistemology, 10-11, 13, 131
        onto-theology, 42, 85
        ontological difference, 41, 131-132, 142
        ontological realism, 7
        theo-ontology 7-8, 102, 115, 120
        transcendence/transcendent 8, 10, 18, 31, 34, 50, 81, 85
    Trinitarian ontology, 129-130
Origen, 97-99, 107, 113
Ortega y Gassett, Jose, 36-37
Outler, Albert, 111, 115

P

Packer, J.I., 90
Palamas, Gregory, 93, 100, 130
Pannenberg, Wolfhart, 64-65, 142, 174
Participation, 10-11, 22, 48, 58, 66, 69, 74, 76, 81, 83-84, 87, 95, 99, 100-102, 104-105, 114-115, 117, 119-121, 123, 129-130, 138, 144, 163
Pascal, Blaise, 115
Paul, the Apostle, 39, 143
Peacocke, Arthur, 58, 61, 90
Peirce, Charles, 58, 62, 91
Phenomenology, 9, 22, 35, 41-44
Philosophical Fragments (Kierkegaard), 38
Pickstock, Catherine, 72, 84, 87-88, 92, 95, 99
Pinnock, Clark, 90, 125, 171
Placher, William, 92
Plantinga, Alvin, 22, 64, 173
Plato, 12, 84, 95, 97, 99, 104, 115
Platonism, 43
Plotinus, 75
Polanyi, Michael, 39, 61, 90
Polkinghorne, John, 58, 61, 90
postcolonialism, 55
postmodernism, 7, 8
    Defined, 9, 26, 47
prevenient grace, 118, 121-122, 127, 155
privation, 108, 132, 142-143, 174
Proclus, 84, 96, 98
Przywara, Erich, 88, 109
Pseudo-Dionysius, 97-99, 109, 113, 130
Pseudo-Macarius, 111
pure reason, 34, 104
Putnam, Hilary, 78, 91

Q

Quine, W.V., 64, 78, 91

R

Radical Orthodoxy, 7, 10, 22, 25, 63, 69, 70-74, 90
Rahner, Karl, 91
Rauschenbusch, Walter, 34
Reid, Thomas, 115, 117
Reno, R.R., 92, 143
Ritschl, Albrecht, 34
Rorty, Richard, 91
Rousseau, Jean-Jacques, 51

S

Sarte, Jean-Paul, 35-41, 75
Saussure, Ferdinand, 49, 65

Schelling, 36
Schreiter, Robert, 147, 153
Schleiermacher, Friedrich, 90
Scientific revolution, 51, 77
Scotus, Duns, 7, 18, 62-63, 71, 73, 75, 76, 81, 83-84, 93
simulacra, 26, 50, 63
Smith, James K.A., 18, 73, 76, 80, 84, 95, 97, 99
Snyder, Howard,170
Spinoza, Benedict, 51, 75, 77
split-level Christianity, 21, 60, 126
Spong, John Shelby, 90
Stephanson, Anders, 54
Stott, John, 90
Stranger, The (Camus), 46
Strauss, David, 35
Strawson, P.F., 67
Strong, Josiah, 54
Stroud, Barry, 67
Sugirtharajah, R.S., 55

T
tabula rasa, 21, 24, 54, 137, 151
Taylor, Hudson, 53
theo-ontology, 102, 115, 120
theologia, 135-136
theological *a priori,* 70, 149, 151-152
Theology and Social Theory, (Milbank), 73
theosis, 13, 85, 101, 104-106, 109, 112, 121–22, 124, 131, 134, 137, 144, 156, 164, 171
theurgy, 84, 98
Tillich, Paul, 35, 65, 90
Torrance, Thomas, 91
transcendental, 33-35, 41-43, 79
transcendental argument, 66-67
transcendental ego, 34, 41-44, 49, 65
transcendentals, the, 19, 88, 108, 133, 137
Trinity, the, 8, 11, 82-83, 85, 124, 130, 146, 154, 164,175
Trinity Evangelical Divinity School, 90

U
Union Theological Seminary, 90
universal witness, 11,22,
univocity of being, 18-19, 24-25, 50, 52-53, 56, 63, 66, 71, 74-77, 81, 83, 93-94

V
Van Huyssteen, Wentzel, 60-61
Voltaire, 115

W
Ward, Graham, 72, 92

Warfield, B.B., 90
Webber, Robert, 91
Wesley, John, 10, 22, 107, 108, 111-128, 155
West, Cornel, 16
Willimon, William, 91
Wimber, John, 57
Wink, Walter, 167
Witherington, Ben, 65, 175
Wittgenstein, Ludwig, 73
Wright, N.T., 65, 90

Z
Zizioulas, John, 91, 130, 138-139, 148

www.ingramcontent.com/pod-product-compliance
Lightning Source LLC
Chambersburg PA
CBHW021829300426
44114CB00009BA/380